KU-486-592

Passing Shots

Passing Shots

Pam Shriver, Frank Deford
and Susan B. Adams

Pam Shriver on Tour

McGraw-Hill Book Company

New York St. Louis San Francisco Hamburg
Mexico Toronto

Copyright © 1987 by Pam Shriver, Frank Deford, and Susan B. Adams

All rights reserved. Printed in the United States of America. Except as permitted under the Copyright Act of 1976, no part of this publication may be reproduced or distributed in any form or by any means or stored in a data base or retrieval system, without the prior written permission of the publisher.

1 2 3 4 5 6 7 8 9 D O C D O C 8 7 6

ISBN 0-07-057177-5

LIBRARY OF CONGRESS CATALOGING-IN-PUBLICATION DATA

Shriver, Pam.
Pam Shriver, a season on tour.
1. Shriver, Pam. 2. Tennis players—United States—Biography. 3. Tennis—Tournaments. 4. Women tennis players. I. Deford, Frank. II. Adams, Susan. III. Title
GV994.S53A3 1986 796.342′092′4 [B] 86-7448
ISBN 0-07-057177-5

BOOK DESIGN BY KATHRYN PARISE

To my two grandmothers, whom I affectionately call Moppie and Gaga. They have both enjoyed a lifetime of tennis and passed on their love of the game to my parents and to me.

And with special thanks to all the players on the women's pro tour. We are a traveling sorority of world-class athletes and we are competitors, but above all we are friends.
Here's to you, girls.

Preface

I always took a special personal interest in Pam Shriver's career because we share a common Baltimore nativity and heritage. But then, as I got to know her, meeting her at tournaments I covered for *Sports Illustrated,* I was delighted to discover that someone I had picked out of the crowd merely for her geography was, in fact, as bright and charming and perceptive as any athlete I'd ever met.

And she liked me and paid attention to me because I was tall.

I remember early on taking an almost avuncular pride in her press conferences, especially those at Wimbledon, which draw the most eclectic crowd of journalists. Pam's conferences there were always popular and crowded, as she entertained the assembled world and worldly press with her candor and humor—often as not creating some innocent controversy in the bargain.

I recall one particular time, as she was about to leave the interview room—her one shoulder all iced up as usual, bulging like a tuberous potato—we got into a gossipy hometown conversation about the love life of some player on the Baltimore Orioles. Suddenly Pam saw all the writers, pens poised, tape recorders going. "Wait a minute, wait a minute," she cried. "This is all off the record"—although the dumbfounded lot of them, from Fleet Street, Sweden, India, and Australia, didn't know a Baltimore Oriole from a robin redbreast.

Late in 1984 I met Pam again, this time in Melbourne where I had gone to record Martina Navratilova's Grand Slam for the year. As it was, Martina got beaten, but Pam was even worse off—beaten, injured, depressed, and anxious only to get home to a sabbatical she had planned for herself. One morning I ran into her at breakfast in our hotel. It was only seven o'clock. Poor thing. I imagined she really must be in more distress than I recognized. Up at such an hour. Unless they have to catch a plane or make some easy money, athletes never see the light of day till the sun is high. Only when I began to read Pam's journal did I realize that she is a champion insomniac who can never sleep in.

Anyway, I had had it in the back of my mind that I would like to work with her on some kind of a diary, and I figured that now was a good time to broach the idea. I've worked with athletes before on such accounts—Ahmad Rashad in football, Arthur Ashe in tennis (he won his Wimbledon the year *after* I helped him with his diary; I trust that is an omen for Pam in '86)—and I had often thought it would be revealing and different to do one with a woman athlete next time. Female athletes must endure many peculiar problems because of their gender, as well as put up with the same experiences that male athletes do. Culturally, women athletes are hybrids, or, at the least, still evolving within the society.

Pam, I imagined, was perfect for the task because she is so observant. As a matter of fact, she probably sees too much, to the detriment of her tennis. Most champions are a good deal more inner-directed than she. It is my own view that when we journalists go prattling on about "the killer instinct," we are really employing a colorful phrase for the more prosaic "self-centered." For goodness sakes, every player wants to beat the other fellow. It is just that some athletes can concentrate more on that task. That doesn't mean they're more bloodthirsty, just more egocentric.

You will see in Pam's journal, for example, that as bright as Chris Evert Lloyd is, as gracious, she has an absolute blind spot when it comes to putting down the players she beats—while, by the same token, she will take extreme offense at the slightest imagined slur upon her own game. Or Martina, ever so generous, wins a tournament—singles and doubles—and immediately starts bitching about how one billboard on court affected her ability to see the ball. Like that, champions often are incapable of seeing one thing—their own game—in context.

Pam, alas, is always in context. She is not necessarily intrinsically smarter than, say, Chris or Martina, but she sees more around her than they do. Is that why they win and she doesn't? Possibly. Also, they may be better players. But, on the other hand, I knew damn well that Pam Shriver could write a much better journal about the life of young women traveling the world and playing tennis.

In fact, never did a breakfast pay off better and faster than that one in Melbourne. Even before she got back to the States, Pam had written several thousand words (some of which were correctly spelled) on airplane stationery. And she kept on writing. I imagine she sensed early on that she happens to be a naturally gifted writer. She has a fine sense of pace, of setting things up; she has a good turn of phrase; and she is not afraid to say things. She was so enthusiastic that she even went out and began taking writing lessons from a former teacher of hers at McDonogh School. And she *wrote* every word in her journal. Longhand. For the original two selections of her work that ran in *Sports Illustrated* in September 1985, I served as an editor. For this book, Susie Adams and I shared that task—but that's all we were, editors. Pam wrote the words.

Of course, it does help an editor to have an insomniac writing a journal—an insomniac tennis player best of all. Most of Pam's words seem to have been written either on airplanes or at 3:30 in the morning.

The idea for the book grew naturally out of the original magazine concept, but Pam also wanted to keep the journal for the whole year just to satisfy herself. During the course of the year, we talked often on the phone, from all over the world, and we met at various places—at her home in Baltimore, mine in Connecticut, in New York and Paris and in other more prosaic locales. It was scarcely hard work for me—mostly a matter of me looking over what she had done, and perhaps suggesting a few additional topics for her to examine. We tried to establish a few obvious themes and to concentrate regularly on a handful of main "characters" in order to give more flow and continuity to what must be such a stop-and-start form. But, of course, there's only so much planning you can do with a diary, and the "plot" was forever at the mercy of forehands and drawsheets and whimsy (and the love interests were even more open to the vagaries).

The traveling cocoon that is the women's tour is a story unto itself. Even for insiders, tennis politics is both boring and Byzantine, so we made every effort to keep references to that to a minimum. But there are a couple of names you must know. The Women's Tennis Association is the players' union, and a powerful force it is. Billie Jean King was the first president, Chris Evert Lloyd is the current one, and both Martina Navratilova and Pam are active on the board. Then there's the Virginia Slims tour, which comprises most of, shall we say, the regular season. Slims originally bankrolled women's professional tennis and remains the single most important financial source in the game, even though everybody is a little skitterish about a cigarette company supporting a sport. Slims produces an important championship, at Madison Square Garden, but nothing in men's or women's tennis approaches in value and prestige the four Grand Slam championships. These are the national titles of France, Great Britain, the United States, and Australia, which are known colloquially as Roland Garros, Wimbledon, Flushing Meadow, and Kooyong.

It's also wise to keep in mind that in a world of AstroTurf, where most baseball stadiums now have the same architecture and dimensions, where even new golf courses look identical, tennis retains the charm and diversion of several different surfaces. This not only adds flavor to the game but also injects more variety into the results. A player like Pam, who prefers to attack the net, play serve-and-volley, has an advantage on faster surfaces, especially on grass, where the balls skid and juke coming off an uneven lawn—so the player who can hit volleys, who doesn't even *let* the ball bounce, has an edge. As you will see, Pam searches the world for grass courts as diligently as Diogenes ever took his lantern after honest men. And Pam is lucky, too, in that while grass is a disappearing luxury, two of the four Grand Slam events—Wimbledon and Kooyong—are still played on the turf, although the Australian is expected to move to some form of synthetic hard court in another year or so. The U.S. Open is contested on just such a hard court, one that tends toward being "fast," while the French is played on slow red clay—or, simply, "dirt," as it was once dismissed by many condescending American players. Pam plays on dirt as little as possible, and invariably to her disgust.

But the diversity of the tour is part of its appeal—and that is increasing as more and more young women from the Continent, even South America, are becoming contenders in what was once very much a game of English-speaking nations. Also, it seems, the tour gets younger and younger as kids from all over the world smell the big money (or, anyway, are led to this fragrance by their parents). Since girls mature earlier than boys, yet are not allowed the same independence, the women's tennis tour now features an admixture of children and parents, coaches, chaperones, agents—as well as an increasing number of boyfriends and husbands. There are a few girlfriends on tour, too, although as Pam explains so perceptively, there aren't nearly as many homosexual tennis players as is routinely, snidely assumed. Still, the cross section is a wonderful one, made all the more intriguing by the fact that the women must look to the very people they are playing—and trying to beat—for much of their comfort and friendship.

As Pam writes so achingly, her goal in tennis is to win a Grand Slam singles tournament. Certainly she is capable of that. Pam is, by any standard, of the class of Virginia Wade, Nancy Richey, Karen Susman, Ann Jones—players of the previous generation who all won a Grand Slam or two. Pam's problem is that she is cursed to be playing at a time when not one, but two, great champions are reigning and driving each other to greater heights. There is not that much left over. Also, the irony to Pam Shriver is that she made a Grand Slam finals, the U.S. Open, when she was barely 16—which is itself something of another curse. Since then, by any fair measure, she has had a lot of plain old bad luck at Grand Slams. Then too, I think she lets those big tournaments get to her even more than they affect most contenders.

On the other hand, she's still only 24 years old. We forget. It's just that tennis players start out so bloody young. Twenty-four is approximately the age when most football and basketball players *reach* the pros. Only a handful of major league baseball players are under the age of 24. And here Pam is, a biblical era of eight years of touring already under her belt and writing an elder statesman's book of sage observations.

Anyway, whether or not she attains her goal in tennis, I am confident that we will all hear a great deal more from her in the balance of her life. Good grief, the Republicans are already urging her to run for Congress, when she's not yet even old enough to run. That's how young 24 really is. Pam also already has entrée to a career in television journalism, and she is clearly picking up the executive instincts that would qualify her for any number of management positions, in or out of tennis. So this book is really no more than a first chapter of a life, and I suspect that years from now the fact that Pam Shriver once won a Wimbledon or a U.S. Open or an Australian Open will be only a footnote to a life that has been full and rich in many endeavors.

FRANK DEFORD

December 7, 1984—Melbourne

I've only got three more days to go before my tennis year is over. Then I'm taking 2½ months away from the tour. Boy, do I need the break. I'm a 22-year-old wreck: My arm hurts all the time, I'm playing terrible tennis, and my attitude is lousy. I figure I'm at the midpoint of my career, and I need time off to evaluate what I've done, what I hope to do, and how I can do it. I've been playing the tour for six years, and the longest I've ever been away has been a month—and that was because I had an arm injury. Why can't tennis have an off-season like other sports? It's too demanding, but there are too many opportunities to make money all year long. I'm tired of tennis, tired of the lifestyle, tired of the other players, and tired of myself most of all.

I should be so carefree, but now I'm so scared when I play. I fear failure at every corner, every decision, every shot. I'm constantly second-guessing myself and asking other people for their opinions, which mixes me up further. How long should I practice? Should I find a new hitting partner? Will I ever fulfill my potential? Can I survive the loneliness and pettiness of the career that I've chosen? Did I choose it or did it choose me?

I'm going nuts with all these questions. Unless I free myself of my doubts, both on court and off, I know I'll never attain my goals. My career now stands at its most crucial stage. Gone is the young girl who got to the finals of the U.S. Open when she was barely 16.

Now there's only a young woman who struggles with her lucky life—and with an arm that hurts.

December 10—Melbourne

Martina and I made history today. We won the Australian Open doubles to complete a Grand Slam in one calendar year. That's never been done by any team! Someday I hope to make history on my own by becoming the first 6-foot, duckfooted Luthervillian to win Wimbledon or the U.S. Open singles title. To do that I may have to make adjustments in my tennis life.

One of these adjustments may be in my relationship with my long-time mentor. Don Candy has been my traveling coach and my best friend for the last eight years. An Aussie transplanted to the suburbs of Baltimore, he gave me my first lesson when I was 9. I've worked exclusively with him since I was 13, and since I was 15 and started playing women's tournaments, Don has gone to virtually every tournament with me. When you consider what we've done, all the ups and downs we've had with my career, all the laughter and the tears, Don has been the major influence in my life. But something's changing in the relationship; we're not getting as much out of each other as we should and as we have in the past. Maybe after ten years it just had to happen.

Don played the tour in the '50s after winning the Australian Junior title when he was 17 years old. Like me he was known as more of a doubles specialist, winning the French doubles with Robert Perry in 1956, losing in the finals of the U.S. Championships with Merv Rose in 1951 and getting to the finals of four Australian doubles championships in the 50s. During the time when Aussies dominated the game, Don was ranked in Australia's top ten for eight years but in some ways he feels he came up a step short and a shot long. Of course sometimes I feel the same way about my tennis, but that's no one's fault but my own. When Don blames himself for me not winning more often I get upset and say "Shoot Don, don't look at it that way. Look at what we have accomplished." Why can't people (me included) see what I have done, not what I haven't done? The pressure of feeling high expectations is crippling.

I do know this, if Don hadn't been around, I doubt I'd still be playing and I don't think I'd be as stable a person. Emotionally, he's been able to help me through the peaks and valleys of the tour lifestyle, and tactically, he's made me one of the smartest *players* around. But in the last year our practices haven't been as productive and we've been bickering a lot.

I've been at No. 3 or 4 in the world for the last six months and yet I'm not even close to really challenging Chris or Martina. I know I have shortcomings in my game and my work habits, but most can be corrected. Don's molded me, and now it's my job. If I can't take what he's given me and go the rest of the way, then I'm just not good enough.

December 11—En route

At this moment, I'm 42,000 feet above the Pacific and it's bumpy as hell. We're going through clouds. . . . I didn't think there were clouds up this high. The trip from Australia to Lutherville is interminable, and I know the inside of this airplane is all that I'll see for the rest of my life! I can't wait to get home.

I'm so patriotic. Not just about my country, but about my city. I love Baltimore and I guess I've kind of put Lutherville—which is 5 miles north of Baltimore—on the map. Well, some maps. Everywhere I go, people say, "You still live in *Baltimore?*" And then they repeat it, as if they can't believe it. "Baltimore?" But, gee, just because the Duchess of Windsor left Baltimore, doesn't mean every girl should. Blaze Starr, the stripper, is still there.

Still, I guess it is kind of funny for a world-ranked tennis player to be from Baltimore. In 1978, I remember looking at the U.S. national women's rankings and discovering I was the only one in the top fifteen who was not from California, Florida, or Texas. And I guess it's even stranger for a world-ranked player to still choose to live there, but Maryland is part of me and it wouldn't be natural for me to live anywhere but in the Baltimore area. I have a real hometown, and they can't take that away from me.

One of my favorite quotations is by Christopher Morley, who grew up in Baltimore: "To be deeply rooted in a place that has meaning is perhaps the best gift a child can have. If that place has beauty and a feeling of permanence it may suggest to him unawares that sense of identity with this physical earth, which is the humblest and happiest of life's intuitions."

Women tennis players lead such a strange life. Every week we're in a different city, meeting and mixing with different people, with no real chances for male friendship, and with strange limitations placed on our friendships with each other because of the competition. I'm close to Martina because of the doubles and all we've been through, and to Elise Burgin because we grew up together in Baltimore, but that's about it. Sure, there are plenty of people to go out to dinner and shoot the breeze with, but there's almost no one to share your deep secrets with. I guess it's the competition; you keep a subconscious wall there.

That's why having a real home base is so important. I get kind of sad when I see all these players like Andrea Jaeger, Kathleen Horvath, Bonnie Gadusek, Jimmy Arias moving to Florida, taking their fathers and mothers to live on an acre near some tennis factory, Bollettieri's or Hopman's. I think you need to have stable things. I've had a stable family life, a stable coach who's helped me remain on keel, a family who loves me no matter how many matches I win or lose. I hate to be unstable, and I think that's why I've felt a little uptight the last couple of months.

I just wish people would understand my personality enough to separate what goes on on court and off court. Off the court, I get along so well with most of the players and everyone thinks I'm funny, and then if I say one thing that bugs them on court, that's it! The end of a beautiful friendship!

Look, everyone's stretched in the line of work they're in, but unfortunately tennis players are physically, mentally, and emotionally stretched twelve months of the year. Sometimes my way of getting rid of all the tension is saying the odd four-letter word. It's never personal, but, God, women are so sensitive. I think people should understand human nature: Everyone is going to screw up. Well, everyone except maybe Chris Evert Lloyd, and let me tell you, she has a bit of the devil in her that she rarely shows the public. Take the men's locker-room incident at Kooyong, for example.

This happened just last week during one of those tedious rain delays at the Australian Open. I walked into the women's locker room and heard Chris say to Andrea Temesvari and Andrea Leand, "I dare you. . . ." They shook their heads, and I said, "Dare what?" And Andrea Leand said, "Chris bet us $100 that we wouldn't go into the men's locker room right now." I said, "No way, not for $100." So Chris arched her eyebrows and said, "O.K., $200." I figured for that kind of money it would be a great way to pass the time. Besides, maybe the guys would actually talk to us for once if we actually stormed their locker room.

So I marched down the hall, took a deep breath and opened the door. My head was down because I didn't know if everyone was going to be dressed, and I said, "You all, this is part of a bet. Chris Evert dared me that I wouldn't come in here unannounced." And they said, "Oh, well, have a seat." So I sat down on the floor and started watching television. They all had their clothes on, and I don't know whether I was disappointed or relieved. Probably relieved. But anyway we started having a little community chat, and then there was a little knock on the door, and Chris poked her head in and said, "Is Pam Shriver in here?" With that she led the rest of the girls into the room and we had a fine old time. Ivan Lendl told a story he'd heard on the radio, some ethnic joke with sexual connotations. And Martina and Chris chipped in with some off-color jokes of their own. Brad Gilbert won the prize for raunchiest. The Swedes are supposed to be so liberated, but they never said two words because they're so shy. They were listening to everything, though. I was right: It was a terrific way to pass a rain delay.

Later that day, Chris handed me a personal check for $200. To the left of her signature, she'd inscribed the words: "For a crummy bet." And that is only the smallest glimpse of one side of Chris Evert Lloyd that people rarely see. There is much, much more.

I've never cashed the check, either. You see, unfortunately, it's still the only time I've ever beaten Chris.

December 13—Lutherville

When I saw Mom at the airport, I realized my voyage was finally over. Mom's always been there for me, in every sense of the word. She's a professional mom and I mean that in the complimentary way. I can't remember a day throughout the school years when she wasn't at home to praise a grade, laugh at a story, or listen to my tearfully told battles with classmates or teachers.

In tennis she spent most of her prime years on the highway, driving me to lessons and junior tournaments. She has loved tennis all her life (she even played Maureen Connolly when they were both kids in San Diego!), so she loved watching me play. But she never got so wrapped up in my tennis that she pressured me, and she never caused a scene. You'd be surprised how many tennis parents do.

There are lots of tennis mothers on the tour, and with a couple of them it's as if they've caught a disease. They get so competitive about their daughters' practice courts, practice balls, everything. I used to think I was the most competitive person in the world until I met some of these mothers. And some of them are so tight with their money. They'll take food from the players' lounge for dinner or for breakfast the next day, and here their kids are making a couple of hundred thousand dollars a year. I'll tell you, there's so much of the tour life that I don't even want my family to be involved with.

I know how much my parents have cared about my tennis and I know they would like to come to more tournaments, but the worlds are so different, light years apart. I almost dread them at tournaments, yet I love them dearly. Parents have a way of getting in the way when you're young, but they—especially Mom—backed away from all that when I started playing women's tournaments. They trusted Don and they turned my tennis life over to him. I'm sure Mom would have liked to continue traveling with me, but she knew that wasn't the best thing for my tennis and besides my 8-year-old sister, Eleanor, needed her at home.

Unlike Dad and me, Mom can be reserved with her feelings, but I've always known where she stood about the "disaster area" my room became when I was home between tournaments. She never harped about it, though, and now that I've got my own house she doesn't have to put up with my mess. I've learned to live with it by shutting my door and sealing off the area. Just as I did when I lived in Mom and Dad's house, five minutes from where I live now.

December 14—Lutherville

It's 2:30 a.m. and, as usual, I'm wide awake. I've always been a poor sleeper, but with the time difference between here and Australia, I'm lucky if I sleep more than a few hours at a time. I don't know why I'm such an insomniac; my mind just never seems to rest. Unfortunately, my lifestyle doesn't help. I don't sleep in the same bed for more than a few nights in a row, and my night matches mess up any sort of bedtime routine. I've traveled for years with a prescription for mild sleeping pills, but I hate to take them. One good thing about my insomnia: I have a lot of time—maybe too much?—to reflect on my life and career.

I don't consider myself moody, but the pressure of expectations has always been a problem for me. Since September 12, 1978, the day that I baffled everyone by reaching the U.S. Open finals, people have told me that (a) I'd be the next Margaret Court; (b) I'd win Wimbledon; (c) I'd be No. 1 in the world; (d) all of the above. I bought the whole nine yards. After all, if you get to the finals of a Grand Slam tournament at 16 years and 2 months, playing your first U.S. Open, winning six consecutive matches—including beating Martina Navratilova in the semifinals before losing to Chris Evert in a good final—then surely you'll win everything in a few more years. Right? Wrong! I've never made it to a Grand Slam singles final since then.

So the 1978 U.S. Open still remains my proudest moment, and I think of it often. I remember most details of that first Open as if I'd played it yesterday—the subway rides to Flushing Meadows, the St. Moritz Hotel, the draw, the matches, the rain delays, the planes, the crowds, the attention, the upsets, the finals, and the drive home. Most of all, I remember my innocent, almost virginal, response to winning. One by one: Candy Reynolds, Sharon Walsh, Jeanne Evert, Kerry Reid, Lesley Hunt in the quarters. Then Martina, then Chris.

Did I really expect to beat Chris and win the Open? No. Actually, I was scared stiff I wouldn't get a game. In front of 18,000 screaming New Yorkers. On national television. Against Chris Evert. In the final. "Game, set, and match, Miss Evert 6–0, 6–0." I could just hear the umpire saying those awful words at the end of the match.

As it turned out I had nothing to be afraid of. I really could have won that match. I led 5–4 in the first set, and Chris seemed more nervous than I was. I remember her double-faulting three times in one game in the first set. I haven't seen her do that since. I lost, but I lost bravely, 7–5, 6–4.

Three points stand out in my mind as dramatic, peculiar, exhausting—and more. The first occurred with Chris serving 1–2 in the first set. We had a long baseline rally before she hit a short ball. I hit a backhand crosscourt approach to her two-fisted backhand. She returned with a short, sharply angled dink to my backhand. I scrambled to my left and reached down with my racket just as the ball bounced. As I hit it, I spun around quickly to get back to the center of the court. I never saw the ball hit my racket. I only hoped it had gone over. In fact, it won the point for me. I had never before hit a shot like it, and I haven't hit one like it since: a blind half-volley slice, angled drop-shot winner! Chris shot me a look of astonishment, disbelief, and disgust. I shrugged my shoulders and turned away: I hit that shot all the time, Chrissie, baby.

The second shot took place at about 2–2 in the second set. I was serving, ad in. I aimed up the center and fired a hard slice serve. ACE! No, the umpire called a let. I heard it too, no argument. Back again to serve. I decided to try the same spot. Whack! ACE! The crowd roared with approval. I swaggered to my chair, grabbed my towel, and laughed. I had 18,000 bozos in the palm of my hand.

The third memorable point happened in the last game. Chris's serve, 5–4. A long point. I approached the net, hit a volley, retrieved a lob over my head, hit a few more groundstrokes, sliced another approach, retrieved another lob, barely returned it, and watched Chris plop one last drop shot over the net. I sprawled on the ground, spread-eagle with exhaustion. I'd lost the match, but I'd won the war: The crowd adored me. Sweet sixteen.

I must have made interesting impressions on people because I received commercial, tennis—even show business—inquiries. Reporters from *People* interviewed me, and their photographers hassled me to pose in Central Park, on top of the Empire State Building, silly things like that. When I turned them down, they apologized for the harassment and asked for my address so that they could send me some of the photos they did take, in appreciation for my cooperation. Of course, stupid, naive, innocent me blurted out my address in Lutherville. Well, *People*'s pictures never arrived, but *People*'s people were on our doorstep in Lutherville at 8:00 a.m. the morning after the final.

All I wanted to do was resume my anonymity at McDonogh School, where I was the only girl voted onto the school's executive committee. (I guess they figured if I got to the finals of the U.S. Open, I could be on the student council.) I was combining my last two years into one—so that I could hurry off and go play for pay—and I just wanted to knuckle down and enjoy my last year of high school. Fat chance.

The *National Enquirer* sent a reporter to school after Mom, Dad, Don, and I had explicitly turned down all interviews. Well, this guy drove out to McDonogh in a black Camaro, unannounced and unwanted, as I was walking from the soccer field to the Allen Building. "Excuse me," he said, rolling down the window of his car, "do you know where I can find Pam Shriver?" Didn't he know what I looked like? Should I lie and tell him I didn't know where she was? I panicked and told the truth: It's always been a bad habit of mine, especially with the press.

"You're talking to her," I said.

He looked genuinely astonished. What a ruse!

"Can I ask you a few questions?" he said. I wanted to say no, but how could I and just walk away from the guy?

"OK," I said, "but only a couple because I've told *People* and everybody else no interviews for a while."

The interview lasted about five minutes and all I could think of was how weird it was to be interviewed by the *National Enquirer* in front of the Allen Building. When it was over he jumped into his Camaro and pulled away. I went home and got into the first major row with my mom about the press. She'd been handling twenty-five calls a day with a polite, but firm "no" and here I was granting an interview to the *National Enquirer* no less. Oh well, my first mistake.

Unfortunately, the success I had on court at the '78 Open pursued me like some kind of golden yardstick, measuring everything I did against those two perfect weeks. Still, I can smile when I look back on that time. Imagine a guy from the *National Enquirer* driving onto the campus of McDonogh School and interviewing some curly-haired kid in front of the Allen Building. Life is a howl.

December 15—Lutherville

People ask me what I'm going to do for the next 2½ months. I don't think I'm going to have time for everything I want to do. First I'm going to consult with my doctors and set up a program to treat and strengthen my aching arm. Then I've got to find a new practice partner/traveling companion for when I go back on tour. I also plan to take an active role in the business of my career. I'm thinking about enlisting a sports management company to market me. In the past, Don's handled my endorsements and exhibitions, so that will be another way his role will change. I hope he won't be too upset, but I know he'll take it personally.

I'd also like to take a minicourse in writing, or business, or history at one of the local colleges. I don't know enough about U.S. history. And Orchard Indoor Tennis, the club that I own, is going to get some of my personal T.L.C.

But most of all, I want to establish a social existence at home. I can count on one hand the good, solid friends my own age I can hang out with here—my older sister, Marion, who lives in my house, Liz Nuttle, my next-door neighbor, and Laura DuPont, who manages the club. And I want to meet some fun young guys.

I haven't gone out much at home and people hear stories about homosexuality on tour, so they must wonder about me. I've never fit into the group of girls that gets asked out a lot. You know the type: cute, blonde, long hair, nice boobs. In high school, I never knew whether it was my height or my tennis or my outspokenness or the fact that I didn't dress up and wear makeup, but guys seemed intimidated by me.

To an extent, I think they still are. I don't regret being a 6-foot tennis player at all, I just wish more guys would widen their thinking about girls. Why do the obvious ones always get asked out? Do they flirt?

Marion's going to help me meet some nice guys. She's two years older than I am, and she has a great base of friends here. Marion's also cute, blonde, has long hair and nice boobs. We're going to have an open house for about 100 people on Saturday, and she might even teach me how to flirt. I don't flirt very well. I'm not even sure I *know* how to flirt.

December 16—Lutherville

Maybe it's all the decisions I have to make that wakes me up. It's 2:30 a.m. and I'm thinking about tennis management companies again. Don has always felt that the management groups couldn't care less about my tennis, that they're only interested in me making money so they can make money. Besides, early in my career, Don and I agreed that I should concentrate on improving my game without the distractions of personal appearances and non-tennis endorsements. Don handled all the tennis endorsement stuff, and we kept a pretty low profile in the marketplace.

Now I feel my game has a solid foundation and I'm interested in branching out. I feel I have a lot to offer a company as a spokesperson and I'd love to do a TV commercial. For that to happen, I need a group like ProServ or International Management Group, the two biggest tennis management firms, to beat the bushes for me. Don just doesn't have the time or the contacts to do it.

I know Don won't like me expanding my commitments. He already thinks I take too much time away from my tennis, that I give too much time to the media, to the Women's Tennis Association, to the tournament promoters, to the other players. He even calls me "the Florence Nightingale of women's tennis" because I've subbed for others at press days, tournaments, and even a pro-am or two. He thinks I've got to be more selfish and reduce my outside interests if

I want to reach my potential, but after six years on the tour I think I know what's good or bad for my tennis. I'd go crazy if I just played tennis and ate and slept.

December 17—Lutherville

We're all early risers in my family. It must be the hunter's blood in my dad; in me, it's permanent jet lag. Yesterday Dad and I were off on our hunting trip by 5:20 a.m. We've gone hunting together since I was 13, and I'm still knocked out by being so close to nature. Maybe it's cruel to shoot things, but nothing we've ever shot has gone to waste. And Dad is a sportsman: He'll chase a crippled goose for hours, while most hunters let them go.

I sometimes think hunting is something Dad should be doing with a son. He's only got three girls, and I guess I'm like a surrogate son. I love doing things with him and our personalities are so similar. We both communicate well with people, have a good sense of humor and terrible tempers in competition. When people at home first saw me play tennis they said they knew I was Sam Shriver's kid for two reasons—by the way I walked and by the way I yelled. One year Dad and I made it to the semifinals of the Maryland mixed doubles together, and a noisy passage it was.

In the past month, we've grown closer than we've ever been. Dad sees me as a grown-up, and it's easier for me to talk to him about guys. All my friends say how comfortable they feel with Dad. I'm just beginning to realize how much alike we are. Of course, he's a better hunter: He got two geese today, and I had trouble just getting up out of the pit without having camouflage draped all over me.

December 18—Lutherville

Pamela Howard Shriver has successfully reentered Lutherville society. The party Marion and I gave was great, over 100 people all talking and laughing until God knows what hour (I collapsed around

1 a.m.). What a contrast to my two days of hunting! My architect brought me a mannequin's right arm with a wristband and a red ribbon around it. "Here's your new arm, Pam," he said.

Somehow that silly gift made me think back to those innocent days when I played tennis without any pain, at least without physical pain. There was some psychic pain, of course, in being a 14-year-old girl playing on the boys' tennis team. I was the first McDonogh girl ever to compete against Gilman, our archrivals. Our first team match was in the spring of my freshman year, and I was playing No. 2 behind Bernie Sandler, my doubles partner. I was as nervous for this match as I'd ever been: The finals of the junior Nationals was a tranquilizer compared to this!

This was war. The McDonogh Eagles vs. the Gilman Greyhounds—"Gayhounds," of course, is what we called them. While I was getting dressed for the match, I realized I'd forgotten my tennis pants. Panic. I thought for a moment. . . . Bookstore! I scrambled down four flights of stairs to the bookstore. The ladies who worked there were always cranky.

"Do you have any bloomers?" I asked, breathlessly.

"What size?"

"Large."

"We only have small."

Why ask me what size, then, I thought. It didn't matter the size, color, or texture; I knew I wasn't playing a Gilman boy in just my underwear. I jammed my legs and butt into these orange (I kid you not) bloomers, grabbed my two Prince rackets, and rushed onto the battlefield.

I relaxed a bit when I saw that Mr. McKibbon, our coach, was even more nervous than I was. He was pacing. Then he'd pause, cross his legs, and bow his head to think. His voice was shaky as he gave us our last-minute instructions. We all wanted to win. Where were the Gilman boys?

They marched down the driveway to the courts single file. What a production. What morons. We all stood casually in a bunch as they strutted over in formation. Then the two No. 1s paired off and walked to their court. I heard the words.

"Playing No. 2 for McDonogh, Pam Shriver." I stepped forward feeling ill. Did I need to go to the bathroom or had I already?

"Playing No. 2 for Gilman, Jeff Himeles."

I reached out to shake his hand, but was stunned to see him pull a plastic rose from behind his back and, with a smirk, offer it to me. What was this? Bobby Riggs and Billie Jean all over again? I regained my composure.

"Thank you very much," I said, taking the rose and my rackets to the middle court. Were my bloomers cutting off my circulation or was I just too numb to feel my legs?

I had known Jeff Himeles since grade school. He had a pleasant face, but I'll never forget his sly, obnoxious, snide expression when he presented me with that rose. Why not a real rose, you twit? Well, I wasn't going to play Margaret Court to his Riggs act. I won pulling away in the second set. First girl to compete, first to beat a Gilman boy. He was gracious in defeat. I gloated in victory. We won the team match 5–2, too, and I was extremely relieved when the whole day was over.

The plastic rose and the orange bloomers were colorful touches, but my first clash with a Gilman team was not my most memorable or controversial. That distinction belongs to the first state high school tournament I played in, which took place right there at Gilman. I was the No. 3 seed and played Peter Brown, Gilman's No. 1, in the semis.

Peter and I had grown up together playing tennis at L'Hirondelle Country Club. We always got along well. I remember having a crush on him as a 10-year-old. By the time I was 13, I was taller than he was.

The day I played him at Gilman he wore a knee brace and was suffering from an alleged virus. He had some beautiful excuses ready. Although he was a guy and four years older, I thought I could win even if the grassy banks around the court were filled with the hated Gayhounds.

From the start of the match, Peter stalled. He repeatedly went back to the fence to towel off. He fiddled with his knee brace, his headband. I complained to the tournament director, who either didn't know the 30-second rule or chose to ignore it. I lost 6–4, 6–3 in a rage. I wanted revenge.

Later in the afternoon, Bernie Sandler and I played the doubles final against, you guessed it, Peter Brown and Jeff Himeles of Gilman.

They were a solid pair and the crowd had grown larger and more obnoxious. Bernie was too nervous and I was too mad to play well. We struggled to split sets. A Gilman guy was yelling after every point we lost: "Stick it to 'em, stick it to 'em."

The guy kept yelling this after points, during the changeovers. Believe me, I tried to ignore it. Keep calm, I told myself. Keep Bernie calm. It was 4–3 in the third. We were changing sides, and the same idiot yelled again. I'd heard that charming refrain one too many times.

"Stick it up yours," I bellowed. Bernie laughed. I felt better. We won 6–4 in the third. We hugged each other. We were the champs!

When I came down from that high, I knew I should apologize.

A freshman girl from McDonogh telling a Gilman guy to stick it up his at the top of her lungs wasn't a very good reflection on McDonogh. I wrote notes to the Gilman coach, whom I'd called an unsportsmanlike jerk (just like his players), to the Gilman headmaster, and to Dr. Mules, the McDonogh headmaster. Very contrite, I told Dr. Mules about the day, the stalling, the crowds, the insult, my insult, our win. Instead of being mad, he burst out laughing. Thank heavens for a man with a sense of humor!

I stopped playing for McDonogh after my sophomore year. I had started playing women's tennis with good results, so I concentrated my energies on adult tournaments. But I'm proud to say that I never lost a high school dual match in two years. That made me proud for McDonogh and for my tennis, but I don't think it helped my social life much. As I said, I think guys were a little intimidated by me.

December 21—Harbour Island, Bahamas

I'm in paradise. It's actually called Harbour Island, and I'm sitting high on a hill overlooking the Atlantic. The palm trees are crackling in a brisk wind. Down below, a rooster just announced the coming of morning. Our cottage vibrates as the hot-water heater clicks on. The luxury of the place is that there's no luxury: no phones, no TV, no agenda. Just sun, sand, water, and the people I care most about: my family. There are eleven of us: my grandmothers, Gaga and

Moppie; Uncle Dick (my dad's brother) and Aunt Barbara; my cousins Rich and Andrew; Mom and Dad; and the three of us Shriver girls—Marion, Eleanor, and me. And that's it for the clan: Good things come in small packages.

December 22—Harbour Island, Bahamas

We went snorkeling today and Eleanor tried it for the first time. She was so brave. I'm eight years older than Eleanor and she's the baby of the family. Sometimes I worry about her as if she were my own kid. She's going through that tough, adolescent stage when nothing seems to fit because of all the puppy fat. I tease her a lot about her weight: She's definitely plump, and no 14-year-old should be that out of shape.

I remember how thin and active I was at her age. Tennis had a lot to do with it. I never thought I was going to be a professional tennis player. It was just something I did to fill my summers. During the rest of the year I played field hockey, lacrosse, basketball, whatever. It was always weird when people came up later and asked me, "Didn't you have an idol?" or "Didn't you always dream about being No. 1?" I never thought about those things; I just had this all-consuming, little-kid kind of love for the game. I used to play for hours. I played my first club tournament when I was 6 and I was in the interclub league at age 7. But I never thought ahead about tennis; I was too busy playing in the present.

How different the game is for kids now. By the time they're 10 years old their parents have created these grand illusions about their children playing professional tennis. With my folks, it was "maybe we'll take you to this tournament this week and maybe we won't." Tennis was never a focal point of our lives.

The only reason I got my first lesson was because Mom stuck a gift certificate for a lesson into my Christmas stocking when I was 9 years old. Actually, that lesson was a pretty traumatic experience. I had very seldom played indoors before and I had never played in the wintertime before. I remember I went out and hit with Mom on an adjacent court at Orchard Indoor Tennis Club for about fifteen minutes before my lesson, because I hadn't hit for four months and I didn't want to embarrass myself. I didn't hit one ball on the strings during that warm-up and I was petrified because my lesson was with this Australian guy who had played the tour. My God, the tour! That was unbelievable to a 9-year-old. And he was a foreigner and he talked funny.

When I finally started the lesson, I hit pretty well, but I can remember Don's voice being kind of abrupt and loud. He intimidated me, and by the end I was almost crying. It's curious because the next winter when I took lessons again, I thought he was the funniest guy I'd ever met. He'd say the funniest things and call me silly names. If I was serving badly, I'd be "serving like a wet hen," and he'd call me "Curly Top." And before my lessons, I'd be doing my homework in the lounge and he'd bang a ball against the glass to see how high I'd jump out of the chair. I can't believe I was afraid of him that first lesson.

Tennis is such a business to me now, such a drag sometimes, I find it hard to recollect the innocence of that time when I was 12 and 13 and I was growing like heck and I was pretty spastic and I wasn't even ranked in the top forty. I was just ranked alphabetically nationally—I just wasn't that good. But then I started growing into my height a little bit and it all began to come together. When I was 13 Don started to show up at some of my matches—this is how I knew he thought I might become a reasonable player. Then I went through an eight-month period when I played great and was ranked No. 2 in the nation in the 14s. But I didn't even win the Maryland state junior championships until I was 14. I remember I beat Elise Burgin 6–4 in the third. We'd been playing each other ever since the day when she was 9 and I was 8 and she creamed me 6–1, 6–1 at Clifton Park in Baltimore City, and she kept on beating me in every local tournament we played. When I got my first Maryland state title over Elise I knew I had it made!

So I didn't win the Maryland States until I was 14, and I was in the finals of the U.S. Open two years later! No wonder I feel so much pressure. I never had a chance to work myself into the idea of being a professional tennis player with a future. My future became the present at the 1978 U.S. Open. That's pretty wild when you think about it.

The first serious conversation that Don ever had with my parents about how good I might get happened when I was 14. I'd just come back from winning the Easter Bowl 16s and I'd beaten Anne White in the finals. I had lost about seven or eight games the whole tournament, and Don thought I should think about playing women's tournaments. That was April 1977 and Tracy Austin was just starting to play some women's tennis. Tracy was my measuring stick because I was going pretty close with her on fast surfaces. So we started making some plans to play some minor women's pro events.

In the process of trying to get into a women's tournament, I got a call early in October when I was 15 from someone named Sara Kleppinger who was with some company named ProServ in Washington, D.C. She asked me if I wanted to play in the local qualifying tournament for the Virginia Slims of Washington. Boy, this was the big leagues, the Virginia Slims tour! I leapt at the chance. I just snuck in geographically. To be the local qualifier, you had to live within a 50-mile radius of the tournament site, and Lutherville is about 49 miles outside Washington, on the far side of Baltimore.

Anyway, I ended up winning the local qualifying tournament and got into the main draw of the Slims of Washington in January 1978. That was my first women's tournament, and probably if Don hadn't thought I'd outgrown most of the competition in the juniors I would never have played a pro tournament that early. I certainly was indoctrinated early in the ways of the pro tour and in the attitude everybody has about upstart 15-year-olds.

I remember showing up for practice at the Virginia Slims of Washington and finding three of the pros just standing around the court. Pam Teeguarden, Laura DuPont, and Janet Newberry obviously didn't want anything to do with the latest 15-year-old threat to their livelihood. Even after Don introduced me to them, they were sort of aloof and snotty. But when we kept standing around, I realized that the reason nobody was hitting was because there weren't any practice balls at the courts yet. Little did I know then that pros don't bring their own practice balls because they're too tight to buy their own. But as a 15-year-old junior I was dumb enough to think that you had to have your own tennis balls to practice, so I had a can in my bag. When I whipped it out, they suddenly became a lot friendlier to me. They actually hit with me, four on a court.

Ironically, it was Pam Teeguarden who became my first win in a main Virginia Slims tournament. I beat her 7–6, 6–0, and she went on to say it was the worst match she'd ever played, which is what every older player says after they lose to a 15-year-old pipsqueak anyway. That, and the balls were too heavy (or too light), the conditions were too dark (or too bright or too hot or too cold), and menstrual cramps came at just the wrong time!

Three weeks later, in January 1978, I won the second pro tournament I ever played in, the Avon Futures of Columbus, Ohio. Winning pro tournaments is a piece of cake, I thought. Wrong, doodoo brain. Wrong! But the Columbus experience was so incredible from start to finish that there is no wonder that my impressions of the pro tour were a little skewed by it.

I had no women's ranking so I had to play the prequalifying to gain entry into the qualifying event, and if I won all those matches, then, hallelujah, praise the Lord, I would qualify for the main draw of the Columbus tournament. Since I was just learning all the rules and regulations of the pro tour, Don and I figured I would play the prequalies and the qualies, achieve a point average that would enable me to gain direct entry into other tournaments, then go home. This way I would only miss one week of school. I had a term paper due and chemistry was giving me fits. I couldn't miss two weeks.

As it turned out, I could and did miss two weeks. I clobbered four people in the prequalies and advanced with seven other lucky ones to the qualies. I lost seven games in three matches and moved into the main draw. How could I leave Columbus without finishing? I couldn't—the heck with chemistry! Two days later one of the biggest snowstorms in the city's history hit Columbus.

I was seeded second in the main event. Renee Richards was No. 1. We were some pair of top seeds. I was a 15½-year-old preppy from Lutherville, Maryland, and she was a 44-year-old transsexual doctor. And we were playing in the cozy, informal milieu of the minor league satellite events: no large, crowded arenas; no heavily laden tables of free food and drink in the player lounges; no new cans of practice balls; no big money; no big publicity; and, as it turned out in snowbound Columbus, no umpires, linesmen, or ballboys for two days.

In the quarterfinals—Sue Mappin vs. Pat Medrado—Don called a sideline and I watched over the baseline. I knew all about being a linesman: Make a quick, loud, firm call and signal with your arm. Occasionally I'd look over to Don between points and he'd make a face. He seemed bored because he hadn't had to make a call. Then suddenly a ball bounced near his sideline. It was either a winner or the ball was out. What was Don's decision? Silence. No call, no arm motion.

"Don, how did you see the ball?" Lee Jackson, the tour referee, inquired from the chair.

"I don't know, Lee, it was awfully close," Don said. I couldn't believe it. Every player hates an indecisive call, and Don had just made the most indecisive call in the history of tennis. Lee finally had to make the call for him.

I'll never forget that tournament either. After fourteen days, twelve matches and two snowstorms, I won my first pro tournament, but the dream final—Richards vs. Shriver—never materialized. Renee lost in the semifinals to Kate Latham. At that time, Renee was still getting a lot of publicity and had become sort of the spokesperson for transsexuals. I remember I was sitting in the player lounge doing my term paper for school when this woman, or what I thought was a woman, came in looking for Renee. She must have weighed about 300 pounds and looked like a refrigerator. I was wide-eyed. I ran to Don and said, "Don! The place is swarming with them."

The locker room would have been frightening enough for me even if Renee hadn't been there. I couldn't get over it. There were naked women all over the place. I mean naked. Didn't anybody in tennis have proper modesty and dress behind the sanctity of bathroom stalls like we did back at McDonogh School? I mean these girls actually seemed comfortable walking around in the buff. And Renee was the most flagrant of all. She knew everybody was really checking her out. I sure was. But I could see that if ever I wanted to become a genuine grown-up professional tennis player, I would have to get used to this. In fact, now I can stroll the locker room buck naked with the best of them.

December 26—Harbour Island, Bahamas

Gimme a break! I'm only fifteen days into my vacation from the tour and my mind keeps coming back to my tennis. Will I miss the game when I retire? Do I have the desire to put in the necessary work to reach my potential? Will everything work out with Don? What about my decision between ProServ and IMG? Will I find a new hitting partner? In four days I start on my fitness and rehabilitation program. I hope I have the discipline not to cheat. On the other hand, I hope I don't worry myself to death.

I think I've always worried too much about what other people said I should be doing, rather than about what *I* thought I could do. Although I wouldn't trade the experience for anything, being the youngest ever to reach a finals of the U.S. Open hasn't been an easy thing to live up to. And now that I'm No. 3 or 4, everybody's always asking me when I'm going to win my first major title.

I try to explain that the reason I got to be No. 3 wasn't because I was beating Chris and Martina but because I was very consistent. I rarely lose to any of the girls outside the Top Ten, and I haven't lost a first-round match in two years. Then I say that it takes time to develop the confidence to beat Martina or Chris, and people say, "Oh, now Shriver's content with No. 3," like I've lost my ambition.

Then I think, "OK, maybe it does help to be a little more positive." So I tell people that if I have a good day serving and volleying on a fast surface, I have a very good chance of beating Chris, and it comes out at Wimbledon that "Shriver thinks Chris Evert is going down the drain," and Chris throws a conniption fit. Or at the Open I goof and say that I'd be a better match for Martina than Wendy Turnbull—after Wendy has knocked me out of the tournament. And I've got to start apologizing in locker rooms from here to Timbuktu.

December 28—Harbour Island, Bahamas

I was reading some of this stuff over, and I better explain something. That is about "girls." Women tennis players call themselves girls. Maybe anything else would be too formal. I don't know. It's the equivalent to male players calling themselves guys.

I break it down this way: If we go to a party or a function where we have to get all dressed up, we're women, but if we're at the tennis club wearing track suits, we're girls—except when we're bitches, of course. You are what you wear, I guess.

Seriously, I'm for women's rights and I think my lifestyle has allowed me to skip a lot of the hassles other women might encounter in the workplace. I feel very lucky that I've never felt subservient to men and that I've never really had to fight for the right to earn my living, but tennis players still call each other girls, and that's that, ladies and gentlemen.

December 29—West Palm Beach

We visited Wendy Turnbull and Ana Leaird, who share a lovely house in Deerfield Beach. Ana works for Virginia Slims and travels on the tour almost as much as we do. Wendy and Ana's house is very comfortable, very modern, very "Florida," but it's not me. When I was looking for my house in 1979, I checked out some of the modern condominium developments around home, but I found them sterile and out of place. They belong in Florida or California, not in Maryland.

Of everything tennis has given me, my house means the most to me. It was built in 1813. I love old places. I wish my house could talk to me and tell me of the babies born in it, the people who died in it, the parties and the quarrels. I hope it likes all the improvements I've made. There couldn't be a prouder owner. Now if I could just keep my room cleaner. . . .

January 3, 1985—Lutherville

I met with Donald Dell of ProServ today. I had pretty much made up my mind that I wanted IMG to represent me, but now I'm not so sure. Donald's a very persuasive guy. IMG—which is the company that Mark McCormack founded after he had his first marketing success with Arnold Palmer—has more of the big names, including Chris and Martina, and they've already set up a big-money doubles challenge for Martina and me against Bobby Riggs and Vitas Gerulaitis later this year.

I've met several times with Peter Johnson of IMG and we get along fine. But, as Donald said, ProServ's smaller size makes it easier for the company to give its clients more personal attention. Also, they've only got the younger women players, like Carling Bassett and Kathleen Horvath, so I'd be the headliner of their women's division. ProServ is also based in Washington, which would be convenient, although IMG's Cleveland headquarters aren't exactly on the other side of the moon.

Sara Kleppinger Fornaciari, a vice president at ProServ, has become a good friend of mine. Sara was the woman who called me to invite me in as a qualifier in Washington that first time, but I really got to know Sara when she was Tracy Austin's agent. Although I was never too fond of Tracy (nor she of me), I always liked Sara. She's straightforward and honest. She's also from Baltimore, having graduated from Bryn Mawr. (She went into the hospital today with labor pains so she wasn't at my meeting with Donald.) I remember when Advantage International (another management firm) split away from ProServ—Tracy dumped ProServ, partly because her brother Jeff went with Advantage. I thought ProServ did a great job marketing Tracy, especially given her personality and her public-speaking ability.

I remember Sara made a one-day trip to Tokyo during the Gunze tournament that year to try to convince Tracy to stay with ProServ. Tracy said no way, but I thought that was a pretty impressive effort to save a business relationship that had obviously been a friendship as well. Besides, Don's always liked Sara and never completely trusted

IMG. But I know IMG would love to handle me. God, I hope I make the right decision.

January 4—Lutherville

I feel terrible. Andrea Jaeger just called and said an article I wrote for the *New York Times* a couple of weeks ago is causing problems for her. In my article, I discussed the reasons for taking this break from competition and the danger of "burnout." Unfortunately, I mentioned Andrea and Tracy, and now the press is hounding Andrea about being exhibit A of mental burnout. She'd been so happy studying zoology at a community college in Florida, out of the limelight, that I hate to think of anyone bothering her again because of me. Damn!

"Yaegs" doesn't think that she's a mental burnout victim, and I must say, she did have a lot of physical problems. She came to visit me for four days in October 1983 and I took her to see Dr. Charles Silberstein, my orthopedist. I watched him do some reflex testing with that little hammer, and Andrea's left arm reacted, but her right arm didn't respond at all. She obviously had some real nerve problems in her arm. The doctor told her she needed to take several months off, but Yaegs said, "I can't take several months off, I have to play this exhibition and this tournament." With IMG and her parents scheduling her into everything, she felt she had the weight of the world on her shoulders and physically she just couldn't do it.

Andrea had by far the most talent of all the young Americans that I've seen. Her anticipation and court sense were incredible for a kid, and her hand-eye coordination was unbelievable. She went through a two-year period where she was ranked as high as No. 2 in the world for a couple of weeks. She was only 16 or 17 years old at the time. As a matter of fact, she came two points away from breaking my record of being the youngest U.S. Open finalist when she lost to Hana Mandlikova in the semifinals of the 1980 Open.

I hope she comes back some day and blitzes everyone, then retires after a year or two. That would be perfect, because Andrea is probably one of the most thoughtful, considerate players I've ever met, and thoughtful people are not made for life on the pro tour.

Yaegs would always remember birthdays and send valentines and Christmas cards. I remember once when Chris got the flu during a tournament, Andrea delivered a get-well card to her hotel room. And when Tracy first had her back injury, Andrea was one of the first to call her. I think as sensitive as Andrea is, the callousness and competitiveness of the tour just got to her. She had problems adjusting to some of the pettiness and cutthroat aspects. If you live and play on the tour, water definitely has to roll off your back. Her feelings were always hurt too easily, but she'd never admit it. I don't even know if she realized how sensitive she was to things. Certainly, she was different because no one else would have done half the nice things that she did.

And now *I've* hurt her feelings. Damn!

January 5—Lutherville

Don comes home from Australia tomorrow. He stayed over to see his mother, Molly. Don and I haven't seen each other in four weeks, the longest time we've been apart since he started traveling with me when I was 15. It's funny how you think you'll miss someone, but you don't at all. I wonder if Don feels the same way about me. I'm surprised I feel this way, because Don has been more a parent to me than my own parents the last eight years. He's been the one I've come to with all my problems; he's been the one who's always been there. It's weird to have someone who's not your family have that kind of influence on you during those important teenage years, but I can't think of a better person than Don to have had that influence.

My parents never had any qualms about essentially turning over the reins to Don. Lots of times when I was younger, I thought I was playing for Don, and whenever I'd come off the court after a big win I'd say, "Aren't you proud of me?" He'd say, "Of course, I'm proud of you, but you've got to play for yourself." Tennis was something that was ours, separate from my family and separate from his family. I remember once I was playing in Dallas. It was my first big tournament and I'd gotten all the way to the semis where I was going to play Evonne Goolagong. It was a dream week.

Then Don's wife, Elaine, and my parents flew in to surprise me and I was livid. Even at 15, I thought, "This is *my* life, and I wasn't even called and asked if I wanted to share it with them." I'm sure my reaction hurt my folks, but on the other hand, I think they came to understand that I really wanted to keep that dividing line between my tennis life and my family life.

It's very difficult for a non-tennis player to understand how consuming the whole life is—to understand that you don't want to go to the nicest restaurant in town, you don't want to go out with people you just met that day, you don't want to go shopping because you have to rest and turn over all your concentration to the match preparation. My family understands why I haven't invited them to more tournaments, and they've never shown up again without calling or being invited. I really love them too much to expose them to too much of the tour. It's like I want to protect them, and I know that Don and I can take it.

Don's way of handling many of the hardships of the tour is through laughter. He's a typical, fun-loving Aussie with a million stories. The one I love the most is the one Gordon Forbes tells so beautifully in his book *A Handful of Summers*. It's a story about a match Don had against an Italian in Rome. The Italian championships used to be notorious for the partisanship of the linesmen and the fans in *Il Foro Italico*. If an Italian went into a match with no chance at all, the crowd would soon even things up by shouting and clapping for the *paisan* and then booing, whistling, and finally throwing coins at the foreigner if he dared to complain.

Well, Don was playing this Italian and he was in a hard-fought five-setter when a ball whizzes by his ear and falls long by a couple of inches. Don doesn't hear a call and looks to the baselinesman's chair only to find that the chair is empty. So Don goes over to the chair and proceeds to have a lengthy, heated discussion with the empty chair! When the chair umpire asks him what he's doing, Don goes over to the chair and starts explaining to the guy in a loud voice, then suddenly continues moving his lips but not saying anything, so the umpire thinks he's going deaf. Well, by the time Don finished with the guy, he was nearly falling out of his chair trying to hear words that weren't even being spoken! Don may not have won the match, but he definitely won the war.

I can't tell you how many times we've laughed so hard we've cried. We're so close that when he starts to tell one of his stories to someone else I'll fill in the one-liners before he does. I can remember just walking down an airport corridor in, say, Cleveland, and just collapsing in giggles over nothing. I don't think I could ever work with anyone who didn't have a sense of humor.

Somehow things have changed between us the past nine months. There's a tension that's never been there before. It's like we're constantly testing each other. I'm a little anxious about seeing him because we left so many things up in the air about my tennis and his role. He said he'd write me but he didn't. What a fink!

January 6—Lutherville

Maybe I'm learning how to flirt? At Nautilus today I spotted the cutest guy working out a few machines down the line. Our eyes met a couple of times over the sit-up boards. Wow, I thought, he's going to start a conversation.

"Are you finished?" he said. (Some conversationalist!)

"Oh, yes," I said. (What wit!)

But I'm no quitter. So when he got on one of those complicated computerized exercise bikes, I hopped on the bike next to him. The only problem was I didn't know how to program the machine. (Perfect, the damsel in distress.) I asked him to help me out and he punched a few buttons and I was set for ten minutes. (I'd have to work fast.) We pedaled and chatted companionably, but I never got his name because before I could introduce myself it became obvious that he already knew who I was. Damn.

But I did discover he works out around 3:30.

I think I'll have my workouts then, too, and work on my technique.

January 7—Lutherville

Today was doctor day. Podiatrist. Gynecologist. Sports medicine clinic at Children's Hospital in Baltimore. A-OK. Charles Silberstein, my orthopedist, gave me the go-ahead to work on my arm. My most recent arm problems have been rotator cuff troubles and tendinitis caused basically by overuse. My therapist has put me on a program of light repetitions with light weights, say 2½ pounds, lifted at different angles to strengthen all the muscles in the arm. I'll start very slowly and work my way up to twenty minutes straight each day.

I'll also go on the Cybex machines, which work on the principle of resistance—the more you push or pull, the more they resist. Those exercises, plus the dumbbells and the wall pulleys, will build my arm back up. I won't even think of hitting a tennis ball for three or four weeks. I can't wait until my arm gets strong enough so it stops hurting when I play.

I've had troubles with my arm since June 15, 1979. I'll never forget that day because, from that moment on, tennis became a job, and often a painful one, for me. I was warming up in a driving wind- and rainstorm during a tournament in Chichester, England. It was two weeks after my graduation from McDonogh, and I was finally out on my own without any school worries. I was hitting with Greer Stevens when I hit an overhead and heard something pop in my right shoulder. I complained to Greer about it, and she assured me that she had the same thing every day when she warmed up. Of course, she had a reputation for being a notorious hypochondriac; I probably couldn't have chosen a worse person to have an injury with. She had everything in the world wrong with her, so a potentially crippling dislocation of the shoulder joint sounded like a mere twinge to her.

Anyway, I went on and played a singles match that I lost 6–4 in the third to Tanya Harford and then lost a doubles match afterwards. I ended up playing five tough sets with a bum arm. I had to pull out of Wimbledon that year, and I lost five straight first-round matches, including a U.S. Open loss to a qualifier. I took a huge dive in the rankings and never got a correct diagnosis until six months later.

Apparently, I had something called a subluxing joint, which means the joint was slipping inside the socket because the muscles around the joint weren't strong enough to hold it firmly in place. I went on a weight program with dumbbells and wall pulleys, and the pain went away for a while, but I'd still have recurrences. Even now, if I don't do my weights religiously, my arm will start to bother me a lot. I travel with a 5-pound weight and rubber tubing. And I also try to find gyms to work out in every place I go.

Before I was given the medical nod to work on my arm, I had confined my workout to my legs, doing four sets of ten repetitions with each leg on the Nautilus machines. Also, I'm doing more sit-ups than I've ever done. Prince Charming wasn't there yesterday. Nuts!

January 8—Lutherville

I saw Don today. It was so awkward. I told him that I'm definitely going to hire a new *traveling* practice partner, but that I still want him to be my coach. No one knows my game better than he does, and I think he's one of the most underrated coaches in the world.

He's only worked with me and he's not a self-promoter like a Bollettieri is, but I know for a fact that Don could take any number of girls on the tour and get them into the Top Ten within six months. He'd be magic with players who have a good serve and a decent volley but have no clue as to what they're doing on the court.

Look at my game: I don't have any flashy shots; my success is built around percentages. Don taught me how to expose an opponent's weakness, what shot to expect from a certain player when you approach down the line to the backhand, things like that.

I'm not really sure if I'm making the right decision about this practice-partner business. I don't know how all the pieces are going to fit in. I hate uncertainty. I like to be in control and know where I'm headed. Now I have no damn idea. I don't know how much I really want to work at this game. I'm sick of so much of the tennis life. I hate the pressures, the questions, the commitments. What the hell am I going to do?

January 9—Lutherville

What a great day! My career seems like a giant jigsaw puzzle: One day I can't fit one piece into the picture, and the next day all the pieces seem to fall into place. I drove down to Washington to meet Hank Harris, who may become my new hitting partner. He captained the University of Virginia varsity and is currently ranked No. 1 in Virginia and No. 4 in the Middle Atlantic area.

I've seen him play before so when this blond guy in jeans walked up and greeted me in a southern drawl, I knew he must be Hank. He seems low-key and he's obviously stifled in his teaching pro job. I know he's a good player, but personalities are the most important part of this equation. If we can't get along or Hank and Don can't work together, it doesn't matter how well he hits the ball.

January 10—Lutherville

My heart just sank today when I picked up the newspaper and read this headline: MARTINA PICKS NEW PARTNER. The article went on to clarify that Martina had only picked Gigi Fernandez to play with her during *my* time off. Whew.

Never mind how great it is to have Martina next to me in the ad court. She has been such a good friend to me. She's been so loyal, so kind, and she tries to help me with my tennis. Not in big ways, but in subtle ways. Martina seems so powerful and authoritative on the court that most people have no idea how warm-hearted and generous she is. She's just another example, like Chris, of how the public only sees one side of the total personality.

I always feel I can go to her for advice, like the thing with Don, or whether I should take this much time off. She was 100 percent for me taking the break. I just ask for her opinion on a lot of things. It would be easy for her to think, "Well, if Shriver gets too much better, she's going to be even more of a threat." But that's not Martina: She just wants people to play the best tennis they can possibly play.

She's great with the other players. The player ranked No. 100 in the world could be Martina's best friend as well as the one ranked No. 3; ranking has nothing to do with it. I get so upset that people don't know how kind and nice Martina can be. Sure, occasionally she can be rude and she can take some things too personally, but if people could just have dinner with her once, see her laugh, and hear her tell her jokes, they'd see what a good person she is.

And now Gigi is going to be the lucky one to find out what a great partner she is. Jeez!

January 11—Lutherville

I saw him again. Don Juan of the sit-up boards. I checked him out while he lifted weights. His muscles are well-defined, not bulky, and he's what I'd call gently masculine, not macho-rugged. He has brown eyes and, of course, there's a twinkle in them.

We exchanged greetings. I blushed.

We chatted at the sit-up boards. I laughed.

We got downright chummy at the bikes. I stalled and stalled and stalled. Finally I had to leave. But I peaked at his workout card: His name is Terry.

January 12—Lutherville

I've been thinking of buying property on the Eastern Shore, so Dad and I took a break from our hunting trip to check out a farm for sale. Although $800,000 is slightly out of my price range, the piece had over 2000 yards of breathtaking waterfront. Real estate is my favorite kind of investment. Right now I own my house, a condominium in Florida that I rent out, and my tennis club. I think a farm would round out my holdings nicely.

On the drive back along the river, Dad spotted a crippled goose. Its left wing was dragging pathetically, and its neck was limp and stretched low. Dad immediately grabbed his gun and set out after the poor thing. It reminded me of the first time I shot a goose.

I was 13 and already a licensed hunter. We went down to the Eastern Shore and hunted all day. Someone in our group had crippled a goose and I saw my chance to get my first bird, so I chased after it with our dog, Barney. We finally caught up with the goose and I shot it twice. Barney brought it back, but it was still alive. I hated this part, but I twisted its neck to put it out of its misery.

I dragged the goose back and proudly set the poor thing on the picnic table. Dad was out in the water bringing in the decoys when he suddenly started swearing at me. The goose had staggered off the table and was swimming away. After forty-five minutes of cussing and running, Dad finally killed that bird. What a lesson: Geese can play dead. Sort of like tennis players.

January 13—Lutherville

I'm a good boss. As a matter of fact, George Steinbrenner could learn a thing or two from the way I handle my club. For me, Orchard is more than a club, it's part of my childhood. Don gave me my first lesson there in 1971. He was the club pro then. Now I own the place. That's weird, isn't it? But it also makes me appreciate it all the more. It's a friendly, gentle place. Maybe that's why there's such a strong loyalty among my staff.

Mrs. Ennis is the one who symbolizes this spirit most. She's been with Orchard for sixteen years and, at 71, she may look frail, but don't you believe it! She walks a mile and a half to and from work Monday through Friday, through snow, rain, or freezing cold because "I like the exercise." She answers the phone, makes court reservations, bills people, makes coffee, keeps the books. If she comes up a dime short in her deposits, she'll peer through her thick glasses and recount until she finds the dime. And if she has to make a personal call, she'll go use the pay phone in the back. When we raised her weekly salary to the minimum wage, higher than it had ever been, she said, "Did I hear right? That's too much."

People like this are an endangered species.

January 14—Lutherville

I spoke with Steve Stone on the phone tonight. He won the Cy Young award in 1980 when he pitched for the Orioles. Steve and I went out a few times a couple of years ago and had a lot of fun, but the age difference (he's 35) or the social difference (you know what they say about baseball players chasing skirts) got in the way.

Steve's now a baseball commentator for the Chicago Cubs. He invited me to visit him in Chicago in February. I'd like to see him; he's great to talk to and we always have fun, but what would be expected of me? Who cares what's expected of me? I do what I feel comfortable doing, and if he or anyone isn't happy about it, tough!

Should I go?

January 15—Lutherville

My room is a mess. My clothes are strewn on the bed, the floor, the chest. A pink-striped sock is hanging out of a drawer. My wastebasket is in the middle of the room. It doesn't belong there. I should get out of bed and clean up, but it's too warm and cozy here.

My bed is my friend. Pink sheets, electric blanket, down comforter, bedspread decorated with fruits and vegetables. I don't want to move. So what if a pink-striped sock is hanging out of a drawer? Let it stay there forever!

Why am I discussing my bed?!

Hugh Burgess, my English teacher during my senior year at McDonogh, has been giving me a private class in journal writing the past few weeks. He said if I couldn't think of anything to write about I should describe something that means a lot to me.

My bed is an extremely private part of me. My bed is queen-size, which means I can spread out, toss and turn, have clothes on it without feeling cramped. I've never fallen out of my bed. It's always waiting for me. My bed is loyal. I love my bed.

The end. (I wonder what Mr. Burgess will make of this!)

January 16—Lutherville

Am I being tested for patience and perseverance? It's 5:00 a.m. I just woke up. My elbow is hurting, a stiff, sore, dull pain. I played yesterday for about fifteen minutes. That was it. I did everything I should have done to prevent this: I took two aspirin a half hour before I played; I stretched and warmed up my arm with a moist heating pad; I hit mostly forehands (my backhand has caused my elbow problems since last March). When I was finished, I immediately packed ice on my elbow and shoulder. My arm should not feel terrible.

Dr. Silberstein has suggested cortisone injections before, but I've cringed at the thought of that big needle being shoved in my joint and turned all around so the juices can ooze into all the nooks and crannies of my elbow. Now I've exhausted all other avenues. I've rested for five weeks and I've been diligent about doing my exercises at the sports clinic. Why does my arm hurt?

My right arm has become a focal point in my life, and I hate that. The other day, I found this note I wrote myself at a tournament in Arizona in 1979. About three months before, I had hurt my shoulder for the first time in Chichester. The note was my brave attempt to put mind over matter. It said:

"I'm so worried about my shoulder, which aches now as I write. The pain is so frightening because of its intensity. I want so much to get rid of this pain. I must be strong. I must be strong."

I was 17 years old when I wrote that. I don't think it's good that a game brings kids to writing things like that. I don't think it's good when young adults are still writing the same things five years later.

January 17—Lutherville

God, just when you start feeling sorry for yourself, life has a way of putting your problems into perspective. Brian Gibbons's girlfriend died of leukemia last week. I'm trying to write him a condolence letter. I don't remember if I met Mandy, but I've known Brian for ten years. We played each other two or three times in high school competition. We also met in a much-publicized match for the state high school singles championship my sophomore year.

Brian was the No. 1 seed, No. 1 in his age group, and I was seeded No. 2 and a top-ranked women's player. Battle of the sexes, Baltimore-style. Brian had a ridiculous amount of pressure on him. If he lost to a girl in the state finals, he wouldn't be allowed to forget it.

He was attractive, tall (my height), and, like most tennis players, he had muscles in all the right places. He was also obnoxious. On the court, he yelled (so did I) and knew all the tricks. When we started the match, the court was lined with a couple hundred people, some hanging from trees. It wasn't a pretty match. He started to try to psyche me out by doing things like standing over against the fence while I was serving. Ploys like that are unsporting and he didn't need them anyway. He was a better, stronger player than I was. I double-faulted about fifteen times and he won 6–3, 6–4.

Both Brian and I have matured since that match. He's in law school now and after four years of dating, he and Mandy had decided to get married. Brian had helped Mandy through two years of treatments, remission, and pain. Now she's dead.

So what if my arm hurts.

January 18—Lutherville

Hank Harris drove up from Alexandria to meet Don today. We all went to T.G.I.Friday for a bite. I thought it might be awkward or competitive for them, but they got along well. They both seem to be cut from the same affable, easy-going cloth. There was a funny moment when Don, expounding on his theories of tennis, knocked a cup of boiling-hot tea into my lap and was so wrapped up in his demonstration that he nonchalantly handed me a napkin and went right on with his explanation! Hank's eyes got real big, and it wasn't until a few minutes later that Don came to enough to ask me if I'd been scalded or not! All in all, I'd call it a successful first meeting between my once and future(?) touring partners.

January 19—Lutherville

Well, it looks as if my dilemma about which tennis management company—IMG or ProServ—to sign with has been solved for me. Peter Johnson of IMG called late this afternoon and told me, "I'm going to make the decision easy for you; IMG is withdrawing its offer to you." I was shocked because I had called Peter earlier in the day and told him I was leaning toward ProServ, but that I hadn't totally made up my mind. I was going to go away for the weekend and make the decision in seclusion. I told him I'd give him the final word on Monday. So two hours after I talked to him, he calls back and withdraws IMG's bid. Obviously, these guys hate to lose as much as tennis players do, and he was telling me, in effect, "You can't fire me, I quit."

I was stunned, but now I'm relieved because I don't have to make that tough phone call on Monday; Peter made the decision easier for me. I'm really happy I'm with ProServ now. I'll be the No. 1 woman in their stable and the only one in the world's Top Ten. Donald's a shrewd guy and Sara will be my personal agent. Tracy Austin's former agent is now *my* agent; that's an ironic twist, isn't it?

P.S. Sara had a baby girl, Sara Blake, on January 4.

January 20—Washington, D.C.

I've been part of tennis history, and tonight I was part, albeit a minute part, of political history: I went to an inaugural ball for the President of the United States. It was only one of nine inaugural balls around town on this night, but nonetheless I was close enough to see the twinkle in the Vice President's eyes, close enough to chat with former Secretary of Defense Donald Rumsfeld (he's one of my old pro-am partners), close enough to talk tennis with U.N. Ambassador Jeane Kirkpatrick. She really impressed me: She just oozed intelligence, elegance, and savvy.

I've been a staunch Republican since I was first able to vote in 1980, and I guess some strong political genes run in the family. Sargent Shriver is a distant cousin and my father's brother, Dick Shriver, worked at the Pentagon under President Nixon and has been at the Treasury the past few years under President Reagan. Uncle Dick has been one of my chief sounding boards for questions about our government and politics. I've always been interested in knowing how our government works, and it's been in the back of my mind to maybe break into politics in some capacity when I retire.

Early last year I got in touch with the President's reelection committee to offer my help, and they asked me to be the honorary chair of Women to Re-elect Reagan in Maryland. It was funny because most of the women on this committee were way up in the political or corporate hierarchy, and they were referred to as the "Honorable this" and the "Honorable that," or the "Senator this" and the "Representative that," and there I was—Pam Shriver, Lutherville, Maryland. Anyway I went to a few political rallies and made some phone calls for the reelection campaign, and now I'm on the list of staunch Republicans who get invited to inaugural balls. That's kinda neat.

Today actually started with an inaugural brunch given at the Mayflower Hotel and finally wound down at a cozy little affair for 5000 at the Washington Convention Center. Well, where else are 5000 going to dance, drink, and mingle? My escort for the day was Michael Sonnenfeld, a lawyer who lives next door to my parents and just happens to be 6 feet, 5 inches tall. This was one time I wasn't asking my sister Marion to be my escort!

January 23—Dallas

I've come to Dallas to visit the Belknaps, go shopping at Neiman-Marcus, get my legs waxed, and see John. Not necessarily in that order.

I met John Field last year when I played in Dallas. I never stay in private houses, because then you have to keep your room neat and smile all the time, but in Dallas I make an exception and stay with Ralph and Lucy Belknap and their daughters, Kate and Laura. The Belknaps understand tennis players and they don't make a fuss. Besides, Kate is my age and we're so alike we're almost alter egos. We're both lifelong jocks. We can't stand frilly clothes or gobs of makeup. We like each other and ourselves the way we are.

It's thanks to Kate that I met John, who is the Belknap's nephew. He is the only important male I've ever met on tour, so maybe I should stay in houses more often. I guarantee you, Mr. Right is not hanging around any Best Western piano bar or any Ramada video game room.

Anyway, it was during tournament week last year, and John just happened to like Mexican food and the sound of one of Kate's impromptu get-togethers for a few of her friends at a local restaurant. I remember John joined us late, hopping over a railing to get to our table. I looked him over: a pleasant face, stout build, jeans, and a warm smile. He pulled up a chair and introduced himself.

After dinner, Kate, John, and I drove back to the Belknaps' house where John and I talked for hours. The next night we did the same thing. His life fascinated me: He'd been on his own since he was 17 when his mother moved to Europe and John chose to remain in Texas. His dad had died when John was 6. He seemed much more mature than any other 24-year-old guy I'd met. Not that I'd really gotten to know that many.

Being a woman tennis player—particularly one who's 6 feet tall—is not the greatest insurance, as I've said, for an enhanced social life. You're insulated and isolated much of the time, and if you do meet a young man he's liable to wonder if you're a lesbian. If he doesn't, all he offers you is a quick sexual relationship—as a big favor to you, of course.

But I got a chance to really know John in Dallas, and we started to phone and write. He has visited me three times since last March, and we've had some wonderful moments together. It's just that the distance is so bloody frustrating.

January 25—Dallas

I am not what you'd call a clotheshound. My fashion taste runs toward "preppy feminine," i.e., well-tailored and plenty of corduroy, and my mother would probably faint if I ever wore a skirt except under threat of death. But I do love a bargain and Dallas seems to set off my shopping genes. The semiannual Last Call Sale at Neiman-Marcus is over tomorrow, so I was pawing through the orphans and rejects there today. Three shirts, an overcoat, one pair of pants, one belt, two sweaters, one blazer, and four pair of underwear now have a new home. Just call it Boutique Shriver.

While I was at Neiman's, I also had my legs waxed. For the uninitiated, leg waxing is torture *and* you pay for it. But the torture is worth the pain if the leg hairs don't grow back for more than a month. This is important to a female tennis player, especially one visiting a guy named John.

I'd never tried leg waxing before, but I'll give anything a try once. I hadn't shaved my legs since returning from the Bahamas, so I resembled a leggy bear. (I was told there must be long hairs or else the waxing won't work.) I walked confidently into Madame England's "wax museum" at Neiman's. Actually, it is a large beauty salon with a smaller salon behind it where Mrs. England has been waxing legs for twenty-seven years. Do you believe that? Twenty-seven years of ripping off hairs, causing agony to thousands of women. Why, she's probably ripped out zillions of follicles!

Here's what that sweet little old lady did to me. First she applied a steaming layer of hot wax onto the backs of my calves. She firmly pressed a strip of cloth over the waxed area. Then with one sharp, rapid tear, the defoliation began. She pressed another cloth over the same area and let *it* rip. I looked back at my leg, trying to remain calm. Was there any skin there? Fortunately, I had only requested waxing from the knee down.

Mrs. England tore away at the backs of my legs for fifteen minutes, then she went to work on the fronts. "The shin and knee areas tend to be more painful," Mrs. England said, interrupting my thoughts, obliterating my hopes. Twenty minutes later, my legs were red and stinging, but smooth, and Mrs. England was $40 richer. Forty dollars! What a rip-off! Literally.

January 26—Dallas

This visit has made me realize how special John is to me. He is one of the few men that I have imagined myself marrying and raising a family with. And he has made me feel attractive to and comfortable with men my own age. What a relief.

As a touring tennis player, I only seem to meet older men. And the few times we play tournaments with the guys, I've found male tennis players to be unsociable or shy or both. It's so bad that if a male player merely says hi to me, I think he's wonderful. You have to go so far out of your way to get them to have a conversation with you, it's ridiculous. Like you have to barge into the men's locker room.

I sense a lot of jealousy from the men toward the women players. I can't honestly say I blame some of the guys. If I was a guy ranked No. 100 in the world, struggling to make it, and I saw some woman like Pam Shriver earning almost $500,000 in prize money a year on the tour, yet I knew if I played her I'd absolutely demolish her, *that* would bother me. I guess it drove Larry Holmes nuts in the same way when little Sugar Ray Leonard was getting all the attention in boxing. Oh, well.

Nonetheless, there is some dating between men and women players, but not as much as there was when everybody played the same tournaments. Now we only have six tournaments together, and that makes any relationship that begins a complicated one to maintain. But when you break it down, those eight or ten weeks the men and women play the same tournaments probably add up to as much time as the women players see their non-tennis boyfriends, unless they're traveling together. So I think in the last couple of years, players dating other players has come back into vogue a bit more. Laura Arraya married Heinz Gildemeister, who played Davis Cup for Chile. Liz Smylie's husband, Peter, was a player. Kathy Jordan dated Eliot Teltscher for a while, and, of course, there was Chris Evert and Jimmy Connors and now there is Chris Evert and John Lloyd.

Despite these healthy signs however, most of the guys on the men's tour have stereotyped the women as a whole bunch of lesbians. Last month, when I was playing in Melbourne with the men, one of the guys told me he thought 50 percent of the women on the tour were homosexual. I told him he wasn't even in the ballpark, but he looked at me cynically. I said, "All right, which half do you think I'm in?"

"You play doubles with Martina, don't you?" he said. I should have hit him, but he wasn't worth the effort.

February 1—Palm Beach Gardens

Life's a howl! Last week I thought my career was in jeopardy because my arm hurt, and my attitude was as sore as my elbow. Now everything is stupendous. I've come down to Florida to work out at the Palm Beach Sports Medicine Clinic and to hit a few balls. Every other day I'm driving forty minutes south on I-95 to the clinic to take advantage of the extensive exercise equipment there.

Yesterday I received my first laser treatment. It's not as bizarre as it sounds: A small laser beam directed at the sore area travels deep into the cells of soft tissue and promotes healing. All in ten painless minutes. How it does this, I couldn't tell you. But it sure beats the hell out of cortisone.

I also had a full physical evaluation at the clinic: blood pressure, resting pulse, body fat, flexibility, grip strength, cardiovascular condition, and leg strength. I measured good to excellent in every category except calf flexibility. (Mrs. England probably ripped that out of me in the leg waxing!)

The leg strength test was a riot. I was strapped into a Cybex machine, which works on the principle of resistance: The harder you work, the harder it resists. A computer then measures range of motion, strength, endurance, and differential between right and left legs. You need a master's degree to understand the printout, but it seems I have a 15 percent deficiency in my right leg. I measure 126 foot-pounds of resistance in my left leg compared to 113 in my right. Not to worry, four out of five tennis players have a discrepancy in the strength of the two legs (I bet Martina's the fifth!) because the stronger leg is the push-off leg on the serve. It'll be interesting to compare my measurements after I've been back on tour for six months.

February 4—Palm Beach Gardens

My arm has never felt stronger, and the other aspects of my tennis life are coming together as well. I've decided to hire Hank Harris to be my touring practice partner. He plays well, mixes up his shots, and should be an easy traveling companion. Moreover, he and Don get along fine. I'm glad this is all settled because it's vital to my development to have a practice partner who will make me work on what *I* need to work on. If I have to practice with the other players on tour, I spend half the time hitting shots *they* want to practice.

I've signed the contract with Donald Dell and Sara Fornaciari for ProServ to represent me. When I told Donald that IMG withdrew its bid, he said, "Well, *we're* still very interested in you." That made me feel good.

Maybe it's the rejuvenating effects of the Florida sunshine, but I feel in control of my mind and body for the first time in months. Time is on my side: I don't have to accomplish all my goals in one year. Don is in place as my supervisory coach, Hank is ready to roll, Sara is already at work on the commercial and endorsement fronts. The rest is up to me. I'm ready to take on the world.

February 6—Palm Beach Gardens

I've just heard awful news. Don's mother, Molly Candy, has suffered a stroke. As if that wasn't bad enough, she lives on the other side of the world—in Adelaide, South Australia. Don is on his way back the 12,000 miles to see how extensive the paralysis on her left side is.

Molly is my third grandmother. I remember vividly the first time I met her. It was on November 25, 1979, the day before I played my first-ever match in Australia. I hadn't won a single match since the previous June, and a shoulder injury had kept me on the sidelines for three months. I'd lost five first-round matches in a row, and my ranking was down in the dumps with my confidence. Molly flew in to Melbourne to see me play Janet Newberry. I won the match and Molly won my heart.

I've sat with Molly for hours in one of the three giant chairs in her living room and listened to the story of her life. She is a complex and passionate woman, flamboyant, opinionated, stubborn, generous, and emotional. We have laughed hysterically together, shed tears together. Molly adores tennis and has encouraged me in every conversation, every visit, every letter. She *knows* I'm going to win Wimbledon and the U.S. Open. "It's only a matter of time, honey," she says.

Now I wish I could talk to her and be the one to encourage her. Don and I are going to see her in May because I have two tournaments in Australia then. But that's still months away, so I sent her a card signed by Chris, Martina, Wendy Turnbull, Virginia Wade, Sharon Walsh, and me. Please, Molly, get well. I love you.

February 8—Palm Beach Gardens

I played my first set of tennis in two months. I've been hitting 1½ to 2 hours every day for the past four days. Occasionally, my elbow or forearm hurts a little, but I think that's from the frequency of play and not an injury. Soreness is fine but lasting pain means trouble. My shoulder feels 98 percent, elbow 90 percent. I miss the competition and am looking forward to my return to the tour.

I went over to Delray Beach where the men and women are playing a new big-draw, huge-prize money event, The Lipton International Players Championships. It was fun to see everybody again and dispel the rumors (there are always rumors in the tennis world) that I was retiring. I also got a lot of well-meant, but unsolicited, advice about my game. Why am I such a charity case?

Fred Stolle said I should learn to hit a flat backhand passing shot. Pancho Segura suggested working with him on my forehand. Roy Emerson told me to forget topspin and just get into the strongest possible shape because endurance will win the most matches when you play as smart as I do. John Newcombe couldn't get away from the subject of sex long enough to tell me how to improve my game. Or maybe he was suggesting that sex might help my tennis? Hmmm.

All these guys are friends of mine, and I respect them so much because they achieved everything in the game *and* retained their dignity and camaraderie. It's funny how much better I get along with these older guys than I do with today's male players. I think part of me would love to have played back then. Of course, that's silly because there wouldn't have been any money. But they had so much fun. Sure, they worked hard, but at the end of the day it was over. I've listened to enough stories to feel that I've lived a small part of it.

I like Emmo's advice best because I know I could train much harder. I could do wind sprints and more weight exercises. I'm not sure I can change my strokes this late in my career, even to save wear and tear on my arm. If you start changing technical things around, you might not have an arm problem, but you might not win any matches either.

But Fred also made sense when he said I should learn to hit a flat backhand. I *can* hit a flat or slightly overspin backhand, but often I'm afraid to lose so I use my safe, slice backhand. I must get over the fear of trying new shots in matches, especially shots I hit in practice. If the new shot results in a loss or two early but eventually teaches me to win points in crucial situations, failing now would be worth it. Be bold, Pam. Be bold.

February 10—Lutherville

One of my intentions during my break is to get more involved in activities in Baltimore. I love my hometown and I'm very proud of it. When that creep Robert Irsay, who owns the Colts, stole the team out of Baltimore in the middle of the night a couple years ago, and put them in some city in the midwest, I was so furious I wrote a letter to *Sports Illustrated.* Got printed, too. My publishing debut.

Anyway, Frank Deford grew up in Baltimore, too, and he's the chairman of the Cystic Fibrosis Foundation, so when he found out he was going to speak at a big CF dinner in Baltimore honoring Jim Palmer, he invited me and I cleared my schedule. Not only is Jim a great guy, but he's spent years working for the Foundation, making appearances, lending his name, even contributing the money he makes from those underwear posters. I admire Jim for that. Not enough athletes give enough back.

The reason Frank got involved with CF is that his daughter Alex had it. She died five years ago when she was 8. When Frank started speaking about Alex and all that she suffered, I was horrified. I was sitting between two perfect strangers and I was bawling like a baby.

February 12—Lutherville

I have a problem finishing books. Reading, like spelling, has never been my strong suit. Luckily for you reading *this,* you're getting the corrected version of my manuscript. But anyway, I just finished reading *Alex, the Life of a Child,* which is the book Frank wrote about his daughter after she died, and the only problem I had in reading it was making out the words through my tears. We just don't think enough. I bitch about a sore arm and bad feet and things like that, and here's a little girl who couldn't breathe and who didn't even live to be the age I was when I started playing tennis.

Alex also made me think of my sister Eleanor. They were both born the same year, 1971, and then Alex died on Eleanor's ninth birthday. I was 8 when Eleanor was born, and I remember Mom explaining to me that there were some complications in the pregnancy because of her age—she was almost 37 then. Mom had to spend several months in bed so she wouldn't miscarry, and there were fears that Eleanor might be born retarded. Mom made a promise to herself that if Eleanor was born healthy, she'd quit smoking. And she did, cold turkey. She hasn't touched a cigarette in fourteen years.

February 14—Lutherville

I feel good inside that I spent Valentine's Day 1985 attending a sports banquet at Our Lady of Fatima Church. The church, located in the heart of an ethnic neighborhood in East Baltimore, organized the sports night to benefit their scholarship fund. I was happy to do this appearance without compensation.

I drove over to the church with Chris Thomas, one of the local sportscasters. First we shared a light beer and some hors d'oeuvres with some of the priests. Before we set out for the hall, I excused myself and asked for the "ladies' room." Then I froze: There aren't any ladies' rooms in a priests' house, you dummy! One of the fathers gracefully ignored my slip and led me to a bathroom. There I discovered that my period had come two days early. Of all places to get my period! I could just hear myself saying, "Excuse me, father, do you have a tampon or a maxipad?" I chuckled at the thought, then relaxed and went out to field the questions of a sports congregation.

The people were blue-collar, salt of the earth, so appreciative. I was comfortable with them from the first moment; I hope I can do more with them in the future. I even got payment: One of the priests blessed my arm.

February 18—Lutherville

Reporters are such a pain sometimes. They always seem ready to sucker in the uninitiated and pounce on the unwary. I did an interview with a writer from *Baltimore Magazine* the other day, and before our luncheon was over I'd almost choked on my beef barley soup. You see, I thought I had him pegged, but his effrontery still surprised me.

During the interview, I mentioned in passing that I'd attended the church sports night on Valentine's Day. And the guy from *Baltimore* latched on to that and asked me, "Wouldn't you have rather spent that night with your valentine?"

Aha, a clever way of asking me, "Do you have a boy/girlfriend?"

"That would have been difficult because he lives in Dallas," I said.

Then came the zinger. "Do you worry about people wondering what your sexual preference is because you play doubles with Martina?" I should have hit him, but he wasn't worth the trouble.

February 20—Lutherville

Today I played a practice set against Elise Burgin and won 7–6. We played a lot against each other as kids, but then I turned pro and she went to Stanford, where she got her degree in communications. Elise finally turned pro herself last June, and now she's ranked in the top fifty in the world. I think that's pretty neat to have two girls from Baltimore numbered among the world's top fifty, even if we are totally different types of players. She's a lefty and a baseliner. But Elise is a great friend and an intelligent match player. I was pleased to win today, especially since it was only my third set of tennis since December 10.

For the first time in five weeks, I served at full speed. Although my serve was erratic, I felt no pain in my shoulder. My elbow hurt only a couple of times when I stretched wide on the backhand. I came up with some new shots to win key points, one a flat backhand crosscourt angle return of serve in the tiebreaker. Making shots like that one will mean the difference between raising my game to another level or staying in the same place.

Although my volleys weren't that sharp and my groundstrokes were a bit shaky, I think I'm right on schedule. I should be playing well by the first week of March.

February 24—En route

Right now, I'm sitting in a center seat on a flight to San Diego, and we're forty minutes late. Normally, I wouldn't care, but John is coming out to see me when we stop over at DFW airport, and our forty-five-minute layover is about to become a five-minute layover.

Typical. John drives all the way to DFW, our flight is too late for us to have a pleasant visit, but we're seconds too early to miss the connecting flight and the next flight out is overbooked, so I can't change my reservations. My social life is doomed!

I'm back on the plane, but I am a little more cheered up because I just read the note John gave me. There were also some pictures in the envelope. One was of John and me at a debutante ball. The picture was from the society section. The caption read: TENNIS ACE PAM SHRIVER WITH JOHN FIELD ATTENDING THE TERPSICHOREAN BALL. You know, that's the first published picture of me with a date.

February 25—San Diego

I'm staying with my grandmother Moppie while I get ready for this doubles tournament. Moppie lives in Coronado, and the place is full of the memories of childhood visits: shopping at the naval commissary, visiting Baskin-Robbins for ice cream, playing bingo every Tuesday night at North Island Air Base. Those bingo games were the worst. We were always beaten by seedy old ladies who had eight cards in front of them to our one or two. Moppie, Marion, and I were amateurs compared to those hardened biddies.

February 26—San Diego

For the past two weeks my arm hasn't bothered me. Not at all. So today, as soon as I get back on tour, my elbow and forearm are as sore as they were in December when I quit. My mind is so confused. My arm rules my life, and I resent that.

February 27—San Diego

This is a special "scrambles" doubles tournament, with the teams handicapped to make it more even. There are eight teams, with the top eight players picking their partner by reverse order of their singles ranking: No. 8 picks first, then No. 7, on down to Martina who picks last. I had the sixth pick and chose JoAnne Russell. To be accurate, Russ picked me. She's one of my oldest and best friends on the tour, and now she lives three doors down from me in Baltimore.

I first met JoAnne at the first pro tournament I ever played, that one in Washington in January '78. She came right up to me in the locker room and said, "Hi, I'm JoAnne Russell." I was stunned. Still am. Remember, this was the same tournament where three older players snubbed me until they found out I had the only practice balls in the arena. JoAnne was one of only two players ever to introduce herself to me. Mary Carillo was the other. JoAnne and Mary are still two of my best friends, and I'll always remember their kindness my first year on tour.

JoAnne and I practiced with Hank and Pancho Segura this morning. Pancho is 63 now and so bowlegged some people think he's crippled. But his legs have always been like that, and in the '40s and

'50s he covered the court as few players ever have. He hits with two hands on both sides, and his two-handed forehand has been called one of the greatest shots ever hit. Don has been an admirer of Segura's for years, and I remember his telling me, "Everyone knew that if the little man hit a forehand the point would be over."

Segura coached Jimmy Connors when Jimbo was still a brash teenager transplanted from Bellville, Illinois, to Beverly Hills, and Pancho remained Jimmy's personal tutor through most of his big years. Pancho is a shrewd tactician, and a practice session with him is rich in both substance and laughter.

Segura's nickname is Sneaky, but there's nothing sneaky about his language. After he hits a bad shot, you might hear, "Just like what happens when old people make love . . . nothing." Both JoAnne and I were in stitches out there today.

February 28—San Diego

Chrysler, the sponsor of this tournament, hosted a cocktail party last night, and although it was optional, JoAnne and I decided to go. Cocktail parties are the same at every tournament, and I always get the exact same questions, in order:

"How's your arm?"

"What's Martina like?"

"Do you get sick of travel?"

"Where do you go from here?"

"Can I get you a drink?"

"Where do you live?"

"How long have you been playing?"

Better, thanks; great fun; sometimes; Princeton; no, thank you; outside Baltimore; eighteen years.

Here comes somebody else.

"How's your arm?"

March 1—San Diego

My first tournament in almost three months. It was predictable for me. I wasn't good returning serve or playing the big points, but I never lost my serve. JoAnne and I lost 6–2, 7–6 (8–6) to Kathy Jordan and Alycia Moulton. They've been playing the tour regularly, and it showed. Even though I didn't produce on the crucial points, I faced enough of them in the second set so that I think I'll be prepared for them in my singles next week. Also, we fought our way back into the second set, which was good for my confidence.

But it's going to take me a few more outings before I regain my match nerves. At 6–6 in the tiebreaker, I mis-hit an easy overhead into the middle of the net. I knew I was going to butcher it because I felt ill while the ball was still in the air! That choke cost us the second set.

March 2—San Diego

Today was a challenge for my patience, my nerves, and my arm. We survived two rain delays, a 40-mph wind, and an uncomfortable chill to outlast Manuela Maleeva and Anne Smith in the consolations. I felt much better on the court. Although I lost my serve three times, I feel as if I have a little excuse because I was serving into the wind. I returned exceptionally well; as a matter of fact, I can only remember two returns I didn't make.

JoAnne and I were relieved that we won and will leave here with something in our pockets. This tournament is a winner-take-all, so if we had lost in the first round of the consolation as well as in the first round of the main draw we would have left with zilch, zero, *nada*, nothing. Now the pressure is off, and we don't even have to worry about choking at the thought of playing for $270,000 and a new car in the finals.

March 3—San Diego

It was weird today, because Martina and I played doubles against each other (in the consolation finals) for the first time in 4½ years. Together, we've won our last eighty-two matches, and we've also won eight straight Grand Slam titles, which nobody else has ever done—singles or doubles, men or women.

I can still remember when I first got up the gumption to ask Martina to play with me. It was at Eastbourne in June 1980, and I knew Billie Jean, Martina's regular partner, probably wasn't going to Australia for the year-end tournaments six months later. So I sent Don (I can't believe what a chicken I was) to ask Martina something like, "Would it be OK if Pam came up to you and asked if you have a partner for Australia?" Martina said, "Oh, sure, she can come up to me and ask me because I don't think Billie Jean's playing."

Well, it took me another two days to get up the nerve to approach Martina in the locker room and ask her to play. And she looked at me and said, "Oh, well, if Billie Jean doesn't play I'll probably play with Rosie (Casals)." At that time I still didn't realize how fast things could change in two days on the women's tour! Anyway, I stood there with egg on my face feeling about 2 feet tall.

So I was even more stunned later that fall when Martina called *me* while I was hanging out in the tournament trailer in Deer Creek, Florida, and asked me if I could play Australia with her. In the four months between Eastbourne and Deer Creek, Rosie had dropped out of Australia. It gave me a small measure of satisfaction to explain to Martina that I already had a commitment to play with Betty Stove, but that I could certainly squeeze her in beginning in January. And ironically, the last time I played against Martina in doubles was when Betty and I beat Martina and Betsy Nagelsen in Sydney. It's the only time I've ever beaten Martina in doubles.

Today JoAnne and I lost to Navratilova-Reynolds, but I burned Martina three times with returns hit down her line. I enjoyed those shots as much as any I've ever hit, because Martina wants us to switch sides now, with me moving to the ad court. I just wanted to prove this small point returning from the deuce court, which is the more comfortable position for me. But Martina says she can return serve better from the right side. Also, because she's a lefty, with her on that side both of our forehands will be down the middle and we can poach better with our forehand volleys. OK, but if we lose our streak right away, I'm going to pick my first fight with her.

We get along so well. The longer I know Martina, the more she fascinates me. Of all the people who've been around her on tour—coaches, friends, advisers—I've lasted the longest. And for all that time she's been my most loyal friend. My first summer on the tour, 1978, I beat Martina in the semifinals of the U.S. Open. I actually felt a little sorry for her. She was No. 1 in the world and the Wimbledon champion, and this duckfooted kid had beaten her in two tiebreakers while planes flew over every twenty-eight seconds and rain forced two delays. I remember when her final backhand passing shot sailed long, I just bowed my head and went to the net to shake hands. I told her, "Gee, I'm sorry, the conditions were pretty bad today."

The press even picked up on it. "I just didn't want to rub it in," I said. I guess that's one of my problems. Should a victorious athlete ever feel sorry for a vanquished opponent? I always do.

Then in the '82 Open I gave Martina an even more painful defeat in the quarterfinals when she was going for the Grand Slam. She had some whiney moments, as we all do, but by the time I got back to the locker room there was a note waiting for me. It was from Martina. "Pam: Congratulations. You played well, and since you beat me, win the tournament. You can do it!" In all the years I've played tennis, I've never heard of another loser writing the winner to wish her well. But that's Martina. She's so sensitive, but so misunderstood. The public has no idea what a generous, vulnerable person she is.

March 4—Princeton

One thing I've sensed lately is that the tour is more natural, nicer. For one thing, there are more men around. There's more money in the game so a lot of the girls are traveling with their coaches along. Or agents sometimes. And recently, more of the players are traveling with their husbands or boyfriends. It's still a relatively new concept for a guy to give up his career to travel on the women's tour, but I guess people are beginning to come to grips with the idea. I'm not sure I could get married and have my husband travel with me, though. Ideally, I would like to play another six or seven years and then settle down. Marrying a tennis player doesn't interest me at all. But it's certainly healthier out here with a larger male presence.

The tour lifestyle is too tough for a woman alone. That's when some of the homosexual relationships start. What happens is a girl who's been out on the tour for a few years gets depressed. She's probably had a steady boyfriend, but the distance or something broke that up, and she's vulnerable.

In men's athletics, it seems drugs or alcohol can become a problem when a player is down in the dumps. On our tour, though, it can be another woman—maybe an older one who's already had some homosexual relationships. So she befriends a younger player. And the comfort and convenience of that leads to a sexual relationship.

I'm not passing judgment. Sometimes I wonder if I hadn't always had Don traveling with me, taking me out to dinner or for a beer now and then, maybe I could have been just as vulnerable to another woman's approaches when I was especially sad or lonely.

Still, there's not nearly as much of that stuff as people think, and there will probably be less now that we're getting more men on the tour. You just can't beat good, solid male companionship.

March 5—Princeton

Just before my warm-up this morning I saw Don. He had driven up from Baltimore to give me moral support for my first singles match back. I was so happy to see him, because I'm feeling a bit unsettled for this tournament. I always like to be at the tournament site two days before a singles match, but the rain in San Diego messed up my schedule. Also, playing on the west coast outdoors in a doubles event the week before an east coast singles and doubles tournament indoors is not my idea of good preparation, but I'd committed to both events before I knew the particulars. Don was just the stabilizing influence I needed at this moment.

I gave him a big hug. Well, two big hugs—one for reassurance. He still has doubts about his role in my career, and now that I have Hank to hit with, he doesn't want to come to tournaments and feel like a spare member of an entourage. But he understands I need someone young like Hank to practice with. I like Hank and it is working out well.

Welcome back, Pammy. My first singles match in three months, and I beat Laura Gildemeister two and three. I couldn't feel any better about myself at this moment. And my arm doesn't hurt. I want to open my hotel window and shout, "Watch out, girls! Shriver is back!"

March 6—Princeton

The trouble with the younger players is that they see themselves as invincible. So when they get an injury, they have difficulty dealing with it. Don always advised me to pull out of tournaments when I was hurt, to think long-term, but a lot of coaches and parents haven't been that protective of their kids. Mostly the younger players do it to themselves, though.

One young American player limped off the court the other day, obviously in great pain. Donna Pallulat, our Women's Tennis Association trainer, said she should take at least ten days off. "But I can't take any time off," the kid said. "If I don't play Dallas, I'll get passed in the points, and I won't make the Slims championships." Typical. She'll risk a serious career injury to keep playing and make the bonus pool.

March 7—Princeton

Last night I beat Bettina Bunge in a tiebreaker in the third. It felt especially good because I'd choked the last couple of third-set tiebreakers I'd played. Bunge is one of those players with unlimited potential who occasionally has problems between the ears, and I had to play smart and tough—especially in the tiebreaker—to beat her.

Then today I lost 7–6, 6–3 to Catherine Tanvier, but I'm not upset. I didn't play poorly. What I played like was somebody who'd had to go to 7–6 in the third just fifteen hours before. Tanvier is another one of the young, athletic, aggressive Europeans. Almost all the impressive young players nowadays are from Europe: Claudia Kohde-Kilsch and Steffi Graf from West Germany; Helena Sukova from Czechoslovakia; Pascale Paradis and Tanvier from France; the mopey Maleeva sisters from Bulgaria.

Besides the Europeans, there's also Gabriela Sabatini from South America and Carling Bassett from Canada. Carling is so neat, original, and flamboyant in everything she does. She's even a flamboyant baseliner. She's the only one of the younger players that I can hang out with, and I really got to know her well down in Australia. She had a crush on some Australian junior—in between the times she was pining away over Stefan Edberg—and so one time she decided to go after the young Aussie's heart through his stomach, and she dragged me along to help cook dinner for the boy and his mates. That was the first time in my life I ever was a chaperone. Carling made a pretty good impression on the Aussie, too, but I'm afraid that distance took the measure of a budding romance. It doesn't matter, though. She's always got a crush on somebody new, no matter where in the world the tour takes us.

Sabatini also has a lot of flair—much more than the two-handed baseliners from the States. The young Americans who play from back there never seem to show any imagination. They're Chrissie clones without her genius. It's crazy, but at 22 I'm the youngest American serve-and-volleyer in the top thirty—and already I feel like I've been around forever.

March 8—Princeton

After our doubles match last night, I was with Hank and an old school friend of mine, Craig Fitchett, on the way to the bar. Martina saw me and came over and said, "Why don't you stop by? Brooke is coming over."

Brooke. Just Brooke. But this is Princeton. The two guys really wanted to meet her, and we did. She was nice, but they had to drag me along. I mean, consider this: I've just played five sets, I lost my singles, I pulled a groin muscle, and now I have to meet an American beauty. Martina and I told Brooke little pieces of gossip about some of the players and risqué stories about things that happen on the tour. She thought they were just the funniest things, but she didn't chip in much. We were hoping for a little bit of return info, but we didn't get anything about her personal life.

My groin pull was the source of much amusement. Of course, my groin pull was purely the result of my tennis, but I may have led Brooke to believe that there might have been some other strenuous exercise aggravating the condition. After all, how would she know? Do you suppose girls like Brooke Shields ever pull groin muscles?

March 9—Princeton

Martina's feelings can be hurt so easily. At the Open last year, she cried after the finals, crushed at the crowd's favoritism for Chris. The public hasn't really reached out to Martina. She's very frank, very honest, a lot like I am, but she just comes across as harsh, especially now that she's beating everybody so easily. The crowds seldom cheer for Martina, and she has trouble understanding that it's just because she's so dominant. I think she's conveniently forgotten the U.S. Open finals a few years ago, when everybody was screaming for *her* against Tracy Austin because Tracy was the favorite that time. Everybody, especially an American, loves the underdog.

But I never saw Martina so upset as tonight, when we were playing

Robin White and Ann Henricksson. A few months ago Martina took Gigi Fernandez aside and told her that if she lost some weight and worked out—as Martina had herself—she could really improve. Gigi has a fluid all-court game and great touch, but she's found herself caught between her father's desire that she go home to San Juan, get married, and have babies and her untapped tennis potential. I think Martina saw a bit of herself in Gigi—a talented but overweight youngster—and if there's anything Martina can't stand it's untapped tennis potential.

Then Martina even asked Gigi to play doubles with her in a couple of tournaments while I was away. Gigi lost 20 pounds and gained seventy places in the rankings—much of it thanks to Martina's interest. If the No. 1 player in the world says you can be good, it gives you a lot more confidence than if your coach or your sister says you can be good.

Anyway, tonight, after Robin made a winning shot, Martina looked up, and who was leading the loudest cheers against us but Gigi Fernandez. True, Robin and Gigi are best friends, but Martina was furious. And this time I could understand. But I don't think Gigi did; she can be pretty dense sometimes about other people's feelings.

March 11—Princeton

Martina and I beat Liz Smylie and Marcella Mesker 7–5, 6–2 in the finals, so now we've won eighty-seven doubles matches in a row. Still, it wasn't all roses. This was the first tournament we'd ever played with me in the ad court, and no matter what Martina and her coach, Mike Estep, say, I still think we're stronger with me returning from the deuce court and Martina from the ad. Oh, well, maybe it's just that I'm not used to the new arrangement yet.

Today was a nice win under any circumstances, though, because Liz is an especially good doubles player, and she probably has the biggest forehand in women's tennis. A couple of times, early on, she burned us with her forehand so much that Martina and I decided to go into what's called an Australian formation. That means that both of the players on the service team line up on the same side of the court to start with. The idea was to cut down the angles in such a way that Liz couldn't swing around and bust her forehand. And it worked, too. I don't think she hit a big forehand the rest of the match.

March 13—Lutherville

There is definitely something special about this date for me. One year ago to the day, I met John Field at that Mexican restaurant in Dallas, and that relationship has been the highlight of the past year for me. Then today a White House social secretary called me up and invited me to come to a state dinner next month in honor of the president of Algeria. My hands were shaking on the phone, but I gave her all the necessary information. Then she told me there would be a White House Marine escort to take me into the dinner. I got hold of myself enough to say, "OK, that's fine. Only can you make sure he's over 6 feet tall?"

I can't really believe I'm going to the White House for dinner. I guess I got the invitation because I worked on the President's reelection campaign and everybody knows I'm wild about the Reagans. I first met the President and Mrs. Reagan in 1981 at a special White House reception for the U.S. Wightman Cup and Davis Cup teams. Both American teams had won the competitions that year. I remember that we all gathered at the White House tennis court where Stan Smith and Marty Riessen played a five-game exhibition. The President and Mrs. Reagan welcomed everyone, congratulated us on representing the United States so well, then gracefully excused us to the Rose Garden for refreshments.

Well, Andrea Jaeger had brought a big jar of jelly beans (that's so typical of Yaegs's thoughtfulness), and I'd brought a Prince racket for the President. And now it looked as though we weren't going to get to give them to him. Jaeger said, "You're older, Shriver, do something." So I stepped behind the microphone and said, "Just a minute, Mr. President, we have two gifts for you." He seemed a little nonplussed by this (I don't imagine he gets upstaged very often), but he thanked us politely. The jelly beans seemed to go over a lot bigger than my racket.

Then at the reception I told Mrs. Reagan that the racket I'd given the President was one I had used at the Open two days before. I didn't want her to think it was some impersonal promo thing from the manufacturer's rack. Anyway, when it was time for them to leave, about half an hour later, Mrs. Reagan ran up and whispered something to the President. He ran back down the hill—mind you, this was only six months after he was shot and he was running down the hill towards me—and he stuck out his hand and said, "Pam, I want to thank you very much. I didn't realize it was one of your personal rackets." I was stunned, but managed to get out, "Well, I want you to know what a thrill it is for me to meet the first President I was ever able to vote for."

That was the greatest moment of my life, to meet the President. To me, he's such a pillar of strength and that's what this country needs. You can't rule a country this big and this great through weakness. I was on cloud nine for about a week after that. I've written to him and Mrs. Reagan a couple of times. I also invited him to visit my house; it's part of the oldest restored village in the United States, after all. I guess it's kind of silly, but it made me feel good. And now I'm going to their place for dinner!

March 14—Lutherville

I invited myself to Kenny Rogers's SRO concert at the Capitol Center. Kenny has been one of my favorite singers since I was 12 years old, but it's only in the last couple of years that I've gotten to know him, and that's because he's crazy about tennis. He plays all the time, has a court on his farm outside Athens, Georgia, comes to a lot of tournaments, and has even supported one of the players—Lisa Spain Short—on the women's tour. Before the concert I went backstage and chatted with Kenny. Later, as I sat in the front row singing along to the same songs I used to as a teenager with a transistor pressed to my ear, I realized that Kenny can do the only thing I wish I could do: sing a song. I wonder if he feels that way about tennis.

March 16—Lutherville

The last couple of days I've had some of my best practice sessions ever. The overhead-volley drill is the killer in the regimen. Hank stands at the baseline and mixes up deep lobs with short dinks and sharp angles to keep me stretching and moving at net until I drop from exhaustion. We've also been working on my passing shots, which I haven't exactly been famous for. My hard, flat backhand has improved more than any other shot. Fred Stolle would be proud of me. I've also been concentrating on punishing my volleys more because they've let me down in the past. My preparation for next week's Virginia Slims Championships has been first-rate. We leave for New York by train tomorrow. I think trains are terrific.

March 17—New York City

I'm staying at the Grand Hyatt. Even with a good rate, the rooms for Hank and me will cost me $250 a day. A lot of people assume that tennis players have their expenses taken care of, like athletes on teams. Well, just for the record, we don't. We pay. It's darn expensive on tour, especially when you're paying for two.

March 18—New York City

It's funny how we get a totally different look at the sites we play in than the audience does. It's like we see them before the makeup and the sequins go on, we see them backstage. I was practicing over at Madison Square Garden where we play the Slims tournament. Now, the Garden is one of the world's most famous indoor arenas—the Knicks and Rangers have played there for years, so have Ringling Brothers and the Rolling Stones, not to mention Laver, Borg, McEnroe, King, Evert Lloyd, and Navratilova. But did you know that the Garden's unsung stars are its cats?

Yep, whole feline squadrons patrol backstage to keep the mouse population in check. At least that's what the security guards tell me. I've seen the cats for five years at the Garden, but I've never seen a litter box anywhere, which makes me wonder: Is the Garden the world's largest litter box? Of course, in all fairness to both the cats and their employers, I've never seen any evidence that it is. But what a thought!

My mind seems to be taking some quirky twists today. From cats to cigarettes. Virginia Slims, a cigarette brand, is the multimillion-dollar sponsor of the women's tour. I'm often asked about the impropriety of a company promoting an unhealthy habit being associated with fitness-conscious young athletes. My answer is simple: Tennis players aren't telling people to smoke; we support free choice to smoke or not to smoke. Personally, I hate everything about cigarettes—their smell, their taste, their smoke—but as long as smoking is legal I think people should have the right to smoke or not smoke as they choose. The same way they have the right to watch or not watch women's tennis.

March 19—New York City

Tonight I heard the saddest news I've gotten in a long, long time. It's a secret—I'm not supposed to know—but Carling Bassett's father, John, the man who owns the Tampa team in the United States Football League, has been found to have two inoperable brain tumors. Carling adores him, and I can understand why. Mr. Bassett is a tower of strength and a successful businessman, and he was a fine athlete, Davis Cup for Canada. I've always enjoyed talking to him.

Of all the tennis families that frequent the tour, the Bassetts are by far the classiest and the most fun.

There's a very fine line between being a good tennis parent and an overbearing one. Mrs. Bassett—Susan—tries her hardest to juggle what is best for Carling, the professional tennis player, and Carling, the 17-year-old high school kid. And she does a fine job, even if Carling doesn't always think so. It's a tough job for a mother to know how much to try to protect her kid and how much to let her try her own wings, especially on tour. It seems that the less obtrusive and more easy-going the tennis parent, the more accepted and well-liked the kid is.

Collette Evert has always made a favorable impression. Everybody likes Mrs. Evert, and once they get over their initial jealousy, everybody likes Chris. To this day, the only time Mrs. Evert will ever come into the locker room is at Wimbledon where she'll run in and put a chocolate bar in Chris's bag every day. By contrast, Jeanne Austin would come into the locker room all the time. Why, Mrs. Austin and Tracy would even lock themselves into one of the toilet stalls. I can remember being at tournaments where I'd actually see two pairs of legs under the door! One year at Wimbledon I was scheduled to play Tracy on Centre Court. Now, Centre Court matches go on like clockwork; 2 p.m. precisely means precisely 2 p.m. Well, Tracy was famous for never being able to get out of the bathroom on time, prematch nerves and all that. Before this one match, Tracy and her mother were in the W.C. for an age!

Tracy was never as popular with the girls as she could have been, and I think part of the reason was that we never really got to know her without her mother around.

Of all the kids on tour now, Carling has the most personality. If she isn't talking about her social life, she's inquiring about mine. If I mention that I'm going to see John in Dallas, she'll say, "Oh, hey, Pammy, is he good in the sack?" And then she'll start giggling. Carling's well-liked and funny, but at 17 she's so vulnerable. Now, with her father so sick, I just wonder if she'll be able to cope. I hope I can help.

March 20—New York City

It's late now. I pulled out a hairy match against Manuela Maleeva 6–4, 0–6, 6–4 in singles, and Martina and I beat Kathy Horvath and Virginia Ruzici in doubles. Maleeva is one of those tough young Europeans. She's a baseliner, from Bulgaria of all places, and her mother was nine times national women's champion there. Yulia Berberian is her mother's name (I guess in Bulgaria the woman doesn't take the man's name) and she's quite a taskmaster. She'll drill those kids—Manuela's younger sister Katerina is also on the tour, and there's a promising 8-year-old named Magdalena in the wings—until they're just about to drop.

The combination of mama's determination and the kids' talent has given Bulgaria the best tennis players the country has ever produced. At 17, Manuela is a bona-fide member of the world Top Ten, and 15-year-old Katerina is closing in on the top fifty. But the Maleevas are still shy and kind of sulky off court, and on court they both look as if they're going to burst into tears at any moment.

Manuela had a pretty good reason to look that way tonight. Our match was a seesaw battle that I could have won more easily, but almost lost. I can't remember losing too many 6–0 sets in my life, and I'm still not sure how it got away from me so fast. Once I got down two breaks, I decided to let it go and concentrate on getting off quickly in the third. It worked: I broke twice to go up 3–0 in the third.

Then I almost blew the whole match on one ghastly overhead. She had just managed to get her racket on a serve up the middle. The ball floated lazily towards me, as easy a put-away as I've ever had, but I began thinking how open the court was, how I'd better not miss, how the match was mine. I forgot to move my feet, and I hit the ball into the bottom of the net. The crowd groaned. I grinned painfully. What's one point, anyway?

I lost my serve to love, and Manuela leveled the set at 4–4 before something caught fire in me and I won eight straight points for the match. The win marked two significant steps for me: It's the first time in more than a year that I've defeated a player ranked above me (of course, I had to slip to No. 8 to do it), and it's the first time in my career I've ever gone further in a tournament than Chris Evert Lloyd (she was upset by Kathy Jordan in the first round). I think every tennis player thinks about measuring herself against what Chris has achieved.

I have a 6:30 a.m. wake-up to be on the *Today* show, but I can't stop thinking about Mr. Bassett and his family.

March 21—New York City

For the first time in ages Martina and I practiced singles together. There's only one practice court at the Garden, so players have to double up and practice with each other instead of their coaches. If there's one way I'd like to be more like Martina, it's in practice. She runs everything down, hits hard, concentrates, but also laughs and enjoys herself. I can't remember all the times I've dragged myself on and off the court. Now I'm beginning to enjoy my practices more.

March 22—New York City

Well, now I'm 3–20 against Martina. I'm generally disappointed. It took her an hour and a half to beat me, two and four, but I only broke her once and my own serve was inconsistent. Oh, well, if you paid money I think it was entertaining.

Deep down I know I'm more of a natural entertainer than a natural competitor, and in this day and age of the DSA—the deadly serious athlete—an occasional human exchange between opponents is refreshing. Martina and I know each other well enough to be able to joke around and still maintain intensity.

Tonight I was serving another marathon game in the second set when from high in the Garden a man let out with a tremendous sneeze. Immediately Martina said, "Gesundheit," and the crowd laughed. So I slowly turned, looked up where the sneeze had come from, grimaced, and wiped my face off, pretending that the sneeze's afterfall had landed on me. The crowd cracked up, and Martina doubled over.

Then she broke me.

March 23—New York City

People often ask if it's difficult to play against Martina in singles and then team up with her in doubles. Well, it would be much worse to play against her in singles and then *not* team up with her in doubles. Seriously, I don't think I'd enjoy tennis if I didn't play doubles. I get great fulfillment from singles but I can't say I have fun, because the pressure's so great. If I lost the pure enjoyment I feel playing doubles, I don't know what would happen to the rest of my feeling about the game.

Besides, some of my greatest highs have come in doubles with Martina. Like today's match. We stretched our win streak to ninety, defeating Helena Sukova and Claudia Kohde-Kilsch 6–7, 6–4, 7–6. It was the most memorable doubles match I've ever played. The tennis was so good that each of the twelve points in the third-set tiebreaker ended on a winner. Every shot we hit seemed to come back faster or lower or more acutely angled.

I know someday our streak will end, and I wouldn't be surprised if Claudia and Helena are the ones who beat us, but today we were both braver and more fortunate. At 5–6 in the final tiebreaker, match point for us, Helena was about to serve to me and Martina said, "She's not going to serve hard now so be ready for the kicker. If you hit a good return, I'm going."

I decided that I'd run around and hit a forehand slice hard, low, and wide, and give Martina the opportunity to poach. It worked to perfection. As Helena reached low and wide to volley my return, Martina crossed and drilled the ball down the center for the winner on our first match point. She was so excited she jumped in the air and screamed, and the crowd seemed to rise and scream, too. Then she turned and hugged me. Fred Stolle told me it was as good a doubles—men's or women's—as he had ever seen. I'm so pumped up I probably won't sleep a wink.

Martina always amazes me how she can come back out on court after playing a tense singles match (she came through like a champ winning her semifinal today against Hana Mandlikova) and *then* play a doubles match with just as much intensity and energy. Tomorrow Martina won't even feel stiff. Heck, I'm still stiff from my match four days ago against Maleeva; by tomorrow, rigor mortis will have set in. But at least I'll have died proud and happy. What a doubles!

March 24—New York City

Carling didn't advance in the tournament, but she came into town for the dance tonight because her father's team was playing the New Jersey Generals at the Meadowlands. Since the hotel had given me a suite (same rate), I invited her to spend the night with me. When she arrived this afternoon, she flitted into the room complaining about what she had to wear to the party. I could see why when she changed into the most unusual outfit I have ever seen.

What I thought was a white flannel slip or something turned out to be her skirt. Under the skirt/slip, she wore gray woolen tights with stirruped feet. Her blouse and belt matched, miraculously: They were gray.

"OK, I know this looks terrible, but it's the only thing I have," she announced. "Do the red shoes match? I had a red hat that makes the outfit, but my dad's wearing it." Her father is wearing *her* red hat? Her father is wearing a teenage girl's hat?

I reassured her that the red shoes were fine; it took some getting used to, but the rest of her getup began to grow on me, too.

"If only I had the red hat," she lamented.

My outfit was typically conservative: black silk slacks and a white blouse, but Carling said, "Now *that* looks terrific."

When she started to put on a little makeup, I thought I'd splurge and I asked her to put some on me. Little did I know the comedy hour had begun.

"This color is perfect, because it's subtle," Carling began, sounding like a cosmetics pro as she applied the base with a brush.

Subtle? Invisible was more like it.

"Do you want to go wild, Pammy?" she asked, eye-shadow pencil poised above my face.

"I don't think so."

"OK, let's try this color first. Close your eyes," Carling said, stretching her 5 feet, 4 inches up to meet my 6 feet. I started to giggle at the absurd picture we must have made, until I looked in the mirror.

"Oh, God," I croaked, doubting for the first time Carling's expertise.

"I'm not finished yet," she said, blending some more colors and asking for an eyeliner sharpener. God knows what that is, but my Swiss army knife worked just fine, and Carling began to draw a line under my eye. I started to peek in the mirror.

"Don't look yet!"

I wasn't sure I ever wanted to look again.

She directed me to rub the liner toward my nose. The dark lines under my eyes thinned out and I started to look a little less ghoulish. Maybe I'll even be able to go to the party without washing this junk off my face, I thought. Then she started brushing my *eyebrows* with mascara.

"What are you doing?" I asked in alarm.

"Models do this all the time," my little blonde makeup consultant answered. "It makes your brows stand out better." Now, I might not be known for anything else, but my eyebrows are famous.

I took the brush out of her hands and put some mascara on my lashes. Then I looked in the mirror.

Not bad. The kid has a future.

With a lead-up like this, the dance couldn't help but be an anticlimax, although both Chris and Martina asked me for advice about what to say in their speeches. Imagine that: Two of the most famous women in the world, who make speeches hundreds of times a year, asking little old me what to say. That's kind of neat, isn't it?

Martina and I were introduced as "possibly the best women's doubles team ever" (sounded good to me), and I ended up giving an impromptu, but heartfelt, speech about how special it is to play doubles with Martina and what a smashing friendship we have and how important it's been to have both Chris and Martina to look up to during my years on tour. I actually felt my voice begin to crack and for a moment I thought I was going to cry.

Then Martina finally got her chance to speak. "Well, I really don't know what I'm going to say. I even asked Pam for her advice but she was no help," she began. Good, warm them up with a laugh. Then she said some nice things about me and promised that as long as she plays I'll be her partner. I think that is one nifty idea. I ought to get that in writing.

March 25—New York City and Dallas

Today we had a meeting of the Women's Tennis Association board of directors. I'm on the board for the third year. We meet about five times a year to discuss every aspect of the association, from hiring a new executive director to accepting the resignation of a secretary who is getting married. We also vote on policy decisions: how the computer ranking system should be administered, whether players should be fined or disciplined, whether sponsorship packages should be signed, how many tournaments top players should commit to.

But we also spend too much time discussing things like whether the Virginia Slims of Houston should be allowed to reduce its draw from thirty-two to twenty-eight players for one year to accommodate a court shortage. Subjects like this should be wrapped up in five minutes, but they invariably stretch on and on, so I usually throw in an absurd suggestion like, "Why not make it a draw of seven and play only on Sunday?" I see my role as keeping everybody loose and alert.

Chris and Martina have served on the board for about ten years. The other board members are less well known but just as unselfish in the time they give to running the women's game: Nancy Yeargin, Candy Reynolds, JoAnne Russell, Shelly Solomon, Barbara Jordan, Lele Forood, Kim Shaefer, Leslie Allen, Marcella Mesker. Chris has been president the last three years and Martina was a president for two years. I figure somewhere along the line I'll probably end up being president. The top women have always served as leaders of the players' association, whereas the men have often been led by relatively obscure players. In the last year, John McEnroe and Mats Wilander have joined the board of the Association of Tennis Professionals, but Matt Doyle is the president and before him Ray Moore was the top guy.

With the exception of Diane Desfor, the WTA has always had a name player as president: Billie Jean King, Betty Stove, Martina, Chris. I think that says a lot about our best players and about all women's tennis. How many other sports have superstars who care that much for their sport?

Martina and Chris have meant so much to women's tennis the last eleven years. Every year that I struggle to do one-twentieth of what they've done I respect them more and more. Can you imagine winning at least one Grand Slam tournament in each of the last eleven years the way Chris has done? Or losing one match during an entire year the way Martina did in 1984? When these two retire, the void may never be filled. They are very special people.

After the meeting I flew down to Dallas to see the Belknaps and John. I have a few days to relax and share some precious time with John. Building a relationship is so hard when you're always traveling; you have to keep starting all over again.

March 27—Dallas

John and I drove out to the Belknaps' farm in Frisco, Texas, about forty-five minutes north of Dallas. We had dinner at the Rancher Cafe in Ponder (population 207); John has been eating there since he was a kid. The cafe is famous for its chicken-fried steaks, so I decided to try my first one. Guess what? It's not chicken at all; it's steak fried like chicken, and it came with french fries and rolls. John and I have been jogging every day so I didn't feel totally guilty about the heavy calories and starch, but for dessert I ordered salad instead of the homemade pie. What a sacrifice!

Before dinner a short man came up to me with a quizzical look on his face. Oh, no, I thought, we're going to have to play the aren't-you-so-and-so? game. But this was Ponder, Texas, and the game had a neat American twist.

"Are you a basketball player?" he asked.

"No, I'm not."

"Are you a long jumper?"

"No." I smiled. *That's* a first.

"Don't you go to Texas Women's University?"

"No, I don't." What was this: Twenty Questions?

"Last time I'll bother you. Have you ever been in the Ponder Boat Shop?"

"No, I'm sorry, I don't live around here."

I just know there's a short man lying awake in Ponder tonight wondering who the tall, curly-haired brunette was eating chicken-fried steak in the Rancher Cafe. Poor man.

March 28—Dallas

Today I worked out at the sports clinic at Northwest Texas State in Denton. I ran into Ed Simionini there; he used to play football for the Baltimore Colts. We got to talking about the drug scandal that's shaking major league baseball now. I have a fear about professional sports. The public and the sponsors will only tolerate so many scandals and violations of the law. How many more drug arrests and point-shaving incidents before the fan becomes disenchanted? I just don't understand why athletes—people who are dependent on their physical well-being—would poison their bodies with drugs or alcohol. And how can they endanger a reputation for kicks or money?

Tennis doesn't seem to have any drug problem. Or if it does, maybe I'm naive but I don't know anything about it. I think part of the reason we're clean is because tennis is an individual sport and you just can't keep up a level of performance throughout a match if you're high on drugs. And you can't take yourself out of the game in the middle of a match. You're it and you've got to cut it out there or your ranking will slip and you'll fall off the tour. There are no long-term contracts in tennis.

I have seen pot at two player parties in seven years. There have been rumors of a couple of girls using cocaine, but I think that was more for recreational use. On the men's tour, there have been more rumors, and Vitas Gerulaitis had a pretty bad scare a couple of years ago when a known dealer mentioned his name to the police, but nothing was ever proved. I can think of maybe one name of somebody who has had to leave the tour because of a reputed drug problem. The women players don't even smoke regular cigarettes!

JoAnne Russell has a unique explanation for why there is no drug problem in women's tennis. "Women players are too tight with their money to get high at their own expense," she says.

March 30—Lutherville

I've just returned from my first blind date. Well, I guess I'm the only one who was blind. If I date around here people know what I look like. The date was fine after some shy, quiet moments.

Although I don't think about this constantly, I do wonder how young men see me. I'm outgoing and funny and my clothes sense is getting better. Recently, even without my mother's insistence, I've added a few skirts and dress blouses to my wardrobe. She has been impressed. Unfortunately, I don't see that any men have been.

March 31—Lutherville

Today is Don's birthday. (It's also Mom's; it's interesting that two of the three most influential people in my life were born on the same day.) By coincidence, I worked out for nearly an hour and a half with him at Orchard. I couldn't be happier with Hank, but it was great hitting with Don again.

I'm feeling kind of nostalgic about Don and all that we've been through together. He's such a lovable guy, and he's made life very easy for me on tour because he's made absolutely no enemies. Oh, everybody might get fed up with him every once in a while because he talks a lot and jokes a lot, but who can't like Don? A tennis player can't afford to have a coach who causes problems, because if your coach is a problem, you're a problem. Don's always gotten along so well with the tour people—organizers, promoters, sponsors, players, and coaches.

I think it's been difficult for Elaine, Don's wife, these past few years. She hasn't traveled with us as much as she did the first few years, and she's had to make a lot of sacrifices for my tennis. But the thing she has to realize, and I think she has, is that tennis has always been Don's life and he was wasting away at a club teaching beginners and intermediates. Going on tour with a top player was just something he had to do. Elaine's a very strong lady and a very independent one, and she's been able to cope well.

Don and I have never needed a contract. The first year he must have wondered what the hell he was doing, because that year I only earned about $25,000; I didn't play a lot because of my sore arm and having to finish school and all. So Don got 10 percent of that. Big income, eh? Soon after that I began to get some endorsements and he did all those contracts, so I gave him a percent of the contracts and raised his percent of my prize money. But he'll never get as much as he's put into it.

Don has done everything possible for my game. He earns every cent that I pay him. I don't even think about it from my end, but he's earned so much more with me than he did teaching at the club that I think it's been worth all the sacrifices he and Elaine have made. At least, I hope it's been worth it.

I think every coaching relationship changes over time. It has to or else you get stale and stop making progress. After eight years of hearing this and that about your forehand volley, you just begin to go crazy. That's what happened with Don and me. I'd just get into the I-don't-want-to-hear-it-anymore business, and we'd start bickering. But you just don't change the habits of a lifetime overnight, and I really enjoyed hitting again with Don today.

April 1—Lutherville

The days before I leave for a trip are always hectic, but today was a joke. It started at 8:15 a.m. with several rounds of phone calls from my bed. I was trying to solidify a bid I was making on that waterfront property Dad and I saw on the Eastern Shore.

I must have made ten calls to my lawyer, my accountant, my investment counselor and pension planner (Dad), my financial adviser (Mom), and the real estate agent before I got my bid down. Then Pam Shriver, real estate magnate, slipped out of bed and became Pam Shriver, tennis player.

I went over to Children's Hospital for exercises and treatment, then followed that with 1½ hours of practice at Orchard. After practice Don got on the phone to firm up my air travel plans through Wimbledon. While I was meeting with Laura DuPont about some business decisions for Orchard, the real estate agent arrived from Easton with contracts for me to sign.

After I had signed the bid, which was into six figures, I heard Don's voice pipe up: "Pam, I'd like to talk to you about saving $28 on your airfare." I just had to laugh. How can you not love a guy like that?

I went back out onto the practice court with Hank, and we put in a violent hour. Then, after a phone call to Kenny Rogers's secretary in L.A. to ask if Kenny would be our MC at the WTA awards banquet at the end of August, we played another set and a half. My body and mind had had it by that time. It was 5:15 and I was exhausted, but the phone had just begun to ring.

In shorthand, here's the rest of my day: Home to shower (thank God, no phones); call from Kenny's secretary (sorry, no dice); to Mom and Dad's for dinner; call from real estate agent with counteroffer; call to my accountant to counter counteroffer; dinner; call back from real estate guy accepting my counteroffer, if I threw in four tickets to Wimbledon.

"When did he recognize my name? Those four tickets make up the $2000 difference in our bids," I told Tom, the agent. It was all lost on Tom from the Eastern Shore of Maryland. "What is Wimbledon?" he said. Ahh, perspective.

Then we finished dinner and I went home to pack. I was diverted by the incredible NCAA basketball final on TV (Villanova upset Georgetown) and by my dumbbell falling down the stairs (ouch!). When I finally put my head on the pillow, I slept like a rock. What a day.

April 2—En route

I'm sitting next to a family with two kids on a flight to Orlando where I'll have a press conference promoting an upcoming tournament. Afterwards I'll drive over to West Palm Beach for the tournament beginning there Monday. The kids on the flight have been good, but one of them needs a diaper change. If the ride gets much bumpier, so might I.

April 3—West Palm Beach

I did the press day in Orlando. I enjoy doing interviews and press conferences and I think I'm good at them. Part of the reason is the ego thing: Who doesn't like to see her name in lights? More than that, though, I figure the least I can do is have some honest and colorful answers.

I'm pooped now. I wonder if Don's right and I'm trying to do too much and not spending enough time working at my tennis. But I love to be busy and I think I'd get tired of tennis if I worked too much harder on my game and trimmed down my other activities. Tennis alone doesn't satisfy me.

April 4—West Palm Beach

This is my first tournament on Har-Tru in two years, and I'm really disgusted with the way I'm playing. This morning when I was practicing with Carling, I got so frustrated I heaved my racket over the fence into the parking lot.

A milestone: first thrown racket since I got back on tour.

My tennis honeymoon is over. Gone are the sunny, upbeat moods. I feel like a monkey in a cage with all these vacationers watching every practice and applauding my tricks.

This afternoon I was playing a set with Hank. At 4–all, a woman stopped right behind the fence and started to talk to me. At 4–all!

"You're not letting him beat you, are you?" she asked.

"I'm trying not to," I said through clenched teeth, trying to block her out of my mind.

"I'm not bothering you, am I?" she persisted.

"As long as you don't talk to me you're not," I snapped at her.

Second milestone: first spectator I've offended since I got back on tour.

April 5—West Palm Beach

Tonight was the first time I've felt embarrassed playing doubles in years. I mean totally embarrassed. I was playing with Hana Mandlikova for the first time, and we were awful. But at least you get to know someone better after you play doubles together. Now I understand Hana enough to know that I'll never understand her. I mean, she can turn wacko when you're playing against her, but she seems wackier when you're playing with her.

The other team, Billie Jean King and Ilana Kloss, were hitting lots of lobs, and sometimes Hana would hit a timid overhead back and sometimes she'd let it bounce and sometimes she'd just let me have it—but without saying "yours." Finally, I asked her why she wouldn't take any overheads.

"Well, you see," she explained, "I'm not used to taking overheads."

Great. Number 3 in the world and not used to taking overheads. Is that absurd?

But soon enough she was at net, and this easy crosscourt lob came toward me. As I stepped back to knock it off, Hana suddenly stepped backward and cocked her racket. I scrambled to escape being decapitated, and she popped a weak little overhead into the net. She looked at me apologetically and said, "I heard your footsteps."

"But, Hana, you said you didn't take overheads."

"I know, Pam, but that's me. That's just the way I am."

Then, during another stretch, Hana was getting in about 30 percent of her first serves. In doubles, a high percentage of first serves in is more important than hitting hard, erratic serves. So I suggested she take some pace off and get more into play. I'll often make this kind of suggestion to a partner, even to Martina. But Hana didn't change a thing.

Finally, on an important deuce point, I thought I'd try again. "Look, Hana," I said, "just serve one with three-quarter pace up the middle." She nodded and promptly whacked a hard serve 5 feet wide to the side. When we finally won the game, I asked her about the serve. "Oh, I changed my mind after I tossed the ball up," she said. "I can't help it."

Incredible. I'd never heard of a top player altering the velocity and direction of a serve after the toss. But that's Hana.

April 6—West Palm Beach

I was thinking about that crazy doubles match yesterday and couldn't help wondering how many times Billie Jean has beaten a stronger, younger player. I played her many times in singles, but never at her prime, and she always beat me in three sets. What a competitor. What an inspiration. What a bitch.

I've never respected anyone more than I respect Billie Jean. She and Rosie Casals were the players who barnstormed and bullied and battled for women's tennis until it began to get some of the attention (and money) it enjoys today. But more than all that stuff, I respected the way both Billie Jean and Rosie played.

When I was growing up I identified with them. They are a good 6 inches shorter than I am and covered the court like a couple of jackrabbits, but we shared the same serve-and-volley style and some of the same character, too. They played the aggressive, gambling, net-rushing style that most young Americans have forgotten about since Chris came along to dominate from the baseline. King and Casals were also feisty personalities, not above heated exchanges or more subtle confrontations with opponents.

As I was coming up, I clashed with both Billie Jean and Rosie because I refused to behave like a timid kid. I dished it out and cussed like a veteran. We traded insults with each other, and I remember one time at Wimbledon I called the referee to the court because BJK kept questioning calls and the umpire kept changing them in her favor. Not that my protest did much good: Billie Jean came back from match point down in the second set and beat me 10–8 in the third!

We bear no scars, no resentments from our clashes. I think Billie Jean and Rosie think I would have fit in nicely with the group of rebels that helped start the women's pro tour fifteen years ago. I'm a great throwback.

April 7—West Palm Beach

Last night's singles match against Hana was a tough one to lose. I played well enough to win at least a set, but I couldn't come up with the right shots at the right time. I played two lousy tiebreakers and lost 7–6, 7–6. On the positive side, this *was* my first singles match on Har-Tru in two years and my first singles on any type of clay in almost two years, and I gave a solid performance against the world's No. 3.

The match was not without Hana-type incidents. At 3–3, 40–30 in the second set I served a letcord that looked out but was called good. Hana questioned the call several times, and even approached the linesman, who isn't supposed to talk to a player, and started berating him. She kept yelling at him, "Did you see the ball?"

Finally the poor guy had taken enough abuse and he yelled, "No!" at the top of his lungs.

Then I lost three straight points and my serve to fall behind 4–3. The next game I broke her back, but, still, Hana shouldn't have been allowed to hold up play for as long as she did. The umpire wasn't strong enough.

April 8—En Route

Today is Easter, and along with Thanksgiving they are two holidays that I usually spend away from my family. This morning I attended Easter service alone at Bethesda-by-the-Sea Episcopal church in Palm Beach. The church was beautiful and I was pleased with my ability to follow the service without my mom's help! I was even more surprised to be recognized by a lady two pews up, but no autographs.

It's 6:30 p.m. and Hank, Carling, and I are headed north on the Florida Turnpike towards Hilton Head, South Carolina, the next stop on the tour. Hank is behind the wheel of an enormous Oldsmobile Delta 88. The trunk is larger than most cars! Carling is sitting in the back seat, singing and munching sour-cream-and-onion potato chips. She just tried to peek at what I'm writing. "Later, Carling."

I lost 6–2, 7–5 to the squirt in the back seat this afternoon in a typically uninspiring third-place playoff. These playoffs are essentially for the fans; all the players hate them. I had two game points to break at 2–2 in the first. Instead I lost that game and the next six in a row. I was hot, mad, and tired, but at 2–6, 0–3 I thought about what a pitiful performance I was giving and won the next four games. I had four game points on my serve in the next game to go up 5–3, but blew the game and match. Well, the two singles matches will help me immeasurably at Hilton Head, and for finishing fourth in singles and third in doubles I won $16,000. That's a small consolation.

The light is dying now and it's time to sing along with Carling for the next 500 miles.

April 9—Hilton Head

We were on the last leg of the overnight drive from West Palm Beach to Hilton Head. Carling was her usual silly self, sticking gum in Hank's hair and falling into the front seat looking for a neck rub. We stopped and had breakfast for $9.11. I mean, all three of us ate our heads off for $9.11 total. We picked up some newspapers there, and when we got back in the car, I took the wheel and Hank flipped through one of the papers. Carling was snoozing in the back, and suddenly Hank nudged me. When I glanced over, there was this headline that read, BASSETT UNDERGOES RADIATION TREATMENT.

I nodded at Hank. "I already know," I said. I snuck a look back at Carling. I decided we better let her know, because after we got to Hilton Head the press or somebody might bring it up. "Hey, Carling," I said, "there's an article about your father's treatments in the paper."

She sat up. "You're kidding," she said. "Let me see." She seemed surprised to see her father's condition become public knowledge, but she didn't say anything else. I just wondered what she was thinking. It all made tennis seem so small.

April 10—Hilton Head

I beat Kerry Reid one and one in what Chris referred to as "your easiest clay-court win ever," just another example of that sly Evert Lloyd wit that the public rarely sees. Kerry was a world Top Tenner in the early '70s, but she's pretty much retired to raise a family with her husband, Raz. They live on Hilton Head, so I think she got into the tournament as the sympathetic, local wild card. She was definitely rusty and not in tournament shape, but it's not easy to beat anyone one and one on Har-Tru, especially not for a 6-foot serve-and-volleyer.

Ros Fairbank and I won our doubles match. I'd never played with Ros either, but she plays doubles nothing like Hana. Ros and I make a solid, high-percentage doubles team. Even so, we struggled to hold her serve today. I must learn to poach more, especially when you-know-who isn't my partner. Martina spoils me in doubles.

Ahmad Rashad is down here for a vacation. We're old friends from when the tour stopped in Minneapolis and he was a wide receiver for the Vikings. When I was 17, I double-dated with Ahmad, Betty Ann Stuart, and Steve Dils, a Viking quarterback. I remember the date vividly because when I missed my 10 p.m. curfew, Don blew a gasket. I can understand: He was my father and mother on tour and here I was running around with football players and high-spirited divorcées. Ahmad and I laughed about it at the cookout tonight.

"I didn't know you were only 17," he said. Sure, Ahmad.

People sometimes ask me if there are any man-chasers on the women's tour. Betty Ann Stuart came the closest. She had been married a couple of times and would marry again in the time that I knew her on tour. If you used all her names she'd be Betty Ann Grubb Stuart Hansen Dent, and Mike Lupica once wrote about "Betty Ann Grubb Stuart Hansen Dent Pierce Fenner & Smith" in *World Tennis*. Anyway, she was lots of fun and going out with her and the guys was a seductive experience. But Don was right to clamp down on me. One promising young player who used to run with Betty Ann, Linda Siegel, basically got mixed up with boys and disappeared from the circuit. But not before she made quite an impression on the media.

Linda Siegel was a young girl from California who had beaten Tracy and then me to win the 16-and-under Nationals in 1977. She was ranked No. 1 in the nation and was going to be great stuff. Linda had a big forehand and moved incredibly well for a big girl. She came to net occasionally, but basically she just ran around back there and whacked that forehand, and she *was* quick. She was a free spirit and had a wild streak in her, which I think is something you have to have on the circuit, but she went boy-crazy, and I think Betty Ann was a big influence in that.

As a matter of fact, it was Betty Ann's halter dress that Linda wore at Wimbledon in 1979 when she had the memorable burlesque incident. Linda was playing Billie Jean, no shrinking violet herself, on Court 2, and Linda just fell out of her dress reaching for a serve or a forehand or something. That picture was on every front page of every tabloid all over the world. That was Betty Ann's dress and Betty Ann's influence. I often wonder what kind of an impact Linda would have had with her tennis had she not gotten sidetracked.

April 11—Hilton Head

I had to come from 3–5, 0–30 down to beat Katerina Maleeva 7–5, 6–3. God, those Maleevas are the mopiest players you ever saw on the court. Somewhere along the line, they've been tagged "Boo" and "Hoo," which is a perfect description. Manuela is Boo and Katerina is Hoo. Pretty soon little Maggie, who's 8 or 9, will be on the tour, so before I retire I know there's going to be a little Boo-Hoo.

So, now I've beaten a 15-year-old for the chance to play a 14-year-old. That's Gabriela Sabatini. I played her in doubles once, and she's the best of all these kids.

The happening of the day was Andrea Temesvari's defaulting in the middle of her match just because she had her period. I'll admit that having cramps during a match is a dreadful feeling, but can you imagine what would happen to women's tennis if everyone defaulted every time that happened?

Of course, the crowds always cheer for Temesvari because of her looks. She spends more time putting makeup on than the rest of the girls combined. Her wraparound skirts barely cover her tennis pants, which barely cover what should be covered. However, what guy cares what I think on that particular subject?

Carling lost to Virginia Ruzici, so I went up to her place to cheer her up. Her dad was coming in, and I was talking to Mrs. Bassett while Carling was changing for dinner. Suddenly I heard Carling yelling, "Daddy!" at the top of her lungs.

At the moment I felt very awkward being there, because Carling hadn't seen her father in ten days. Those treatments must be hell. His hair had all but completely fallen out. But Mr. Bassett was in high spirits. He never stopped talking about tennis or the USFL or real estate or the twenty deals he seemed to have going.

April 12—Hilton Head

It's late in the afternoon. I had Sabatini down 7–5, 4–3 when the rains came. We'll finish tomorrow. The courts have absorbed much of the moisture and are playing much slower, and her topspin shots are made for the conditions. I must get more first serves in and mix up my shots more if I'm going to win. Her backhand seems to be her stronger side, but unfortunately that's the side I'm more comfortable hitting to. Rain delays are never fun, but when you're in midmatch, they're excruciating.

My hotel room is a disaster area—like always. Clothes are strewn all over the other bed; shoes, socks, newspapers, and dirty laundry litter the floor. I ask myself why I don't neaten up. But why should I? I don't expect to entertain anybody. Besides, I feel more at home this way.

For some reason I was thinking about a women's golf tournament I saw on TV last week. We compete for the same sponsors and audience and, from my nonpartisan, disinterested point of view, there's no comparison between the physical demands of the two sports. Tennis players, without a doubt, have to be in much better physical shape than golfers. How else could you explain the fact that the first-round leader in a recent golf tournament had had a baby only ten weeks before? I can't imagine even playing a tennis tournament ten weeks after having a baby, much less being in contention to win a major championship. Then again, I can't imagine even having babies at this point. . . . I'm too busy playing against them!

April 13—Hilton Head

This tournament is great practice for Wimbledon: It's been raining from the moment I opened my eyes at 6:50 a.m. It's now 3:45 p.m. and play has finally been canceled for the day. Ever wondered how players spend rain delays? Eating, reading, sleeping, watching TV, trying to stay calm, getting nervous, and generally going crazy being cooped up inside with no way of releasing energy or tension, that's how.

Since I'd expected to be on court most of the day to complete my other singles matches after I'd beaten Sabatini, I ate a bowl of spaghetti and an English muffin before 8:30 a.m. Distance runners are not the only athletes who load up on carbohydrates; so do tennis players expecting a marathon day. There have been times that I've eaten three bagels in the hour before a match, just to make sure I have enough of an energy source to draw on during play. But Martina is the only one I've ever seen actually eat *during* a match. Bagels, oranges, and protein bars are her regulars, and one time we were playing doubles after she had played a long singles and she actually got someone to bring her a ham sandwich on the changeover! Can you believe that?

By noon today I had read every newspaper I could get my hands on—the *New York Times*, the *Savannah Morning News*, the *Atlanta Constitution*, and something indigenous to Hilton Head called the *Island Packet*. I'm a news nut so I also watched the morning news shows, the financial reports, and, of course, the weather reports. (I've outgrown the morning cartoons.)

Some TV movie with Charlton Heston seemed to be on for hours as I dozed off and on. By 2 p.m. I still hadn't been outside my condo, and I was more than happy to do a TV interview with NBC. They showed the tape of my suspended match with Sabatini on national television. That was the high point of my day, challenged only by Carling's coming over to the condo and blowing bubbles with her gum. The bubbles were bigger than her head!

April 14—Hilton Head

Great. I not only lost to a 14-year-old, but it took me forty-five hours to do it. Sabatini and I finally got back on court at 8:45 this morning after a day and a half of watching raindrops. She was loose from the start, while I was so uptight I had no rhythm on my serve and a queasy stomach throughout the match. It didn't help that four games after we resumed the match, at 6–5, 15–all to be exact, I did something I've never done before: I hit the net with my racket during a point. I had hit an overhead that she barely reached. But her shot had wicked backspin on it, and when I reached over the net to put it away, I hit the net on my follow-through. I was so unnerved I lost the next five games and ultimately the match.

When I came off the court, I realized that it was more than nerves that had tied my stomach into knots: I'd just started my period. The irony hit me that Gabriela, still two days short of her fifteenth birthday, probably doesn't get her period yet. I think I would have beat the little twerp if it hadn't rained for two days, and the balls hadn't been heavy, and we hadn't had to play at 8:45 in the morning, and I hadn't just gotten my period. And, of course, it was the single worst match I've ever played in my life. (See Pam Teeguarden, December 22 entry.) But I'm a generous, mature veteran; I don't make excuses when I get beaten by 14-year-old pipsqueaks.

Seriously, since I've returned to the tour, I've been handling my losses in a much calmer, more rational manner. Maybe I'm growing up, gaining perspective, or maybe Chris's example is rubbing off on me. Losing is never fun but I'm beginning to realize that there's always a tournament next week where I can try to redeem myself. In the past, I've smashed rackets, belittled Don, yelled at my friends, and cursed a blue streak after losses. I don't know if the new me is here to stay, but it's certainly made life quieter for my friends . . . and my rackets.

A champion deserves good luck, but Chris Evert has *great* luck. Take today, *pul . . . lease*. If Chris has a mental weakness, it is playing a teenage opponent for the first time. Two years ago she nearly lost to 15-year-old Carling Bassett, and Chris still talks about how nerve-racking and unpleasant her first match against 14-year-old Tracy Austin was. Her finals here against Sabatini had all the elements that Chris hates: a talented 14-year-old with nothing to lose, swinging from the heels and spurred on by media hype and national TV.

So, get this: By the time Chris played Gabriela, the kid had already played $3^1/_2$ sets against two world Top Tenners (me and Manuela Maleeva); thirty-five games and one 11–9 tiebreaker. On the other hand, Chris had played one match, an easy 6–2, 6–2 victory over Steffi Graf (to be perfectly fair about this, Steffi's 15 too). The only reason Sabatini was forced into playing a third singles match was because the finals were scheduled live on network television. Anyway, Chris struggled to win the first set 6–4 before wiping out the exhausted teenager 6–0 in the second.

I think everyone kind of took advantage of Sabatini. She could and probably should have declined to play the finals today, but she and her coach, Patricio Apey, didn't want to disappoint anybody. Also, I don't think people think of the fatigue factor as much as they should when a player is only 14 years old.

Gabby is the real thing, though. She's so good that the only thing that can keep her from at least going right to the top five is if she's played right into the ground. Today, because of the rain, she played $5^1/_2$ sets of singles: That's way too much for one day. And next week she's scheduled to play her fourth straight tournament. If I were Gabriela (or her coach), I wouldn't play tennis next week, no matter what.

April 15—Lutherville

Income tax day, and it's raining. How appropriate. With my corporate and personal taxes, I owe well into six figures, but the real estate investments help trim that some. I also rent the ground floor in my house to Marion, so that helps, too. I'm not comfortable with high-risk tax shelters like oil or racehorses, because I don't know enough to really be in control. I'm thinking of hiring a financial consultant for PHS, Ltd. My financial portfolio is getting too complicated for the combined family wisdom.

April 16—Chicago

I flew here to meet with Bill Ylvisaker, chief executive officer of the Gould Corporation, which owns the Palm Beach Polo and Racquet

Club. I've never met with a CEO in his office before. Sara Fornaciari of ProServ says that the club wants a touring pro to lend the same kind of pizzazz that polo has brought to the place. I've been to PBPRC, and it's a first-class development with exclusive, high-priced homes, eleven polo fields, seventeen tennis courts, and two golf courses. I think I'm the pizzazz they need for their tennis operation.

April 17—Washington, D.C.

Ho, hum, typical day: Tonight I went to the White House for a state dinner in honor of His Excellency, the president of Algeria. It all began this morning when I drove over for coffee and doughnuts in the East Wing with a star-studded group invited by Mrs. Reagan. I arrived and, feeling slightly awkward, found a vacant seat in the corner beside the coffee cups where I could follow the proceedings. Cheryl Ladd and Jennifer O'Neill took to the scene like the actresses they are, but Joe Namath must have been feeling as odd as I was, because he made a beeline for the coffee cups. We had a deep conversation:

"Hi, Joe, I'm Pam Shriver."

"I thought I recognized you."

Then we were ushered into the Rose Garden where we waited with Vice President Bush and his wife, Barbara, Secretary of State Schultz, White House Chief of Staff Donald Regan, and several hundred Marines in parade dress carrying musical instruments. Finally, the President and the First Lady and President Benjedid and his wife walked in to the strains of what must have been the Algerian national anthem, followed by the Star-Spangled Banner, followed by a twenty-one-gun salute. After the speeches, we adjourned and I hooked up with my Uncle Dick, who is doing a consulting project for the White House.

We had reservations for lunch in the White House staff mess: I've never tasted pan-fried trout, corn fritters, and salad quite as good. On our way out, I heard the Vice President's voice. "Hi, Mr. Vice

President, I'm Pam Shriver," I said. I'd met him twice already, and he'd called the week before to see if I could play tennis, so he knew me, but my mom always says it never hurts to overintroduce.

"Oh, hi, Pammy, you missed a great game the other day," the Vice President said. "Did you get the message we tried to get you?" He said he'd give me a rain check, so I'm going to drop over to Camp David sometime soon for a little lunch and tennis. Wow!

Then, on our impromptu tour of the West Wing (a friend of Uncle Dick, Claire O'Donnell, who works for Donald Regan, did the honors), the Vice President popped up again. He invited us into his office—on a table over by the window was a picture of him playing tennis with Bjorn Borg, which Bjorn had autographed for him—and he showed us the guest list for the state dinner.

"You're sitting at a very important table," he said. I got all nervous when I scanned the names: Mrs. Reagan, President Benjedid, Jennifer O'Neill, fashion designer Perry Ellis, architect Richard Meior, magazine publisher Anthony Mazzola of *Harper's Bazaar*, and Mrs. Richard Merriman, who is the president of Garfinckel's, the department store. What on earth was I going to have to say to these people? "Listen, President Benjedid, on your second serve, you've got to take a little of the pace off and try for depth"?

To soothe the butterflies in my stomach, Claire, Uncle Dick and I took a tour of the Rose Garden. We looked up an old school friend of mine, Mina Wright, who is working at the White House as an architecture historian. She gave us a peak at the Vice President's office, the ceremonial one, in the Executive Office Building. Apparently, he uses it quite a bit because of the tradition. One of the traditions is that all the Vice Presidents sign their names under one of the desk drawers. Claire wanted to know if Bush signed twice, once for each term. Funny girl, Claire.

By this time it was almost 3:30 p.m. and I had to get ready for dinner. A trip to the beauty salon and three hours later, I was shampooed, cut, blow-dried, styled, sprayed, made up, and decked out in pearls, diamond-stud earrings my grandmother gave me, an aqua lace evening gown, and white sandals with—uh, oh—2-inch heels. But yes, my escort, a Marine captain named Tom Gilroy, turned out to be, as promised, tall—and handsome, too.

We drove over to the White House and I took the time to notice the china on display. Every President and First Lady has had their own set of china except the Carters. Why Mrs. Reagan got so much flak for choosing new china I'll never understand. Tom guided me upstairs to the reception area to await the guests of honor. I positioned myself behind a cluster of people talking to Donald Regan. He isn't what you'd call a barrel of laughs; he obviously isn't a political being, but we chatted pleasantly.

The tension grew until finally the two couples were announced and a receiving line was formed. "Tom," I told the captain, "I'm not going to make it." He looked at the rapidly disappearing line and took a warm glass of Perrier from my hand. He gave me a confident look and said, "I'll pick you up on the other side."

Tom had explained how I was to give my name to a Marine standing behind the dignitaries. The messengers then whispered the names into the ears of the dignitaries so they would know whose hand they were shaking. I felt as if I were getting closer and closer to jumping off a cliff. I remember saying something illuminating to Mrs. Reagan: "I think I'm eating with you." Good, Pam; everyone was eating with them tonight.

I found Tom and we followed everyone down a long hall which led to the dining room. Once again Tom left me on my own; he hadn't been invited to the dinner. "We get to eat in the Cabinet room," he said as he told me he'd meet me back here after dinner. My place card was between Perry Ellis's and Anthony Mazzola's, two seats down from Mrs. Reagan.

The Vice President's table was behind ours, and we talked again about playing tennis. Then no sooner had the last person sat down than fourteen waiters appeared, bearing food to the tables. Cold lemon sole with dill sauce. Rack of veal with rice and yellow squash. The conversation naturally enough turned to fashion. Mrs. Reagan felt right at home. I tried to act intelligent. Finally, I loosened up and told Mrs. Reagan I was looking forward to her fund-raising tournament for drug-abuse prevention. I also asked President Benjedid if he played tennis. Through an interpreter, he told me he played several times a week, but I don't think he's quite the enthusiast he claims to be, because he didn't even know what kind of racket he uses.

After the dinner, and a little ballet performance, I was watching the President and Mrs. Reagan on the dance floor. Suddenly this arm comes out from behind a plant next to me and I hear a familiar voice say, "C'mon, Pammy, I'm not much of a dancer, but let's give it a go." It was the Vice President. No matter how bad a dancer he was, I knew I was a lot worse, but what the heck. He said, "Have you met the President?" I said, "I did in the receiving line." And he said, "Well, let's waltz over there and have a chat." The next thing I know he's tapping the President on the shoulder. We had a nice little chat.

Two dances later I danced with Tom Gilroy, my Marine captain, and he told me that it was the first time he'd ever danced at the White House. Just think, it was my first time too, and I'd danced with the Vice President and had almost cut in on the First Lady! It was the most memorable day of my life . . . at least until (if?) I win a Grand Slam singles.

April 18—Lutherville

I made the *Washington Post* in a picture with my escort, Captain Gilroy. That's the second published picture of me with a date. I'm on a roll.

April 19—Lutherville

I've put on 8 pounds since I went back on tour in February. Too many big restaurant meals, too many sweets, too much nervous nibbling in the players' lounge. So far today I've eaten half a grapefruit, an English muffin, a banana, and a cracker with cheese. I'm starving.

April 20—Lutherville

My left Achilles tendon has been bothering me since Hilton Head ten days ago. Now it not only hurts when I play but also when I'm walking up and down stairs. Nagging injuries like this usually disappear quickly, but my foot pain hasn't. Dr. Silberstein has suggested heel lifts. Apparently, when I changed from one model of tennis shoe to another, my heel must have been raised or lowered a fraction, and this caused my Achilles to stretch and become sore. There are so many little things that can affect an athlete's fitness! We're sort of modern-day heroines in reruns of "The Princess and the Pea."

April 22—Orlando

I've been working with Hank for two months, and I can honestly say that there are only two things about him that annoy me. He's mellow, consistent, hard-working, and fits in well with both sponsors and the other players. *But* he talks too much on the phone and he leaves the lights on. He's usually out with friends when I go to bed, and when I get up he's still sleeping . . . and the lights are on in the kitchen.

If we hadn't been staying in so many condominiums lately, I probably wouldn't know these things about him. I've been running around after him turning lights off for weeks. I'm sure I do a lot of things that rattle his nerves, like miss a lot of forehands, but electricity costs too much to waste.

April 23—Orlando

Tomorrow once again I play Katerina Maleeva, the 15-year-old, the younger of the Boo Hoos. At that age, she's played five straight weeks on tour—and all far away from her own country, Bulgaria. I've never played five straight weeks of tournament tennis in all my life. That's too much tennis for anyone, much less for a kid.

There's talk that the International Tennis Federation will limit the number of tournaments a young player can enter. The trouble is, I've been around tennis long enough to know that a lot of parents and coaches and agents will then just find some promoter and schedule the kids in lucrative exhibitions the weeks they're supposed to be taking it easy.

These kids have no idea that they could be on the road to burnout. They should look at the example of Bjorn Borg. He was one of the most famous athletes in the world when he retired at age 26. He was only one year off winning five straight Wimbledons, and suddenly the guy doesn't want to play anymore. But if you start playing at 15 and tennis is the only thing you've known, it's very easy to lose your enthusiasm at 26.

You can get good at tennis at such an early age—there are no Masters golf champions at age 16—that I think it's possible to win too much before you learn how to handle it. Everybody has varying degrees of burnout at some time during the year, so it's not the exclusive problem of kids. However, the serious kind of burnout—stage three, if you will—seems more likely to hit people like Bjorn who have played intensely and continuously from the time they were 14 or 15.

Borg notwithstanding, you don't see the burnout thing so much in foreign kids. I think this has something to do with America's love affair with No. 1. There's just something in our society that says if you're not the best, if you're not No. 1, then who and what are you? It's very destructive. Look what it's done to Jimmy Arias and Aaron Krickstein, who have suffered physical and mental strain and have watched their rankings drop significantly.

Physical burnout and the mental kind go hand in hand, because if your body's hurting it doesn't take long for your mind to slide downhill, too. When you have burnout, you just lose interest in practice, in keeping physically fit. During matches your interest, your determination, and your competitive pride start to go out the window. A malaise hangs over you. You get irritated at little things. Off court you're not happy and on court you're a mess. This is what I was feeling last December in Australia, and I'd like to protect kids from ever feeling that way—or worse. It's a horrible feeling.

April 24—Orlando

Why do I even play tennis?

Tonight I lost in three sets on my worst surface to a 15-year-old. We didn't even get on court until after 10 p.m., and the score, 7–6, 3–6, 6–4, was as painfully aggravating as the match. I couldn't have played more uptight if I had stuck a gun to my head. The lights neutralized my overhead and I totally whiffed one smash—I can't ever remember doing that. That error was especially distressing because it came off an easy lob and the point would have given me three points for a 5–3 advantage in the first set. I played abominably in the first set, but I still had a set point. I played the point well, set myself up for a winning volley, then dumped an easy backhand into the net.

I'll say one thing for old Hoo: At 15 this kid is a veteran at stalling and interrupting the flow of play. She knows all the tricks. Now, I'll admit that I was obnoxious myself at times, but I'm 22 and I've been playing for seven years. I'm allowed to be obnoxious.

The match didn't end until 12:20 a.m., and then I made poor Hank go into the bar with me. I'm not that much of a drinker, but I started with a black Russian and followed that with a strawberry daiquiri. You can tell I'm not much of a drinker if that's what I'm ordering back to back.

I remember thinking in the middle of the match how easy team athletes have it. On a tennis court there is nowhere to hide, no bench to sit on, no substitutes to call in. I hate the nervousness that goes with playing these matches. I can't perform when every part of me is so tense. How do I learn to relax? Should I practice more? Should I go to a sports psychiatrist? Should I quit? I'm definitely thinking too much about when I'm going to quit and what I will do after spending the better part of my life playing tennis. I always have these thoughts after I play a shockingly poor late match. I haven't been out of a singles on a Tuesday in years.

Now it's 2 a.m. and I can't sleep. I'm writing this on the toilet because I'm rooming with JoAnne Russell, who's asleep. Given the state of my game, it's an appropriate place for me. Just think, a week ago I was at the White House; now I'm in the outhouse.

April 26—Orlando

Tennis players are not immune from the stresses and tragedies of life; as a matter of fact, I sometimes think our lifestyle places such a premium on our looks and health that we become more vulnerable to emotional problems. We don't respond by getting involved with drugs, but we can hit some mental troughs. There's a rumor going around that one of the girls has bulimia; I remember being in the locker room one time when she went into the toilet and forced herself to throw up after a big meal. She's always been a big, sturdy girl, not fat, just big. Now she's thin. She's lost so much weight that I hardly recognize her, and I've known her since the juniors.

Another girl who's gone through some really tough personal problems is Regina Marsikova. She was forced to leave the tour three years ago when she was charged with vehicular manslaughter in Czechoslovakia, her home country. Last week she returned to the tour. Regina looks the same, except her blonde hair is shorter and her teeth seem stained yellow, perhaps from smoking. Her absence from the tour has robbed her game of its pounding topspin power. I can only guess at what the ordeal has done to her mentally. I'll be interested to see how she does in matches.

April 27—Orlando

Martina beat little Maleeva 6–1, 6–0. Katerina sure didn't have the nerve to hold up play and stall against Martina the way she did against me. Boo to Hoo.

April 28—Camp David

More in the saga of Pamela H. Shriver, fodder for teenagers one day, partner for the Vice President the next. Marion and I drove the one hour and fifteen minutes from Lutherville to Camp David. The turnoff for this peaceful mountain retreat isn't obvious, but the red "Do Not Enter" signs give it away. It's a perfect place to get away from it all: The squirrels play, the birds sing, and behind the double security fences the VIPs relax. As we approached the formidable 15-foot-high gray fence at the entrance, two Marines inspected the car. They wheeled a mirror around under the bumpers to check for bombs.

Vice President Bush greeted us in his golf cart. "Pile in and we'll go over to the courts," he said. I've never had a more impressive chauffeur. When we got to the courts, the introductions began. It was a real Bush League: Patty Bush, Bucky Bush, Marv, Jeb, Johnny, Barbara, Neil, Sharon, another George, and a Prescott Bush. Then the Vice President and I got down to the business of beating the Bushes.

During the warm-up I realized these guys were not hackers. Son Jeb was particularly strong, and the Vice President himself could be a solid, consistent player if he had the time to play regularly. I knew by the tone of his voice that he really wanted us to beat his son Jeb and his brother John. I knew I couldn't let our Vice President down. It would've been unpatriotic. We beat them 7–5, then played another set and a half with some other Bushes.

Afterward we all had a dip in the pool. I even dove. ("Degree of difficulty: 1," in the Vice President's opinion.) Marion and I showered and on our way to lunch stopped off at the souvenir shop. The Navy guy behind the counter said these things aren't sold anywhere else in the world except Camp David. I took the pitch: I ended up with $104.95 worth of Camp David glasses, mugs, shot glasses, cards, and plates. You can't get these anywhere else in the world! Where were the T-shirts and bumper stickers?

After lunch we sat around the large living room of Laurel, the main dining and conference cabin, and talked about tennis. There were seven telephones in the room. Out by the pool there had been five more phones. The only place I didn't find a phone was on the playground. I guess the President doesn't spend much time on the swings.

Late in the afternoon, we shot some skeet; the Vice President hit nineteen of twenty-five targets, while I was nine for twenty-five. Vice President Bush is one of the nicest important people I've met, and his family are just as natural and relaxed. About 4:00 p.m. the Vice

President and his family headed back to Washington in his helicopter.
Second most memorable day.

April 29—Lutherville

I wasn't too keen for my exercises today, but I ran through my routine at the sports clinic. For eight minutes I rode an upper-body exercise cycle. When I felt my arms were warmed up, I did six sets of thirty repetitions as quickly as possible on the shoulder machine, which offers resistance whether you're pushing or pulling the handles. By contrast, Nautilus is slow weight work, more beneficial for strength and endurance training. Tennis demands more quickness than strength.

Then I worked on a forearm machine that has helped my elbow problem. I finished by lifting 2-pound dumbbells, which at that point in the workout felt like about 20 pounds each. Chris Evert told me a few weeks ago that she uses a 30-pound dumbbell for her forearm exercises. She's deceptively strong, especially in her arms, but I find that impossible to believe. A 5-pound weight is more than ample for me.

Anyway, after I'd iced my elbow and shoulder, I took a "contrast bath" for my aching Achilles. I alternately submerged my foot in ice-cold water then 106° water every three minutes for twenty minutes. They used to do this sort of thing to make prisoners talk in the Middle Ages. Then a therapist massaged my foot and gave me an ultrasound treatment.

And that is the life of an athlete in the prime of her career.

April 30—Lutherville

All of my glamorous visits to Washington and Camp David have overshadowed my tennis. My attitude has slipped, and I may fall out of the Top Ten for the first time in almost five years. Practicing with Don today I lost all grip on myself, slamming my racket to the ground and then whacking it three more times to make sure it was dead. If I could have twisted its neck, I would have.

If I saw improvement I wouldn't get so angry, but I never improve. Now I'm feeling vulnerable. I'm a scalp now! Once players see you're vulnerable, they play much more confidently. I can see people getting "up" to play me because they have no pressure. They're loose as a goose because they've reached the spot in the draw where they were supposed to go—the rest is gravy. They beat me, get one big win, and then the next day, where are those great shots? Nowhere, because the situation is reversed and now they're supposed to win. That's why you get so many upsetters being upset themselves the next round.

I wonder whether I'm cut out to be a tennis player. I have such a love-hate relationship with the game, it's not even funny. Sometimes, like now, I feel as if I'm in prison and I have to stay in for another six or seven years. Sometimes I'm so frustrated, so enraged, so discouraged that I'd like to run away and hide.

Here I took all those months off and my body still feels the same. My arm hurts. My mind is always uptight on court. I'm just lost in the tennis world, wondering when I'll get out. But what about the money? What about the big titles I might win? What about people thinking I'm a quitter? No, I must keep going in this crazy lifestyle. My next tournament is in Australia, a country I love second only to the USA. I can't think of a better place to find my game and rekindle my confidence. There's grass and Wimbledon six weeks ahead. Press on, Pamela H. Shriver, press on!

May 1—Lutherville

More frustrations today, but I played through them for $3^1/_2$ hours. Hank drove up from Washington and we played two sets, both of which I lost. Don watched, and then he lectured me on my attitude. He thinks I'm lying to myself when I say I don't want to play anymore. I know he disapproves of all my off-court activities, but he also knows they're important to me.

Don is coming with me for the two Australian tournaments. If anyone can dig me out of my hole, Don can. We haven't been together much since the first of the year so I even look forward to the thirty-five-hour flight.

These tournaments could make or break my year. If I play up to par I could play seven or eight singles matches. I need to play enough singles matches so I'll feel comfortable on the court with the players ranked below me. I used to know I would win certain matches; now I have doubts. I must get rid of the doubts and Australia is the place to do it.

May 3—Sydney

Don and I just arrived from L.A., fourteen hours. Apart from the space shuttle, I think that's the longest nonstopper around. We're about to board another plane to Adelaide to see Don's mother, Molly. The last time I saw Molly she was a vivacious, bubbly, strong, and active old lady. Now she's in a nursing home in Adelaide and can't take care of herself because of the paralysis in her left side. Oh, Molly, hang in there.

May 4—Adelaide

Don and I practiced on some school courts across the street from the nursing home so Molly could watch. She's always been so interested in my career, and her partisanship has embarrassed even me at times. Like when she told me, "Turnbull is too fat and too old to be playing tennis." Wendy Turnbull, too fat and too old, was ranked No. 5 in the world and earning $300,000 a year at the time, but you couldn't shake Molly from her opinion, no matter what you said. Now when she saw me, she just cried. She won't read the paper or talk to people at the center.

Maybe we can snap her out of her depression. The least we can do is put up with blacktop courts that turn the balls into lumps of charcoal after twenty minutes, a net that's about 6 inches too low, and a short fence. Practice has never seemed so important before. Please get well, Molly.

May 5—Adelaide

Don arranged for me to practice with a few local pros. Cost me $85 U.S. I can't imagine Martina or Chris paying anyone to play sets with them.

Tennis players are notoriously tight with their money, and some of the Aussies are legendary for being cheap. "Short arms with deep pockets" is their expression. Here are the Five Commandments of a tight tennis player:

1. Thou shalt always return a tournament car's gas tank on empty.
2. Thou shalt never buy sodas during a tournament, but take freebies home from the players' lounge.
3. Thou shalt avoid buying tennis balls at all costs.
4. Thou shalt attend sponsors' parties for the free food and not the socializing.
5. Thou shalt use the WTA phone for long-distance calls.

May 6—Sydney

Don stayed on with his mother in Adelaide, so I ordered room service. I hate eating alone in a restaurant. There's nothing sadder than seeing a woman eating alone on the road.

My fashion shoot for *The Australian*, the national paper, was a hoot today. The designer was there so I wasn't about to poke fun at the red feathers or the strange fur hat or the bizarre hemline or the long black gloves or the 4-inch red, spiked heels I had to wear. Suffice it to say, Carling would have loved the whole outfit. One of the guys who helped with the shoot looked as if Carling had applied his cosmetics, and he couldn't resist trying on the clothes after I was finished with them. And his sidekick wore a wig and five necklaces.

I wish Molly could have seen the whole thing: *This* would have made her laugh. And she would have appreciated the fact that these guys and I became friends; she always had an eccentric streak in her.

May 7—Sydney

I arranged practice for 7 a.m. with one of the Aussie juniors. Barbara Potter had the court from 5:30 to 7. Only Potsie would have set up a practice for 5:30 in the morning. She's so hard-working that she can be a pain about practice courts, practice balls, and match times. Lefties are said to be weird, but Potsie can be downright bizarre. Like the time she appeared dressed to the nines for a casual dinner date with a tournament volunteer in jeans. I don't think the poor guy knew what he was getting himself into. Even so, it must have been a quick bite because Potsie is usually in bed by 8 p.m., getting her training sleep. And talk about frugal! No morsel of food in the players' lounge is safe when Potsie and her mother are around.

It just blows my mind when I see players making hundreds of thousands of dollars a year doing things like this. I saw the little Maleeva, Hoo, pour a big thing of sugar into a plastic bag, presumably to take it back to their flat. The family is making a fortune, especially in Bulgarian terms, and there was the little girl, emptying the sugar container from the players' lounge. JoAnne Russell was right, women players will never have any problems with drugs because they'll never pay for them!

May 8—Sydney

Tonight is my first singles match. I've certainly felt better about my tennis than I do at the moment. I need to win a couple of matches. It will mean the world to me. Since my break I haven't really felt confident. I'm drawn to play Barbara Gerken, a buxom baseliner from Santa Monica, California. It's a good first match for me, but

I'm nervous. If I play positively, attacking second serves and going for my shots, I should have an easy time, but at this point nothing seems easy. I've tried to go to two health clubs I've used here before, but both have gone out of business. I've had to rely on my dumbbells to exercise my arm, which is adequate but not great.

My elbow has been bothering me again because the balls are heavier here than in the States. I'm really sad because I've done almost everything possible for my arm and it still hurts. I'm not sure how much longer I can live through these problems without going berserk. Finally, after our warm-up tonight, I just went over and sat next to Don and cried.

My match against Gerken started off with a bang. I led 4–0 before I started to miss a few shots. She picked up her game and before I knew it the score was 4–4. I was livid: I needed a routine match and here I was blowing a two-break lead! I pulled myself together and won the set with some clutch serves and volleys. Then in the second set, I again blew chances to run away with the match. I lost my serve from 2–0, 40–15 after butchering two approach shots. I was incensed.

On the changeover at 2–1, I actually remember thinking about smashing my racket, hitting myself, throwing a cup of water, yelling at the ballgirl, or tipping the umpire out of his chair. Why did I have to make the match more difficult than necessary? The anger turned out to be cathartic, and I regrouped to win my first match 7–5, 6–3. Yea!

May 9—Sydney

Liz Smylie and Kathy Jordan have made a pretty good team since they got together last year. But Kathy was late entering here, so I'm playing with Liz and we just won our second match. In a while, I'll go back over to warm up for my singles against Ros Fairbank. I lost to Ros the last time I played her, but my attitude and desire were at an all-time low. Although I'm not playing my best here, I want to win so much I can taste it. That should be enough.

May 10—Sydney

After six months I've finally reached the semifinals of a tournament. I struggled to win the first set 7–6, which was good because I haven't played a good tiebreaker in quite awhile. But the second set may have been a breakthrough of sorts. I played aggressive, positive tennis and cruised past Fairbank 6–2.

Next I play Alycia Moulton, who serves a ton. She's another one of those players who have wonderful talent but just don't know how to play the points. She beat me 6–0, 6–1 in the 12-and-under Nationals one year, but she says she doesn't remember me. (I wasn't too memorable then.) Alycia graduated from Stanford in 1982 and is well respected by the players. Maybe she'll learn how to get the most out of herself one day, but frankly it's fine with me if she doesn't. Especially not today.

I beat Moulton as easily as I ever have, 6–3, 6–2. I was never nervous and wasn't afraid to try any shot. I broke Alycia's first service game with some fantastic lobs. You might say, big deal, but Alycia's almost 6 feet tall and these lobs were carefully planned and difficult to execute. She crowds the net too much and I knew I could lob her effectively, but to do it in a match situation is a wonderful feeling.

May 11—Sydney

Yea, me!! I won both the singles and the doubles. Now I know how Martina feels. I played eight tough sets of tennis in twenty hours. I never felt so confident. My singles match against Dianne Fromholtz Balestrat was the best finals of my career. My serve has never worked better in an important match. I never lost my serve and I broke hers three times to win 6–3, 6–3. Why, if I serve at Wimbledon like I did today, there isn't a player in the game who won't have to struggle to beat me. Why would I ever even consider leaving tennis? Even my arm feels rejuvenated.

© Melchior Digiacomo

Pam Shriver

Carling's rainy-day activity in Hilton Head. I think this is how you get the press to call you bubbly.

© Carol L. Newsom

Martina, Chris, and I play dress-up, like real girls. We're at the Waldorf-Astoria at the March of Dimes–Women's Tennis Association banquet on the eve of the U.S. Open.

Ana Laird

WTA and Virginia Slims staffers pose with a clean Martina and a piqued Chris. This was when Chris said she was irritated because I didn't invite her to my birthday party. Hey, Chris, nobody said life was a piece of cake.

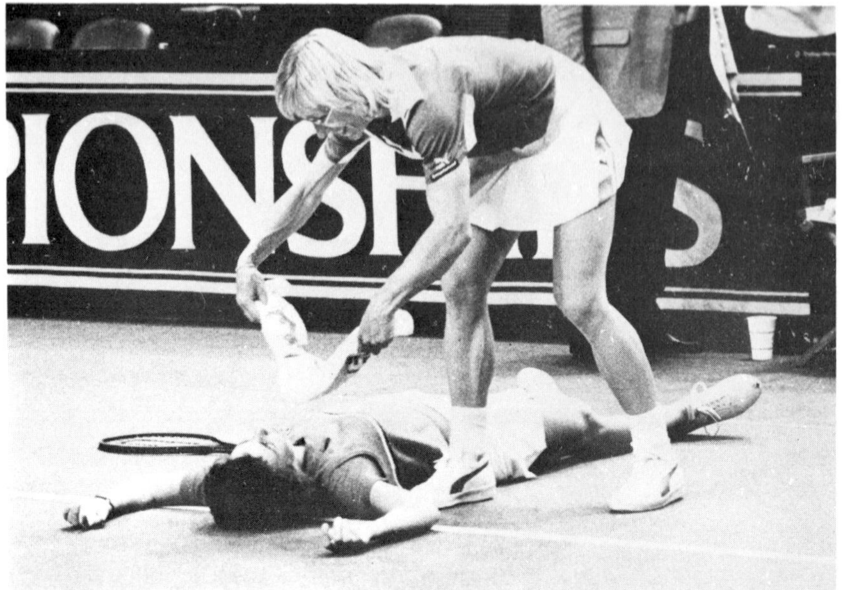

© Carol L. Newsom

Martina revives me after we beat Kohde and Sukova 7–6 in the third in the finals at the Garden to keep our streak going. It was the greatest women's doubles match ever, if you want my opinion.

© Russ Adams Productions

Walking out with Chris and Mike Blanchard, the referee, before the finals of the '78 Open. Would my nightmare come true and I'd lose love and love?

© Carol L. Newsom

This must be a doubles match because I'm happy and relaxed.

© Melchior Digiacomo

A sweet, young, innocent schoolgirl saying hi and thank you to 18,000 people who were in the palm of her hand for a while.

Don Candy and Mike Estep with their charges.

© Carol L. Newsom

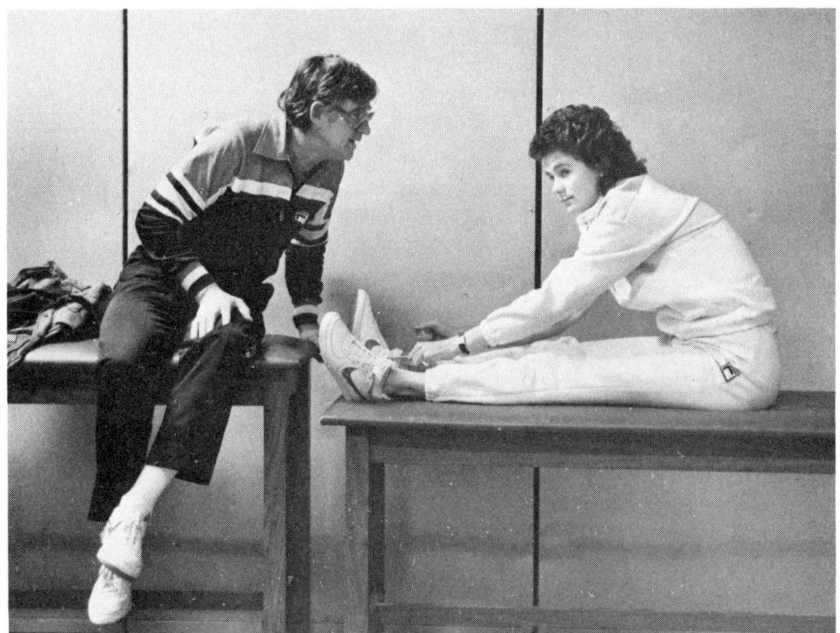
© Melchior Digiacomo

A quiet moment with Don before a match in Chicago in 1984. I won the tournament.

© Carol L. Newsom

Liz Smylie and Kathy Jordan (hidden behind Liz) after stopping our streak at 109 in the Wimbledon finals.

So I got lucky and hit a topspin forehand winner.

© Carol L. Newsom

© Carol L. Newsom

My mother always told me to "keep your legs together on changeovers." Now maybe I'll listen.

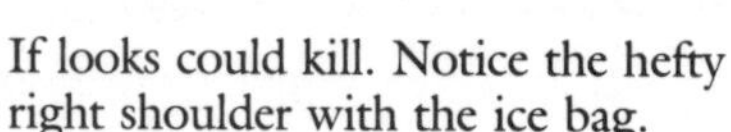

If looks could kill. Notice the hefty right shoulder with the ice bag.

© Melchior Digiacomo

© Carol L. Newsom

© Andy Hanson

ABOVE: John and I at a black-tie dinner in Dallas. This was the first time this jockette ever made the papers with a date.

LEFT: The big gag—after losing 6–4 in the third to Jordan at Wimbledon, 1984.

BELOW: This is at Newport the summer of '85, and the sad fact is that the only people watching me play are paid to do so.

© Carol L. Newsom

© David Walberg

ABOVE: Little sister Eleanor, with Brie, one of our three Labradors.

RIGHT: The most loved tennis parents on earth. Low-key support—just what I need.

© David Walberg

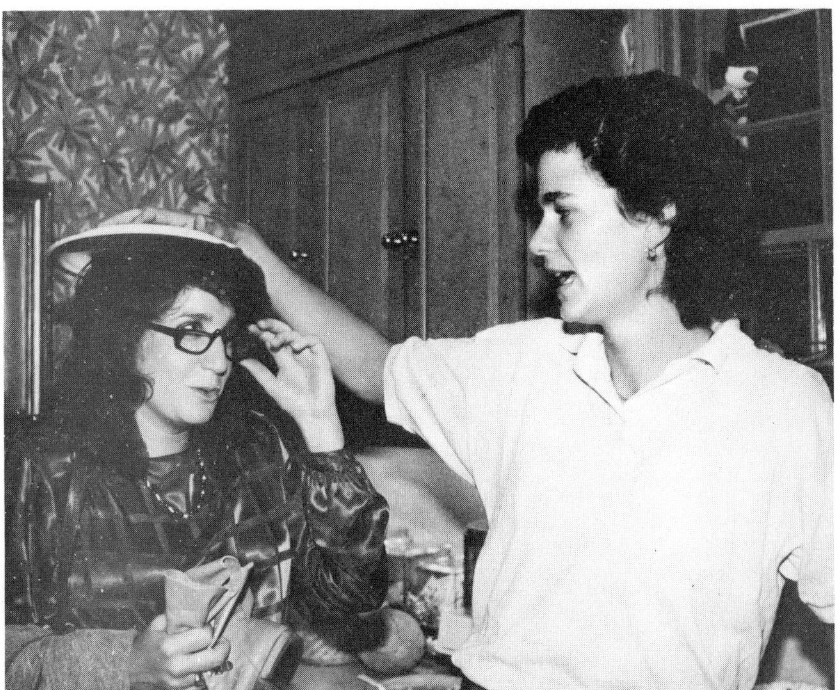

© Carol L. Newsom

Elise Burgin and I doing what we've been doing for 14 years, horsing around. This was in Dallas.

© David Walberg

Don finally finds a way to shut me up . . . temporarily, anyway.

© David Walberg

Hank and Don in the players' box at Wimbledon watching me struggle against Our Ginny on center court.

© David Walberg

The talented, gifted, athletic, and wacky Hana.

Andrea Temesvari: queen of topspin and make-up mirror.

© David Walberg

© David Walberg

The late, great Tracy Austin. Did you hear the one about Tracy making a comeback? Miss ya, kid.

© Carol L. Newsom

Could this be my next career?

© David Walberg

Hank, Don, and I at practice during the middle Sunday of Wimbledon.

My best friend and big sister, Marion.

Don Candy

Official White House Photograph

Unless . . . until? . . . I win Wimbledon or the U.S. Open, this may be the thrill of my career.

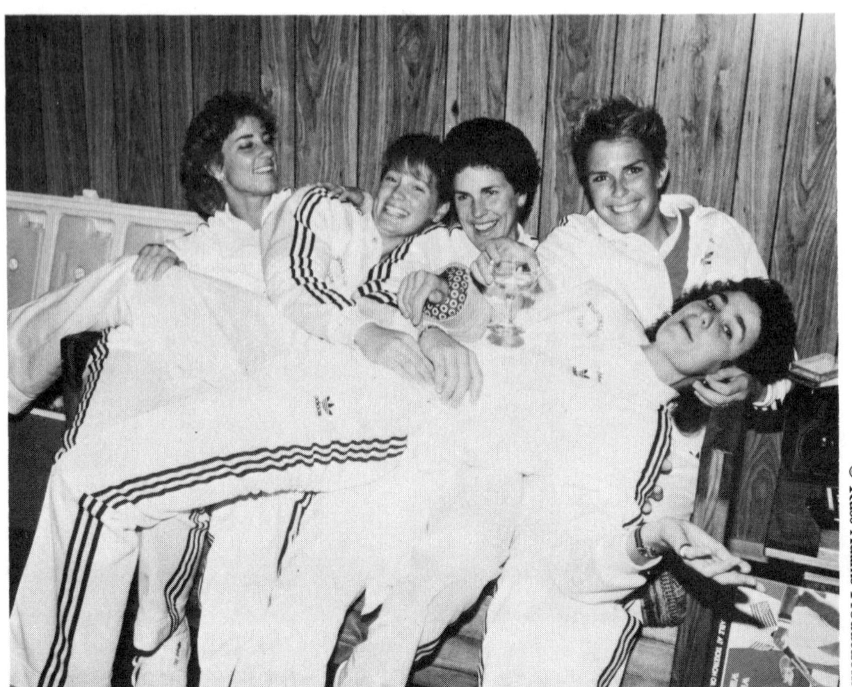

© Russ Adams Productions

Our oh-so-serious Wightman Cup team. But, hey, we won.

Pat O'Connor / Virginia Slims

Backstage with Tina after the Virginia Slims. With us from the left are Kathy Jordan, Marcella Mesker, Chris Evert Lloyd, (me), Tina, and Wendy Turnbull.

May 12—Sydney

When I checked out of the hotel I discovered my only extravagant expenses were nightly binges at the minibar in my room. I spent $32 on juices, drinks, imported chocolates, and macadamia nuts, but I won $40,000 U.S. in prize money and another $30,000 in performance bonuses from Prince, my racket company, and my two Australian endorsements, Kraft cheese and Hoover.

The desk clerk told me one of the players had asked the hotel to empty her minibar so she wouldn't be tempted. Before I could respond, the clerk said, "I think it was Potter." Of course, it was. Potsie's a fun-loving person underneath that deadly serious demeanor. I do admire her dedication, but sometimes she can take it all a little too far.

May 13—Melbourne

Confidence means everything in tennis, and it had a lot to do with me turning my first-round match around after losing the first set. I was playing Csilla Bartos, a big, strong Hungarian who plays with the same heavy topspin as her countrywoman, Andrea Temesvari. My stomach had been feeling queasy before I went on court, and that first set gave me more indigestion, but after she held for 1–0 in the second, I took twelve straight games and won 3–6, 6–1, 6–0. I can't ever remember doing that before.

Now that I'm confident, I wish I could bottle the feeling. I've gotten to know quite a few players ranked outside the top fifty on this trip, and the difference in their games and mine often comes down to confidence. You can see the tension in their faces and bodies. I was watching Lisa Spain Short play last night. She's a tall girl with an all-round game and a big serve, but since winning the NCAAs for Georgia last spring she's lost seven first-round singles matches in a row, and her ranking has slipped from No. 60 to No. 104. I remember when I lost five first-round matches in 1979. I was so uptight. I can see the same tenseness in her. Certainly, with her talent and her big forehand, she can do a lot better than she's doing. I can only sympathize with how she must be feeling now—like a sad, lost dog.

May 16—Melbourne

Evonne Goolagong Cawley has messed up more tournaments in Australia with defaults and early losses. Yesterday she defaulted with a bad foot. I don't know why she bothers entering because she's not really a threat to win matches after two years away from competition. I guess she plays mostly for her business interests in Australia: The public adores her here. But it's not really fair to the tournament and the other players. One year she played the Australian summer tour when she was four months pregnant. Another time she got sick, held up her first-round match two days, then defaulted. This time she's played only one match and she's defaulted again.

That kind of business can't be good for tennis.

May 17—Melbourne

I've managed to pull out three three-setters in a row. I've finished my matches around 11:30 p.m. three nights running, and you can imagine what that does to my sleeping habits. I'm exhausted. My legs have been stiff and sore since Sydney and they're getting worse. But I'm winning. What a great feeling!

May 19—Melbourne

The Shriver juggernaut keeps on rolling. For the first time in my life I've played in a singles final two weeks in a row, and I've won, too. I beat Kathy Jordan four and one. Kathy and I have always gotten along as kind of a sisterhood. We're both aggressive serve-and-volleyers on the court. We're both from the east coast; she's from outside Philadelphia. We've both had depressing battles with injuries. She's always been a great doubles player. As a matter of fact, we've played doubles together a couple of times. One of us would try to calm the other down; when one of us wasn't yelling, the other was. We were an interesting team. She's been fined *so* much through the years because of her temper.

She'd have to be different off the court or else everyone would hate her. But she is popular off the court, although she has her prickly moments when she offends people. She's always been very much a rebel, which I think goes hand in hand with her on-court personality. One thing you can't see on court is her sense of humor: She's been one of the moving forces behind the player skits at Eastbourne. I've been the butt of some of those, but even I've had to laugh.

Over the years she's had so many injuries simply because she's not strong enough. She can't help it that she's built so lean, but her unorthodox style places even more strain on her body and has prevented her from really making it big. Still, as far as being a competitor and an athlete, she's one of the best on tour. The second set I played against KJ today was one of the finest tactical sets I've ever played.

Everything has come into focus here as I hoped it would. I've begun to realize what I'm all about as a tennis player, which is: Get the hell to the net behind a big serve, approach with deep shots, and attack the other guy's second serves. Don is unbelievable at straightening out my game. He's prodded me to forget about rallying from the backcourt. I sometimes forget that the reason I'm a good player is because I serve, volley, and smash very well.

Almost every champion has had a great strength and also a weakness. Tracy Austin won two U.S. Opens before she was 20 with the worst serve I have ever seen. Bjorn Borg won Wimbledon five times without a really solid volley. Ken Rosewall had a terrible serve, one John Newcombe called "a piddly little thing." Billie Jean King's forehand was pretty dodgy; Goolagong's forehand was dicey and her second serve was the pits. Chris has done all that she's done until recently without a serve or a volley. Martina, as all-around as she is now, used to choke her forehand volley something awful. And Lendl's volleys aren't too magnificent.

All these champions lived by their strengths and lived with their weaknesses. If I'm ever going to win a Grand Slam singles, I must depend on my serve more, and that will give me more courage to hit better forehands from the baseline.

My entire game lifted several notches this week. Will it be a turning point? If it is, I'll swear it was my match against Fairbank in Sydney that turned me loose. Going into that match I felt like crap. I swore I had to lose. Fairbank had beaten me the last time we played, and the first set looked like more of my same tentative, uptight stuff. But I got it into a tiebreaker, won the tiebreaker 7 to 2, and then played perfect percentage tennis in the 6–2 second set. I still wasn't playing great but I was thinking great. That match got me back on track and gave me the confidence to start going for the big shots.

May 20—En route

The friendly skies of United are on strike, so as we approach L.A. I've been traveling for 22½ hours. By the time I get into Baltimore tomorrow morning I will have taken off and landed seven times in forty hours—Melbourne, Sydney, Auckland, Honolulu, L.A., Indianapolis, Pittsburgh, and Baltimore. This will be a record for me.

May 22—Lutherville

We had our quarterly board meeting of PHS, Ltd. On the board are my accountant, John Garrison, my lawyer, Lou Ditch, Mom and Dad, Orchard's manager, Laura DuPont, Don, and the president, Yours Truly, ahem. We laugh and tease and have a great exchange between the fiscal conservatives (Mom and Lou) and the liberals (Dad and John). We talk about club business, tax problems, possible shelters, money management, pension plans, and endorsements. The president, ahem, tries to steer a conservative-liberal course. Today we decided to search for a financial planner to put my capital to work more creatively.

May 25—Washington, D.C.

Another day at the office. Back to the White House. This time it's a tournament for Mrs. Reagan's youth drug program. We raised about $400,000, and I talked to everyone from Michael Jordan to Tom Selleck to Mrs. Reagan herself. Also in attendance—although I didn't know she'd be there—was Tracy Austin.

She didn't play, just umpired. Tracy won two U.S. Opens by the time she was 19, but then she came down with sciatica. Except for a brief and abortive comeback, she really hasn't played since '82. Tracy was as gutty a player as I've ever seen, and it's obvious she has had a serious physical problem. But now it's also apparent that she doesn't seem to have the nerve to step back onto the court, or even admit she's scared. Tracy was always petrified of any physical problem.

Of course, I know that lots of people will take anything I say about Tracy with a grain of salt, because it's not exactly a secret that we never hit it off. You want to know the first words we ever uttered to each other? Well, it was the 12-and-under Nationals in Savannah, and I was playing cards with a bunch of other players. Tracy was standing behind me, watching my every move. When I played a card, I heard this squeaky voice behind me say, "That was stupid." Her first words to me. Instinctively, I shot back, "Shut up or I'll step on you." My first words to her.

Through the years, that warm relationship has deteriorated further. The culmination came when we played each other in Toronto in 1981. The chair overruled seven calls, five of them for Tracy. It got so ridiculous I actually lay down on the court after an overrule cost me a chance at a tiebreaker. When Tracy won and jumped in the air, I just couldn't take it. I came to the net to shake her hand and I called her a four-letter word. Then I threw in another four-letter word. Tracy broke into tears . . . although she did compose herself enough to tell the press every word I had said to her when the two of us were alone at the net—or, at least the first letter of every word I had said. Can you imagine Dan Marino saying, "Mark Gastineau called me a word that begins with *s*!"

Mrs. Austin was even more upset. She said that even her three sons had never been around such language in all their lives. Very sheltered family, the Austins.

The incident made the front page of the Toronto paper and screaming sports-page headlines all over the rest of North America and the free world. The best thing was that a few weeks later I got a letter from a guy named Bulldog Joe, who was serving time for assault with a deadly weapon in a prison out west. Bulldog Joe sent me a clipping of the incident, said that he liked my style and that he wanted to be my bodyguard when he got sprung from stir. I haven't heard from him since then, though, so I guess he's still in the slammer.

Anyway, at the White House today, I'm introduced to the Secretary of State, and Mr. Schultz says, "It's nice to meet you, Pam. Did you hear that Tracy Austin's making a comeback?"

Well, I thought that was the introduction to a joke, like, "Did you hear the one about the shaggy dog?" So I said, "Hey, it seems to me I've heard that one before." Sure enough, right behind me I hear this familiar voice say, "Oh, Shriver, you always needle me." Speak of the devil.

May 27—Lutherville

Tonight must have been my 200th goodbye dinner at Mom and Dad's. It's a ritual before I take off for almost any tournament, and tomorrow I leave for France and England for six weeks. Hank will be with me the whole time, and Don will come over for Wimbledon. Also, my sister Marion is staying with me in Paris. We're not just sisters. We're great friends. I need some intragender support in Paris; the place is swarming with male chauvinists.

May 29—Paris

The French Open is the rare tournament that provides free accommodations. Unfortunately, you have to stay at the Sofitel, which the players have nicknamed the Sofisteal because many had valuables ripped off from their rooms in 1983. I've been lucky. The only time I was ever robbed was when Martina and I were playing an exhibition in San Antonio, and I caught this guy going through my bag in the locker room. I chased him, and a cop caught him. It turned out that the only thing he'd stolen was our underwear. Actually, it was kind of flattering that somebody would want my underwear, but then I had to fill out the police report and put down: "Two tan Olga bras, size 34B, two size 7 beige panties. . . ."

In a way, Martina's exhibition tours—a.k.a. Pam Plays the Pigeon—are a rip-off too. I've played exhibitions with Martina about five times. These matches are difficult for me because Martina is as loose as a goose hitting every shot known to man. I'm trying to win a few games and entertain the crowd. Sometimes she forgets the main purpose of these exhibition matches and beats my brains out.

I remember one time in Greensboro, North Carolina, I went out on the court a little flat but determined to stay with Martina and put together some high-quality points. Well, Martina could have kept me in the points by hitting some drop volleys for me to chase down. At least we could have started some fun points that way. Martina has great touch, she can time the ball more easily in a new atmosphere, she's a better athlete, and she can get into more of a groove with her topspin groundies. But, no, *I* was the one trying to play touch shots.

At one point she ran down one of these soft, hit-me dinks and absolutely blasted it by my right ear. I'd had enough and hit her with the most withering look she's probably ever seen from me. I finally got through to her: She gave me a little nod and snapped out of the let's-pound-Pam-into-the-ground routine. And I should give her some credit: She did allow for two baseline rallies. I can't believe anyone in the crowd enjoyed the match that much. I sure didn't.

The next night she was better. We had three baseline rallies.

May 30—Paris

I didn't sleep well last night: terrible cold. The French Open has a reputation for germs, because it has 150 girls using a locker room that should only hold 50. I'm spoiled because all the other Grand Slam tournaments have a separate changing room for the seeded players and past champions.

May 31—Paris

Because the red dirt is my worst surface, I'm only playing doubles here, and Martina and I won our second match today. I have a problem because I have all this yucky stuff in my throat and I want to spit all the time. But I don't think girls are allowed to spit on tennis courts yet. Only boys can spit.

June 1—Paris

Just by chance, I practiced next to Chris today, and it's not hard to see why she has been so successful. She benefits from every second on the court; her concentration is constant. She was practicing with her husband, John Lloyd, and he ran her from side to side. Chris never gets credit for how well she moves—almost incredibly graceful, always in position, her weight always perfectly transferred with each shot.

Of course, John doesn't get enough credit, either. He's commuting back and forth across the Channel, helping her on clay, then going back to England and working out for himself on grass, preparing for Wimbledon. Obviously, this is not good for John's tennis, but he's willing to sacrifice for Chris.

June 2—Paris

Ken Flach and I lost to Paula Smith and Francisco Gonzales, 9–7 in the third. I always feel nervous in mixed because we women are obviously the vulnerable ones. The guys hit the balls so much harder than we do. Today my volleys were tentative and my returns inconsistent. Paula held up much better.

People always wonder how a woman pro would do in a match against a male pro. A guy should be able to annihilate me because of his natural advantages in strength and speed. But for some reason, I'm more than holding my own against Hank in practice. We played two solid hours, $1^1/_2$ sets, and I won them. Either he's toned down his shots to match mine or else he's being incredibly diplomatic so I don't lose confidence. I'd rather he'd beat me. The better he is against me, the better I will become.

June 4—Paris

It's nice having the men's and women's tours together, but a lot of the guys have their girlfriends along and there isn't much mixing. I'm sure some people wonder who Marion is, especially since we don't look like sisters. She's a straight-haired blonde and is stacked, and I'm neither of those. So every time I introduce her I make sure I say, "This is my *sister* Marion." I know the way people think on this tour.

I talked to John on the phone. I miss him. He's special, but I'm not sure I'm ready to have a boyfriend traveling with me. There's enough pressure without having to worry about a companion.

Martina's incredible that way. Besides her coach, Mike Estep, and his wife, Barbara, and Pam Derderian, who helps with her business, Martina is traveling with her good friend, Judy Nelson, and six members of Judy's family. They're all nice, but I'd go nuts with so many people around. Martina, though, thrives on it. She can shut out her surroundings better than anyone I've ever known. I've seen her in tears, emotionally torn, right before a Wimbledon final, and then go out and win in a breeze.

June 5—Paris

Tonight was the International Tennis Federation's Champions Dinner to honor Martina and John McEnroe, the No. 1s of 1984. This dinner is always a treat for me because the game's grand old guard shows up in force: René Lacoste, Jean Borotra, Don Budge, Fred Perry, Frank Sedgman, Tony Trabert, Fred Stolle, and Maria Bueno were on hand tonight. And of course, Ted Tinling was the *chargé d'affaires*.

Ted has been a fixture on the international circuit for over sixty years, ever since he used to umpire for Suzanne Lenglen's matches on the French Riviera in the '20s—even though he was barely a teenager at the time. He's British and was, from all reports, what the British call "a useful player." He combined his two passions, tennis and fashion, into one career and is probably best known outside of tennis for putting the lace on Gussy Moran's panties at Wimbledon and the sequins on Billie Jean's dresses in America. His bold and flashy designs became just the bright signature that the fledgling women's pro tour needed in the early '70s. Ted has always been ahead of his time, and he's always known it. "You all are going to miss me when I'm gone," Ted says, and I'd believe him except I think the 74-year-old guy with the bald head and the diamond in his ear is going to dance on all our graves.

Anyway, Ted lent his usual touch of class to the affair tonight. It even rubbed off on McEnroe, who seemed as comfortable in front of a crowd as I've ever seen him. He made special mention of his girlfriend, Tatum O'Neal, saying, "I want to thank Tatum for being here with me and for making me a better person." She must be something to make a guy as intensely private as McEnroe say something like that at a dinner for 300 one block off the Champs Élysées.

June 6—Paris

Martina and I beat Chris and her young French partner, Pascale Paradis, today, and I was far more nervous than I should have been. But I'm always nervous when I play Chris in doubles, because that's the one area where I'm her superior. I don't want to lose that advantage even for an instant. I know she feels the same way in singles. It's amazing how easy Chris is to get along with everywhere but on the court. As soon as she even gets near a court, she can put on a special air and make me feel insecure.

Sometimes my mouth gives me a few problems during matches, but I'm mostly just yelling at myself, releasing tension. Chris, however, doesn't understand that sort of emotional imperfection, so I always end up apologizing to her in the locker room. Then she gives me a little lecture on my character deficiency.

I always want to yell at Chris: "Hey, not everybody can appear to be as controlled on the court as you." The reason I say *appear* is that underneath that visible graciousness, there is the fiercest of competitors. Just once, I'd like her to scream out a dirty word on the court or snap back at a reporter or call an umpire an s.o.b. Just once. I know it's in her, but to the public she's always the lady.

Fans even have the impression that Chris doesn't question calls. But she does. Only Chris will never lower herself to *say* anything. She'll just very discreetly stare at the linesman—and sometimes even the umpire—freezing her movement for a couple of seconds. Her eyes say it all. Those eyes can really do quite a job on the officials. Ultimately, the thing about Chris is she always handles herself with class, but she has nastiness in just the right way. Classy nastiness—a terrific combination.

June 7—Paris

Martina gave me her new autobiography yesterday, and I just finished it. She reveals almost everything in her life—her bisexuality, all that. That will make it a lot easier on me when people ask me personal questions about Martina. Now I can just politely say, "It's all in her book. Read it."

Personally, I don't care what Martina chooses to do in her private life as long as she's healthy and happy. But in the back of my mind, I think about her meeting the right guy and being swept off her feet. Martina is extremely sweepable, so I think it's only a matter of time before she gets married and has kids. Good. I'd make a great godmother.

Something else is interesting about Martina and Chris. Chris brought out her autobiography a couple of years ago, and the two books are a fairly accurate reflection of the two personalities on the court—the one charging and open, the other playing it safe and solid.

June 8—Paris

Chris and Martina played their sixty-fifth match today, another Grand Slam finals. Chris edged Martina 6–3, 6–7, 7–5 in one of the most dramatic matches I've ever seen. Technically, Martina served poorly and hit short an incredible number of times, whereas Chris was clocking the ball and never looked like losing until 5–5, 0–40 in the third. Chris could have won in the second set when she had two points for a 4–2 lead. But Martina hung in that set and the match on the strength of her legs and her heart.

In the last set alone there were seven service breaks, partly because of a strong wind that made the ball difficult to time and to read. Chris's backhand passing shot was clean and accurate throughout, so it was only fitting that one last Evert Lloyd two-hander up the line ended the terrific struggle after two hours and fifty-two minutes.

I've never seen Chris so thrilled. I'm sure if this match had slipped away, she would have wondered if she would ever beat Martina in a Grand Slam finals again. Chris was playing on her best surface with favorable conditions against a rival who wasn't playing her best. At 5–5, 0–40 in the third, Martina was ahead for the first time in the match, but then Chris dug deeper and found a champion's pride and mettle. Martina won only two more points the rest of the way. But I think she won a lot of the fans when she came around the net after it was over and gave Chris a hug. Then Martina struggled through a short runner-up speech in halting French. The crowd didn't know whom to love more: the champion for her dignity and graciousness or the vanquished for her valor and sportsmanship. Those two certainly know how to play Grand Slam finals.

I think the reason why the rest of us can't do better against Chris and Martina in Grand Slam tournaments is that we seldom get into a finals. That creates a snowball effect. The more Chris and Martina play big matches against each other, the more experience they deny the rest of us. I'm sure Martina and Chris still get nervous before one of those finals, but the rest of us would probably be throwing up. I would so much like a chance to throw up before a Grand Slam finals.

I've only been in one Grand Slam finals, and I was so young I can hardly remember how it felt. As I watched Chris and Martina today, as good as they are, I saw so many things that they did wrong. So you don't have to be perfect to get to a Grand Slam finals, but it helps to be gutsy and lucky. I mostly identify with Martina because we play the same kind of game. Today she hit way too many short balls. Hana or I would have approached on every one of them. Chris approached quite a bit and took the net away from Martina. Sometimes.

Martina is hitting with too much topspin now, and on television Mary Carillo said out loud what several people have been whispering: that Mike is trying to turn her into a female Mike Estep with a big kick serve and heavy topspin. Of course, Martina's weaknesses are our gains, but the fact is that a female Mike Estep isn't nearly as good as the old Martina Navratilova. Her serve used to penetrate more, but now the kicker acts just like a right-hander's slice, and her forehand, which used to be a cannon shot, is landing around the service line. Maybe she'll start playing more like her old self on the grass. And maybe she won't.

And maybe I'll win Wimbledon. Well, who knows? I spoke to Don on the phone tonight in Baltimore and I told him that, for the first time, I honestly believe I can win Wimbledon. But I'm not going to tell anyone else. It'll be our secret.

June 9—Paris

Marion is going back to the States today. She'd started to climb the walls the last couple of days because the tennis scene has gotten to her. She can't understand how I do the same thing every day. The horrible thing is, I didn't realize how monotonous my life in tennis is until someone else came along and told me.

It rained today, so they moved our doubles final with Helena Sukova and Claudia Kohde-Kilsch off center court. That meant only about 150 people watched us become the first team ever—men or women—to complete a run of eight straight Grand Slam tournaments. It was difficult, too, but after we lost the first set we won the next two rather easily for our ninety-ninth win in a row.

There was only one sticky moment. That came in the second set after I botched an easy volley and we heard one person clap enthusiastically. Martina looked past my shoulder to where the clapping was coming from. "It's Kohde's father," she said, and cursed.

I turned around to see Mr. Kilsch standing on the balcony, laughing at us and smoking. Tennis parents can be such a pain when their kids are playing. Mr. Kilsch is Claudia's stepfather. When he adopted her, she took his name to go with her blood father's, and now Mr. Kilsch travels everywhere with her. Her tennis seems to be the focal point of his life. I don't understand why parents change their lives in order to travel with their kids, but I have seen how being so wrapped up in a child's career seems to warp adult perspective. Lots of parents succumb to tour pettiness; tennis fathers will hit you over the head, while tennis mothers will stab you in the back. Thank God, my parents aren't a part of that.

Anyway, after the match I passed Mr. Kilsch, and before I knew it, I'd called him a jerk. In the locker room Claudia questioned my behavior, which she had every right to do, and we called each other a name or two. Then everything settled down, and I went off to collect my prize money. Wouldn't you know it, of all the people in the world, who's there but Mr. Kilsch, picking up his daughter's check.

This time I told myself not to say a word, and I didn't . . . until he started to scold me. "You are just another ugly American," he said.

That did it. "Oh? You want to talk about an ugly heritage? Let's start with the Germans." Then we started to go around, until finally I said, "You shut up and I'll shut up." A nifty compromise, I thought.

"I shouldn't shut up, I'm older than you," he said. "You shut up."

I finally left. I'll have to apologize to Claudia. Maybe.

June 11—Birmingham, England

Elise Burgin moved in with me because she couldn't find other accommodations. It's amazing we'd be in the same room in 1985 after growing up together in the juniors in Baltimore. Remember, she clobbered me in our first match at Clifton Park in Baltimore. Elise didn't concentrate on tennis full-time until she got out of Stanford. Now she's in the top thirty, and I love having her on the tour. She is one of the easiest players on the tour to tease because she doesn't take the jabs personally. She's funny, spirited, and as good-natured as they come.

June 14—Birmingham

Oh, great. Here I was so keen for Wimbledon, and it's been raining every day. Now my serve has disappeared. Rhythm just gone, only where to? I wish I knew.

June 15—Birmingham

Wouldn't you know: I haven't played Elise in singles in nine years, we room together for the first time, and we have to face each other in the semis. I'd always heard how Stolle and Emerson used to fix breakfast for each other before their Wimbledon finals, so I figured Elise and I could manage before the Birmingham semis. But last night she nearly drove me nuts, what with a late massage, then a bath, then doing laundry, the midnight phone calls from the States. Then I awoke this morning to the sound of Elise rattling the icebags strapped to her sore arm.

Once we got on court, I began to feel more comfortable with the situation. She's not a natural grass-court player, and even though I struggled with my serve, I beat her four and two. The highlight of the match came in the second set, when I blew a lob volley. I forgot my head was raised and when I said, "That was a f------ horrible effort," you could hear it all over Birmingham. The umpire gave me a warning for "audible obscenity," which it sure was, audible and obscene both.

"Well," I said to the umpire, "how else would you describe that shot?" The crowd broke up, but Elise didn't think it was so amusing.

When we shook hands, she said, "God, you're weird on court, Pam."

I said, "I'm the same as always. You just haven't played me in nine years."

I find the women's tour such a contradiction at times. On the one hand, it's blood-and-guts competition and the women always want to be treated like the men—equal prize money, equal press coverage, equal everything—but then they go and take remarks made on the court so personally. I mean, you just can't have it both ways, but that's the way we women often seem to want it.

June 16—Birmingham

I called Don last night and he made a few suggestions about my serve. So I went out today and threw my toss a little more to the right and out in front . . . and killed Betsy Nagelsen 6–1, 6–0. I've won fourteen matches (and three tournaments) in a row on grass going into Wimbledon. Maybe I've forgotten how to lose.

And this too: This was my first tournament victory without Don Candy at my side. Hank was really pleased with *our first* win.

June 18—Eastbourne

Today Navratilova and Shriver did it—100 straight wins, the first time in modern tennis history. We went into this match with a little more intensity than we usually have for a first-round match, and cruised past Gretchen Rush and Camille Benjamin 6–0, 6–3. They made us sweat a little: We lost twelve straight points to go down

1–3 in the second before winning the last five games in a row for our century.

Tonight there was a dinner party in our honor. I had a glass of champagne or two or three and got very giggly. About thirty people came to celebrate our century. Martina stood up and reiterated what she had also said at the Virginia Slims banquet in March: She never wanted to play doubles regularly with anybody but me. This time I was ready. I grabbed a menu and drew up a contract on the back:

"I, Martina Navratilova, promise always to play doubles with Pam Shriver."

Then, suitably armed, I got up to speak and promptly found my head in the lampshade hanging over the table. Once the laughter had subsided, I read the contract aloud and made her sign it. I even had George Hendon, the tournament director, sign as an official notary. I'm never going to lose this contract.

June 19—Eastbourne

The practice-court situation the week before Wimbledon is abominable. There are only eight courts for about ninety players. Trying to get a court alone for an hour is almost impossible. The stakes are so high, and both Hank and I have been touchy. My arm doesn't feel terrific, and I'm torn between serving more to find my rhythm or serving less to get rid of the soreness.

Here is the last word on tennis mothers, I swear. Abe Segal, who used to be a tour player, Betsy Nagelsen, and I were sitting at breakfast a couple of days ago when Annabel Croft and her mother walked by to go to the buffet table. Now Annabel is 19 and English, but she definitely has an untamed seductiveness about her. In our WTA calendar, for example, she posed in a leopard skin something—I thought that went out in the '60s, but with her long, wavy, chestnut mane and good looks, it seemed to work. And her mother is definitely from the same pride. Anyway, Abie is a healthy male and he took one look at the dynamic duo, dropped his bangers and mash, and said, "*That's* the best package deal on the women's tour."

June 20—Eastbourne

The countdown for Wimbledon is making everybody testy and the rain hasn't helped matters. Needling on the court is never pleasant, but it's miserable when one of your best friends is involved. Today Martina and I played Elise Burgin and Alycia Moulton. We got an early break only to lose my serve at 3–1. Alycia had a game point for 3–3 and hit one of her huge serves, which caught the line. I barely returned it. My return was floating harmlessly toward Elise at net when the linesman called a fault on Alycia's serve. Elise smashed my return away and the umpire overruled the fault call, announcing the game for Burgin-Moulton. I told the umpire that since I'd made the return over the net we had to play a let.

It was bad luck for Elise and Alycia, but the rule book backs me up. They grudgingly accepted the replay of the point, but when we won it, Elise glared over at me and said, "Ya happy?" She'd been muttering to herself since the match began so I knew she was nervous or angry. But so was I, so I retorted, "Don't be a jerk (or something like that). You keep quiet and I'll keep quiet."

Instead, we got crankier and more vindictive. In Martina's next service game, Elise lashed out at one of Martina's second serves and ripped it at me. If I hadn't been concentrating, I'd now be headless. I barely reflexed the volley back and Elise stepped up for another shot at the sitter. She was so overeager that she sent it right into the middle of the net. "Bad luck," I said facetiously.

The last incident came on my serve midway through the second set. I had already lost serve twice and was getting pretty frustrated with it. When my service winner on the centerline was signaled good but then ruled out by the umpire, I botched that point and the next. I let out my first good yell of the match, a loud "God," followed by a quieter "dammit." When I heard Elise mutter something to the umpire about a warning being in order, I almost walked around the net. If Elise wasn't such a good friend I wouldn't have been as angry, but she had criticized my little outburst the week before as well and now she was getting obnoxious.

Martina told me to settle down and talk to Elise after the match.

We finally won 6–3, 6–4, and Elise barely looked at me as we shook hands. Later on in the locker room, our reconciliation began with me throwing crushed ice at her as she stepped out of the shower. The only good thing about fights on the court is straightening them out in the locker room. But sometimes you just don't get to the sanctuary of the locker room.

I remember several years ago I was playing doubles with Kathy Jordan against Rosie Casals and Ilana Kloss at Amelia Island. Jordan and Shriver, the young lions, lost in straight sets and it was the finals to boot. I guess I'd been kind of a jerk during the match, but at the end I thought everything was fine and at the net I extended my hand to Rosie.

Well, she took after me like a terrier attacking the mailman. She called me some choice names and said that I was obnoxious. I finally retreated to my chair, but she came around the net to my chair and started challenging me again. Then I started calling her names.

Meanwhile, two guys came on court with the tables and the trophies for the presentation ceremony. The sponsor came out to present the checks, and Edy McGoldrick, the tournament director, had to step between Rosie and me. That was the closest I've come to seeing two women get into a fistfight on court.

June 21—Eastbourne

Yesterday must have been my day for mending fences because I found Mr. Kilsch in the player tent and said, "I'd like to apologize for what happened in Paris." He couldn't have been nicer. He said, "And you forget what I said to you." We shook hands and, just like that, everything's fine.

Don arrived today and I was so excited to see him. Hank's been doing a terrific job with me, but Don is someone special. I'm not playing singles here, but in doubles and in practice, my serve has been fluid and accurate, my returns low and near the sidelines. I've never approached Wimbledon in such a confident frame of mind.

June 22—Eastbourne

Martina and I ran our doubles streak to 104 matches, winning the tournament over Jordan and Smylie in two tight sets. I was relieved because they're tough and mobile and seem to get better with each match. We never really found a comfortable groove because it was so windy and cold. Those kinds of conditions favor the underdog, and I was worried that we'd lose our streak because of the capricious English weather.

Afterward, Martina remembered to show me a telegram that had been addressed to both of us after we won No. 100. It was from Chris. She called us her "doubles idols." Can you imagine any of the men players sending another player a congratulatory telegram? Well, that's not altogether fair to the men. Not many of the women would have done what Chris did, either. In fact, none of them did, did they?

June 23—London

I've gotten a rotten draw for Wimbledon. I catch Martina in the quarters; I'm seeded fifth. And what makes it worse is that the reason I play Martina in the quarters is because Manuela Maleeva is the No. 4 seed. Boo.

Besides that, my four matches leading up to the quarters are mental testers. First there's Anne White, a big, hard-serving American who always seems to make me struggle even though she's never beaten me. Then, Anne Hobbs to play Virginia Wade: two Brits on home turf. Next, Steffi Graf, the young West German who might forget where she is and plug into her limitless potential five years early against me!

Well, what the heck! I'm playing the best grass-court tennis of my life. My serve has regained the fluid, accurate power it had in Australia. My returns have been consistently low and near the sidelines. I know deep inside that with solid, grass-court play I'll reach my quarterfinal with Martina. I'm not even too ticked that I have to play her. I know I can beat her, especially the way she's been playing recently. At this stage of my career, I'm not too interested in just reaching the quarterfinals. I want to win the darn thing.

June 24—London

The weather has been horrible, even by English standards. Through two days of play only seven matches have been completed. At times like these, with everybody cooped up in the Tea Room or the changing rooms, you hear a lot of stories.

There are the inevitable silly yarns of how Wimbledon's rules and sense of propriety trips up a rookie or two. This year it is Hu Na, the Chinese player who defected to the United States in 1981. Hu Na qualified for her first-ever Wimbledon by winning three preliminary matches at the Rowhampton Club, where they don't observe Wimbledon's white-only clothing rule. She didn't realize that Wimbledon can be pretty starchy about the rule; she had to buy all her skirts, shirts, and socks off the rack! Na shouldn't feel badly: I remember being told that one year Martina had to run out to Harrods to buy a white tracksuit during one particularly chilly fortnight because the only warm-ups she'd brought were red!

But some of the locker-room tales are just so sad. This year besides the talk about the bulimia victim, there's been a rumor about a player who has been so beset by injuries the last couple of years that she's fallen into a deep depression.

June 27—London

Obviously, I'm being tested. After four days of rain, in a tournament that started Monday morning, I finally get on the court at 7:15 Thursday evening. Then my opponent, Anne White, takes off her warm-up suit, and there she is wearing the first full-length white leotard in tennis history. Anne was sweating like a bandit in that thing, too. After almost every point she had to go towel off.

I won the first set with a break, but suddenly she went on a tear and broke my serve twice. I battled back and pushed the set into a tiebreaker. The light was fading with every point. I desperately wanted to get off the court a quick winner, and I had two match points in the tiebreaker. But Anne was too tough: On one of the match points she nailed my serve for a backhand crosscourt winner. She took the tiebreaker 9–7, then darkness took the match away until tomorrow.

I just saw on the telly that the All England Club has outlawed Anne's leotard even if it is white. Good! Wimbledon is tough enough without one of my weirder friends serving a sartorial ace like that.

June 28—London

Coming back on court for an unfinished match is terrible on the nerves. Ann Jones, who's English and won Wimbledon once in the '60s, knows all about the pressure here. I hear she was as gutsy as they come. So it made me feel good when she said before I went out for my third set against Anne, "I'll be watching from the Members' Box if you need any encouragement, Pammy."

I held the serve in the opening game, then broke Anne right away. I managed to hold serve the rest of the way and closed out the match 6–3. What a relief!

When we shook hands, she said, "I hope my outfit didn't distract you yesterday."

"Well," I said, "you might have told me about it."

"I didn't want it getting out." But she got plenty of ink, and she got her first postmatch press conference at Wimbledon. Then they brought me in.

"Would you ever wear something like that?" one of the guys asked.

"Nowhere you could see me," I said.

I guess I kind of ruined what could have been the big news of the day, but then John Lloyd beat Eliot Teltscher in a dramatic five-setter on Centre Court, so Fleet Street had its story after all. Teltscher served for the match, but Lloyd played incredibly well in the clutch. Chris's match followed John's on Centre and she looked like a wreck.

"Are you OK?" I asked. Her cheeks were as red as a beet.

"I was hyperventilating in the last game," she said.

God, I'm never going to marry a tennis player. And if I do, he better promise never to play a torturous five-setter on Centre before my match on Centre.

June 29—London

What do you know: I routined Anne Hobbs 6–3, 6–2. No rain, no leotard, no controversy.

June 30—London

Because it's the mid-Sunday off day at Wimbledon, we had our WTA board meeting. Don was furious that I went. He thought I should be resting and concentrating on my next match. I don't think the WTA officials understand how much these long meetings can sap a player's energy. I'm caught right in the middle: Martina and Chris are good enough that it doesn't affect them, and the rest of the board members aren't contenders so they're willing to sit there forever. If anyone's going to be adversely affected, it's me. Anyway, to pass the time today, Chris, Martina, and I passed silly notes back and forth. And who do you suppose wrote the most outrageous notes? Chris. How different she is away from the courts.

I think I'm cursed. It's not enough that I get the first leotard against me, tomorrow I get the last Virginia Wade on Centre Court. "Our Ginny" has announced that if I knock her out she's through at Wimbledon. You can imagine how popular I am in England.

July 1—London

It was worse than I expected. Our Ginny fanned the flames all Sunday—morning, noon, and night—with brave, hopeful, plucky quotes that the British eat up with their tea and scones. By the time we took the court on Monday the crowd was hushed and expectant, as if they were receiving the Queen or something. And in a way I guess they were: Virginia gave them an emotional binge in 1977 when she won the Wimbledon title on the occasion of the Queen's 25th Jubilee, and the British have treated her like royalty ever since.

I managed to keep the crowd pretty quiet in the first set. I served well and returned well enough to break her twice to claim the set 6–2. But then I started missing my first serves. She started pounding my second serves. I double-faulted a few times. The crowd started to warm to the contest: They would have to root her home. All told, there were five breaks of serve in the second set, three against me. When she hit two return winners in a row and won the set 7–5, the noise hit me like a wall of thunder.

I smiled, or at least tried to. I was determined not to show any pain (my new mature behavior). It got pretty scary in the third set, and my stiff upper lip was beginning to shake when I went down 1–2, 0–30 on my serve. Those nice, sporting, fair-minded Englishers were exploding on every Wade winner and tepidly pit-patting after a Shriver winner. After awhile, on the crossovers, I'd make sure to wait until Virginia went back on court before I did, so then I could pretend that some of the applause was for little old me. Virginia even had one break point against me for a 3–1 lead, but she missed. The collective sigh from the standing-room-only crowd was deafening. After I held on to that service game, she folded and I gained confidence. I swept the next five games for the match. Phew!

Later I had dinner with Ian Hamilton, the player rep for Nike. He told me that Nike is having a party for all the guys who wear Nike during Wimbledon, and one for the Nike girls during the U.S. Open. I hate the way everybody naturally separates us. It's become such a reflex that they don't even think about it anymore. When I brought up having us both at the same party, you would have thought I'd come up with Einstein's theory of relativity. "That's a *good* idea! We'll have a mixed party next time," Ian said.

Just another example of a little female ingenuity. It kills me that we are always the ones trying to bridge the gap with the men players. I storm the locker room in Melbourne; I suggest a mixed party to a sponsor. The best story I heard about this came from Anne Hobbs, who told me she went to the Wimbledon ball last Saturday with one of the guys. "How'd you get him to ask you?" I said. "I asked him," she replied. Good for Hobbit. Maybe I'll try that sometime.

July 2—London

Yesterday I played a 39-year-old past champion and today I got a future champion, one who turned 16 two weeks ago. I'm lucky I played Steffi Graf on the grass. It's her worst surface, and she didn't serve and volley at all. She knows how to, but she just forgot to. That's the difference between Steffi and the American kids. They're not even taught to serve and volley. Graf is going to be a top-five player within a year, mark my words.

But I don't know what it is about these German fathers and me. Today Mr. Graf was sitting right behind the linesman, and when he called one of Steffi's passing shots out, Mr. Graf started yelling, "No, no, no," right into the poor guy's ear.

So I turned to him and yelled, "Shut up!" And he did. There wasn't a peep out of him the rest of the match.

July 3—London

Today is the day: Martina in the quarters. I'm determined to sting my volleys, gamble on my returns, and concentrate my hardest. It's been nearly three years since I beat Martina at the U.S. Open, and these are the matches I dearly need to win if I'm going to win a major. So now, enough writing, it's time to find out my destiny this year.

Well, I tried my bloody hardest, but what can I say? Martina played the best against me that she has in a year. I had my chances against her but failed to capitalize. The key to the whole thing was how I played the tiebreaker in the first set. I played it well and set up two or three points that would have put me in a commanding

5–3 position. But I missed a couple of backhands up the line by inches. I really thought I was going to win that tiebreaker. Instead I lost it 7–5 and the match 7–6, 6–3.

I told the press afterward that I'd have no trouble playing doubles with Martina later in the day. But it was hard to smile; this loss hurt. I'm satisfied that I played the right way, and that the points were of a high standard. Only I didn't win. I wasn't good enough.

July 4—London

Happy Birthday, me! I'm 23 years old. My birthday always causes a big fuss because it takes place at Wimbledon and on our Independence Day, but the timing has also given me my share of painful moments. Last year, for instance, I invited about a dozen people for dinner at my favorite London restaurant, Alexander's. Don and I and Graham Lovett, a good friend from Australia, arrived around 8:00 p.m. and began to toast my birthday with champagne, anticipating the rest of the party. Well, one by one everyone called to say he or she couldn't make it. The three of us drank enough champagne to dull the ache of being stood up by nine good friends on my birthday.

This year I decided not to have a big party, just a few people to dinner. Martina and Elise were the only players I asked, and Martina begged off. She has played fourteen sets of tennis the last two days in singles, doubles, and mixed, so who would blame her for wanting a night of rest? Besides, she gave a little party for me at her flat near the club right after our doubles match.

Anyway, Virginia Slims also wanted to note the occasion so they brought me a cake after our doubles quarterfinals, before I went over to Martina's. (I had a modern record, four cakes today.) We beat Chris and Jo Durie. I didn't say anything, but Chris's selection of doubles partners kills me. For the Australian Open, she picked Wendy Turnbull, who's Australian; for the French, she chose Pascale Paradis, who's French; and here she picked Jo, who just happens to be British. I wonder if she's lined up Carling Bassett for the Canadian Open.

Anyway, in the locker room after the match I cut the cake and offered it around. Suddenly Chris piped up, "Pam, for those of us who aren't invited to your party tonight—can we have a piece of cake, too?"

I was stunned. I almost dropped the piece I had cut. I knew very well that even if I had invited her, Chris wouldn't drag into London from Wimbledon for any birthday party of mine two days before she plays No. 66 against Martina. So she's mad at me for something else. Will you please tell me why we women have to be such sensitive bitches sometimes?

July 5—Wimbledon

I found out what was bugging Chris. In the press conference after Martina beat me, I answered a rather obvious question by saying, yes, I certainly wasn't crazy about always having to play Martina in the big tournaments. The last time I played Chris in a Grand Slam event was four years ago in the Wimbledon semis. Since then, I've played Martina five times in Grand Slams and lost three other times before the round I would have played her. Obviously, on the grass at Wimbledon, I'd rather play Chris than Martina—which certainly shouldn't come as a surprise to Chris, inasmuch as she's lost all five times that she's played Martina in the finals here.

But the press kind of slanted my responses when it reported them to Chris. She got her nose out of joint, and she even sent me a sharp little note lecturing me on "sour grapes."

Can't Chris understand? The questions keep coming about Navratilova and Evert Lloyd. I try to defend myself, uphold women's tennis, and say that the other players aren't that far behind, when, in fact—at least at the majors—we're light years behind. No one likes to admit she doesn't have a serious chance.

And Chris: How could she ever understand the frustrations of chasing opponents you never draw closer to? She's always been No. 1 or 2. She's always fulfilled the expectations of the public and herself. Can't she appreciate those of us who never fulfill expectations and who begin to doubt that we ever will? Can't she try and understand what she and Martina do to the rest of us?

July 6—London

It's all over. One hundred and nine wins. Jordan and Smylie beat us 6–4 in the third. I'm sad. I'm proud. We won 109 in a row like champions and today we lost like champions. Kathy and Liz played the best match of any of our opponents, and they deserve the victory.

The only pain is that we were up 3–0 in the third set and blew it. Martina obviously had had a draining day, though. She had taken three sets to beat Chris—and a partisan British crowd—in the finals only two hours before. I wasn't any rock myself, but this was one of those rare times when I had to get after Martina.

When she was broken in that last set to bring them back to 2–3, she just put her head down. I could hardly get her to move. "Come on, let's go, Martina," I said. "Come on." It was all I could do to get her over to sit down for the changeover. That one game was the biggest momentum switch I've ever witnessed. Up to that break, the points had been weird, but we'd been in control. Then they broke Martina and you could just see them come. From then on, Liz was in the clouds. We didn't even think to try different things to stop Liz. Remember in Princeton, when she was playing with Mesker, and we threw the Australian formation at her? Why didn't we give that a fair chance against her today? Dumb, dumb, dumb.

Anyway, at 3–2 we were still on serve. We could have still won. But then Liz held serve, and on my serve in the next game, she mishit a backhand return up the line *on* the line. That point broke our backs. She had no business trying it, then she mishits it and the darn thing brings up chalk! Jordan won the next point for the break and we never recovered.

For the first time in five years I left Wimbledon a loser all round.

It was so hard. When we came into the locker room I started the usual chore of icing my arm. I looked over at Martina and she was crying. I went over to her. "I always knew that whenever we did lose, I'd cry," she said.

I knelt beside her and shed a tear or two myself. What the hell. We'll probably never see 109 consecutive victories again. I don't know if anybody will. I don't think people comprehend what 109 straight wins over more than two years mean. "Don't be too upset," I said. "It's still a special day for you—your sixth Wimbledon, four in a row."

But that didn't seem to pick her up. I knew how much she cared for our matches and for me. So, after a while, I got out the contract that Martina had signed in Eastbourne. I brought it over to her and said, "Is this still good?"

Martina just let out with one of her high-pitched gales of laughter. "Of course, it is, Pam," she said.

But I knew that.

July 7—London

I went over to pick up my prize-money check at the All England Club. One of the first people I saw there was Peter Smylie, Liz's husband. He was grinning from ear to ear, but when he saw me I could see he felt badly for us. "Don't worry about us," I said, "we've won this thing four times."

"You guys were so great after the match. That meant a lot to Liz and Kathy," he said.

I'm playing with Liz in the next tournament, on the grass at Newport. That's going to feel strange for both of us, especially since Kathy has now decided to enter Newport as well.

July 8—London

I'm really bummed out that Chris is mad at me. I bumped into Peter Bodo, a writer for *Tennis* magazine, and he asked me if I'd taken any grief for my quotes.

"Peter," I said, "I didn't think anything I said was all that offensive."

"It really wasn't, but a few of the guys took a couple of things out of context and played it off Chris. I could see it happening and was tempted to say something to Chris about it."

"Well, would you talk to Chris sometime and explain what happened because she's upset with me again."

Peter is a nice guy, and I know he'll plead my case well if the opportunity presents itself. I hope it does because I really don't feel up to making up with Chris again.

July 9—Lutherville

Home again. Oh, how nice to pick up a paper and read about the Orioles—or to make a phone call to a friend without worrying about the time change. I'm feeling reflective, as I often do after a major tournament. I'm 23 now, which is not old by any means. I could play this game for another ten years. But I don't want to play tennis into my 30s. I keep thinking about Virginia Wade.

Bowing out with a good, tough three-setter on Centre Court is the way to leave the game. What will Virginia do now that I've put her on the shelf? Some TV commentary in England and the United States? Some coaching? Some endorsements? But where does the traditional bit fit in? Does she want to get married? Does she want kids? I want to get married; I want to have kids.

All athletes have fears. The fear of losing, the fear of injuries. My fear is the fear of retirement. I've seen too many people stumble on their way to retirement. I don't want to stumble. I want to leave when I choose, not when my game or my body takes the choice out of my hands. I don't want to grow dependent on the applause or the attention or the high of winning.

I've been extremely lucky to have had Don around since the beginning to keep my head screwed on straight. And I have wonderful parents and a wonderful family to keep things in perspective. I still feel as normal as any traveling world-class woman athlete can possibly feel. I still like myself and my values. I've always said that my goal is to leave the game the same person I was when I entered it. It's not easy, you know, because the life seduces you into thinking that you're grander than you are. But I think I can do it.

July 10—Lutherville

I spent the day in New York at a press conference for our Riggs-Gerulaitis challenge match in August. It's Battle of the Sexes II, and I don't think the guys have a chance against Martina and me. Vitas has definitely lost a step, and he's going to need all his steps to cover for Bobby, whose mouth is faster than his feet by a long shot. Neither of us got a word in edgewise, and neither did Vitas, during the p.c. today.

It was Bobby's show. But that's OK. You've got to give the crazy character credit for still being in the limelight forty-six years after he won the "triple" at Wimbledon in 1939. The story goes that he tanked at Queen's Club the week before to set up better odds, and then bet a bundle on himself to win the singles, doubles, and mixed there. And he came through, too! Maybe he knows something we don't know about Battle of the Sexes II?

Interestingly, Martina is probably the player who will win the next triple. She only missed one this year because of our loss in the doubles final (ouch!). She was telling me today that between 2 p.m. Saturday when she went on the court for the singles final and 8:30 p.m. Sunday when she left it with the mixed doubles championship, she played 12 sets and 157 games! She and Paul McNamee won a 6–7, 7–5, 23–21 marathon over Betsy Nagelsen and Scott Davis in the semis, and that match broke the record for the most games played in a Wimbledon mixed match and the most games ever played in a mixed doubles set. "Those are two records I never thought I'd break," Martina said today.

Some people have all the luck: Martina breaks records even when she doesn't mean to!

But back to the Riggs-Gerulaitis thing. I'm hoping it will be fun, but I'm afraid the whole deal is going to be a nuisance. It's scheduled for the Friday before the U.S. Open starts, which is lousy timing. I cringe when I think that the main reason I'm playing the thing is because of the money. Win or lose, I'm guaranteed $100,000; Martina's guaranteed even more. She's going to give her share back to her Youth Foundation which could put me in an awkward spot. Of course, Martina's resources are a lot greater than mine, and I'm beginning to think how more than half of my career is already over.

July 11—Lutherville

I signed my first non-tennis endorsement contract tonight. My agreement with Guy Laroche watches lasts for sixteen months. I'm thrilled. The watches are sporty, medium-priced pieces, and I'm going to ask everyone I see, "Why don't *you* wear a Guy Laroche watch?" Do you think people will get sick of this?

July 12—Lutherville

Hank came up to practice with me today. I sense that he's having problems with his girlfriend, Kim, and all the traveling he's been doing with me can't be helping any. I knew that his traveling on the women's tour would be a test for their relationship. Kim stays home in Alexandria and Hank's meeting all these fit, young girls on the tour. He's 28 and it can't be easy for him. At Eastbourne, he met Carina Karlsson, a cute, fun Swedish player, and they began to flirt. I don't know what this means to his relationship with Kim, and I really don't want to know.

I want to stay out of it. Hank and I have a business relationship. People probably think we're involved with each other anyway, because anytime anyone travels with somebody on the circuit, especially if they're reasonably attractive, people think there's something going on, whatever the sexes. But there's nothing going on between Hank and me . . . except some pretty mean practice sessions and a helluva long itinerary.

July 13—En route

Hank and I are driving from Lutherville to Newport, Rhode Island, to catch the induction of Fred Stolle, Arthur Ashe, and Ann Jones into the International Tennis Hall of Fame. The drive will take around seven hours, give or take a few hours, so we've left plenty of time. I'm sitting here watching the miles slide by and realizing that for all the traveling I've done I've never seen much of this country. My time as a player is so regulated by the places I've got to be and the commitments I've made to tournaments, sponsors, press, practice, matches, and conditioning that there's never time to stop and absorb a place.

For years I've had a dream of touring the United States in a motor home. That's the first thing I'm going to do when I retire. I'm going to drift off into the sunset with an outdoorsy all-American guy, and we're going to follow the sun. Slowly. Past the Great Lakes and the Great Plains, past the Grand Tetons and Mt. Rushmore. Up the Rockies and around the Grand Canyon. Down the west coast from Washington to San Diego. We'll hunt and ski and skate and hike and cook out and sleep under the stars, listening to the animals and becoming part of this great country. If I knock on your door to ask for directions, be nice because I won't mean to intrude. I only want to get close. To America.

Well, we arrived in time for the Hall of Fame ceremony, and a quickie it was, too! Sometimes tennis seems to do things in such a Mickey Mouse way. After a lifetime of achievement in the game, Fred and Arthur and Ann were given a minute to sum up their thoughts and feelings. One minute! That's not exactly what I expected when I rose at 6:00 a.m. to drive the seven hours to be there in time for the ceremony.

July 15—Newport

I'm worried about getting "up" for another tournament so soon after Wimbledon, and Chris is still mad at me for some things I said to the press there. So I'm a little uncomfortable here, but grass will always be my favorite surface and my arm feels good. The 2½-month break was the best thing I've ever done for myself.

July 16—Newport

Why do I have so much trouble sleeping? I swear, sometimes I feel like I haven't slept in a whole week.

July 17—Newport

I'm more nervous here than I was at Wimbledon. That's ridiculous. I played Lisa Spain Short today and the tension never left me. I won but it wasn't easy.

Then I shot the breeze with Chris, Wendy Turnbull, and Ana Leaird. People often wonder what we talk about in the locker room. We talk about guys, their bodies, and their habits just like the guys talk about girls. Today's topics also covered birth control (no consensus: pills, IUD, diaphragm, rubbers, or chance it) and pot (consensus: who needs it? One day, I'll probably try it).

It upsets me that Chris is still mad at me. I know she likes me, but I guess she doesn't always care for my big mouth.

July 18—Newport

Today I'm a tennis player. Tomorrow, the first woman senator from Maryland? That just shows you what a couple of glasses of wine at dinner can do. I went out with a bunch of Philip Morris execs and got to talking with Len Saffir. He works for the PR firm that represents Philip Morris, but he's also done some political publicity for a senatorial candidate, and by the end of the evening he'd drafted me. "You wouldn't need a degree," he said, deflecting my reservations. "I bet 20 percent of all U.S. senators haven't finished college." Then he kidded me that he was volunteering to run my campaign for the seat that Senator Charles Mathias, the incumbent from Maryland, is vacating: Can you see it? Pamela H. Shriver (R-Md)?

July 19—Newport

It's happened again. Whenever Chris loses a set or struggles to win, the papers quote her as saying she's "lost her concentration" or "lost her timing," or, heaven forbid, both. Well, yesterday Chris beat Hu Na 6–2, 7–5, and this morning's paper quotes Chris this way:

"My timing was off, and I didn't return well. It's very hard for me to keep up a high standard of play. One match in a tournament is not going to be quite as sharp."

And then, finally, some words of praise for Hu Na: "She's a good little player. She serves and volleys well and moves well and has a good attitude."

To be fair, Chris is invariably gracious and complimentary towards her opponents, but in the papers it doesn't always sound that way. I wish she could understand this about me!

July 20—Newport

Wendy Turnbull has become a difficult person for me to read lately because she's so inward about her feelings. We've had some misunderstandings the last couple of years because of things I've said on court and to the press. I've apologized and tried to explain that I'm cutting myself down and sometimes in doing that I cut other people down too, but I don't think I've gotten through to her.

It's funny that Rabbit would ever be mad at me, because she's the one who sticks out in my mind as a player who's gotten the most out of herself, and I respect her as much as I do anybody on the circuit. She's not very big but she's very quick and she always plays the right shot. She's actually taught me a lot when I've played her, and I lost to her the first nine times we played. Wendy's so professional she doesn't lose many matches from being nervous or getting angry. So much of her game is control, and after a winner, she has this little swagger. That's all she shows. Imagine!

I always have to work hard to beat Wendy, and today was no

different: 6–4, 7–6. So tomorrow I go against Chris in the finals for the first time in $2^1/_2$ years. And Chris is still mad at me. Great.

July 21—Newport

Well, I lost again, four and one. I'm now 0–15 against Chris, and I'm beginning to think she'll never ease up enough for me to get close. I seem to bring out the fire and ice in her. She played great. I didn't. End of story. Well, not quite.

The whole thing was an emotional fiasco. Throughout the second set I kept thinking about how Chris was beating my brains out because she was still ticked at me for those quotes of mine at Wimbledon. The first set had been a typical experience of me getting up 2–0, 30–0 on my serve and losing the vital break and being up 0–40 but failing to break hers. I've lived through those failures before and I learn from them. But the second set was a wipeout.

I was pathetic. As soon as we shook hands I sat down and bawled like a baby. I haven't cried on the court in years, but I can't stand having people mad at me—especially Chris—for no reason. And I can't stand not making any progress against her. This was on grass, for crying out loud!

At least something good came out of the ordeal: I don't think Chris still thinks I slighted her at Wimbledon. In my postmatch comments, I tried to make that clear. In my runner-up speech on court, I said, "People misunderstood what I said about wanting to play Chris after $2^1/_2$ years. I mean, do you think I enjoyed this? I never meant that I'd win or anything, although sometime somewhere I think I will win and then I hope Chris will forgive me. . . ." I nearly cried again.

Chris responded in kind. She told the crowd that she had been oversensitive and that she could understand my frustration. Then she went on to say some nice things about me, but I wasn't in the mood to hear them.

I might have felt a little better if Liz and I had been able to salvage the doubles, but we played badly and lost to Wendy and Chris, of all people! I can't stand losing to Wendy and Chris in doubles, so I was nearly vomiting by the end of the 6–4, 7–6 debacle.

The only solution? Stop at the Pimms booth on the way back to the locker room, of course. The ladies there were only too happy to help me soothe my bruised feelings. Imagine playing in the hot sun for hours, feeling depressed, and then drinking some whiskey-and-champagne concoction, all on an empty stomach. I was reeling by the time about ten of us piled our junk and our bods into four cars and headed towards Worcester, Massachusetts, for a Tina Turner concert.

Of course, by this time, the girls at the Pimms booth had given me a refill, and then I felt called upon to relieve Analee Thurston of her drink. After all, she was driving. Talk about drowning your sorrows! Anyway, I remember rambling on and on about the frustrations of the day and the tennis life and other people's touchy feelings and . . . and . . . and. . . .

The concert was loud and blurry, but I did notice that Tina Turner has great legs. God, she's sexy. Every time I jumped up to dance, someone pulled me back into my seat, so I boogied to the bathroom. On the way back, I saw a fuzzy Chris Evert Lloyd buying something at the T-shirt booth. I walked over and said, "I'm sorry for everything that happened. I didn't mean it." She said, "It's OK, I overreacted." So, not only have we made public amends, but private ones, too.

I feel much better, emotionally. Physically, I'm a wreck. I'm sober now. Sober and wide awake at 3:35 a.m., watching an ad on TV about "the electronic fish caller" and "bonus lures." I've never known thirst until now. So this is what it feels like to have a hangover. I don't ever want to feel like this again. I swear that I will never drink another Pimms as long as I live.

July 22—Lutherville

Captain Tom Gilroy, U.S. Marines, came up from Washington to take me out to dinner. He was my escort at the state dinner in April.

I like him . . . and he's only an hour's drive away.

Liz and Peter Smylie are driving down from Newport to spend the night here. They're two of my good friends on tour. They're both Aussies, spirited and funny. Peter toured with Liz for a year or two before they were married last November. He was a touring pro and then a teaching pro with Tony Roche in Australia. Tony was the best man at their wedding.

Anyway, Peter is still Liz's coach and that must get sticky at times. He can't always tell her what she has to hear from a coach, because he is also her husband. It is a complicated role so Rochie still puts his two cents in in Australia and at different times during the year when they all happen to be at the same tournament.

July 23—Lutherville

I'm working on putting together an exhibition tournament in Baltimore to benefit the Cystic Fibrosis Foundation. I have never played a professional match in Baltimore, and this seems like the best way for me to help in the fight against CF. I would play for nothing and Martina might participate for a reduced fee, but we still need about $100,000 in corporate sponsorship. My agent, Sara, and I made presentations to four companies around town, but the banks seem to be the only ones likely to put up that much money.

My social life is picking up: first the dinner with Captain Tom and tonight Craig Fitchett, my old McDonogh buddy. Craig likes himself, but not in a bad way. He's definitely got one of the finest bodies I've ever seen. During dinner my mind kept wandering. . . .

July 26—Lutherville

Hank drove up from Alexandria to work me over. Our practice sessions are much more physical than what Don and I used to do together. I pulled a butt muscle which really became painful at the end of two hours. Serves me right: I haven't been stretching enough.

July 29—Los Angeles

I called Tom Gilroy tonight and he told me he'd been thinking a lot about me. I didn't tell him, but I've been thinking a lot about him, too. I always figured there would be a time when I'd date a few guys besides John. When I first met John a year and a half ago in Dallas, I couldn't remember the last time I'd met an attractive, intelligent man within five years of my age. I enjoyed his company and we hit it off beautifully. He came to visit me a couple of months later and the two weeks passed quickly (a good sign) and pleasantly. But now our careers make the visits more infrequent than I think a relationship needs to grow and prosper. And my social life is just starting to blossom. John, who went through his "blossoming" in his late teens and early 20s like most normal kids, is readier for a serious relationship than I am. I was concentrating so much on my tennis in my teens and early 20s; now I'm ready to play the field a bit. I don't want to feel uncomfortable or guilty, so I'm going to Dallas next week to let John know where I stand.

July 30—Los Angeles

I just finished writing President and Mrs. Reagan, wishing them a relaxing vacation. God knows, after the cancer operation, they deserve it. I never know if they receive these letters, but I feel better knowing I've written them. After all, the President is as close to a hero as I've ever had.

August 1—Los Angeles

This is the life. Sunshine, warm breeze, the sound of waves, the endless Pacific. Yes, I'm making a rare appearance at the beach in my bikini. You can certainly see that I don't work on my tan very often: I'm fish-belly white from my neck to my upper thighs, and below my ankles my feet are the same shade of pale. Yick! I'm happy I'm not playing doubles because I'll have more time to catch up with the bronzed goddesses on tour. I don't know how they have the time or the patience to lie around getting rays, but more than half the players on the tour are golden brown.

August 2—Los Angeles

My long-lost serve came bouncing back today. I crushed Peanut Louie five and one. Ten aces! Then back to the beach where some guy just walked up and asked, "Excuse me, but do you know where I can get some weed?" Only in California!

August 3—Los Angeles

Tonight I beat Zina Garrison 7–6, 6–4 in a fine, hard-fought match. Zina is as nice an opponent as anyone on the tour. She applauds good shots and occasionally acknowledges your winners with a simple "Yup." After the match, Zina gave me a soul handshake at the net. Hey, I'm cool, too.

August 4—Los Angeles

Claudia Kohde-Kilsch killed me two and three in the final. I could've played better, but from the first game I was looking down the barrel of a German cannon. She didn't miss one ball. Still, five finals in my last six tournaments isn't bad. And somehow it's hard to get upset about losing a tennis match when 137 people lost their lives in the crash of Flight 191 outside Dallas two days ago. Plane crashes are always terrible but this one was a bit close for comfort. I'm taking the sister flight, Flight 192, to Dallas today.

I read the accounts in the paper and was shocked to see Ian Laver's name on the list of victims. He was Rod Laver's cousin and a pro at Laver's Racquet Club in Florida. I didn't know him well but I'd met him. His 12-year-old son, Richard, survived the crash.

Flying has never bothered me because it's a necessary part of my life. But I do hate seats away from the window. I guess I feel more secure when I can see the ground. The only time I've really been scared on a plane I was stuck in the inside seat of a JAL DC-10 on a short flight from Tokyo to Osaka. I kept craning my neck to see out a window. Couldn't see a thing. Thicker than pea soup outside. We were descending. Still no clearing in the clouds. The ground *couldn't* be that far away; the landing gear was down. Suddenly, without warning, the plane's nose jerked up and we started a rapid ascent. "*What* is going on?" I thought. The longer the crew refused to explain, the more my alarm grew. Finally the captain rattled off something in Japanese. None of the Japanese around me seemed the least bit concerned, but that wasn't much comfort. They don't show much emotion anyway. Finally, the translation: We had made a "misapproach to the runway."

A misapproach! OK, I miss approaches all the time, but I don't have traffic controllers helping, and my unforced errors aren't life-threatening. How could he make a misapproach? When we landed twenty minutes later, I nearly ran off the plane.

August 5—Dallas

I'm not as comfortable with John as I was a few months ago. I know he senses this. We had a long but not-too-conclusive talk about "us." He doesn't see the distance as a real obstacle. I sure do. He wants us to keep phoning each other every two days, but I find the conversations a bit tedious that way. Why not call each other once a week so we have a little more to say? No, he thinks our calls will become less and less frequent that way until we don't call each other at all. Another dead end.

I wasn't sure when I arrived here how I would leave John this time—as a boyfriend, an ex-boyfriend, a friend, or a strange combination. I guess it'll be the latter.

I do know I need a couple of years to date as many men as I want. John said he understood, but I'm not sure that he does. Men are showing a lot more interest in me lately. In L.A., a TV producer I'd met during an interview sent me a note with a teddy bear in a tutu. He said I'd made his day. *Sure*. The next day, Captain Tom Gilroy, U.S. Marines, sent me flowers wishing me luck in the tournament. That made *my* day.

John and I had talked about taking a vacation somewhere warm in late December. What if we plan something now and by then I'd rather go with someone else? Oh boy, am I in a mess or what? Sure beats not having any guys around, though!

August 6—Dallas

I phoned Parkland Hospital here to get a condition listing on young Richard Laver. He's serious but stable. I then reached a family waiting room or something to leave a get-well message. I spoke to a man and started to spell my name. "I know you," he said and thanked me. I wonder if Richard Laver knows me. If he did, it might be nice for him to know people are thinking of him.

I played two sets of doubles against Dick Stockton and Courtney Henderson, a nationally ranked senior. My partner was Bill McGowan, the head pro at T Bar M. Dick thinks Martina and I will beat Riggs and Gerulaitis. Dick was ranked in the world's top twenty when Vitas was playing at his best, so he should know a thing or two. He said Vitas's favorite shot is a backhand up the line.

Martina and I play R & G in eighteen days, but *I* seem to be the only one concerned about the match. I called Martina and suggested we play doubles in Mahwah next week, but she wants to take most of that week off. We haven't played together since Wimbledon—and we lost there, remember? The compromise is that I'll go wherever Martina is a few days prior to the challenge. I'll bring Hank along and she'll have Mike. If we can beat those two we'll be in good shape.

This match is a really stupid thing to be worrying about right before the U.S. Open. Maybe her attitude is the right one, but I'd hate to lose to a 67-year-old with a big mouth and a 31-year-old with a big mouth. I don't think *that* would look very good for women's tennis.

August 7—En route

I'm sitting next to Jill, an "almost-8"-year-old from Tyler, Texas. She's decked out in a pink jumpsuit and pink sandals. Her only comment on all my rackets was "My stepdad plays all the time. . . . Likes to watch it on TV, too."

Jill sure beats some of the fat people I've had to sit next to on airplanes who only want to talk about tennis. She's on her way to see her real daddy in Washington and she can't sit still: 2½ hours is a long time for an almost-8-year-old to wait when she hasn't seen her daddy in a year.

Jill and I have helped each other out on the flight. I unjammed the lock on her little green suitcase; she shared her bubble gum and potato chips (sour cream and onion: her favorite). She even offered to scratch my back. I accepted. I wish I had her on every flight.

August 8—Lutherville

I've ducked into a phone booth and hope to emerge as Pam Shriver, businesswoman. Noxell has committed $10,000 to my exhibition for CF in Baltimore, and Black & Decker might do the same, so we're in search of a $100,000 umbrella sponsor. We've got a number of corporate presentations lined up today.

August 9—Lutherville

Hey, what do you know! I read in the paper that Chris is playing in Toronto this week, and guess who she's playing doubles with in the Canadian Open? Yep. Carling. But, gee, they're also scheduled to play the U.S. Open together. I guess Miss America wasn't available for Chris. Just kidding, Chris. Just kidding!

August 10—Lutherville

Maybe Don's right. Maybe I am stretching myself too thin. The last two days I've been from CF business meeting to photo shoot for Cybex (the people who gave me my exercise bike) to lunch with Don to practice with Hank to Washington for two newspaper interviews to dinner at Sara's to the Marine Parade and a night on the town with Captain Tom Gilroy, U.S. Marines. Then more practice, this time in northern Virginia with Hank and Kim Shaefer, a photo session with *USA TODAY*, and finally a picnic with my family out in Dad and Mom's orchard last night.

And oh, yes, a conversation with the Vice President, whom I'd called to get permission for *Sports Illustrated* to use (in my diary excerpt) the photo of us dancing at the state dinner. The article is due out in August. Would you believe Mr. Bush asked me to Maine for the weekend for a little lunch and tennis? Sounds like a great idea, but I don't think I can swing it.

I'm not sure what will happen in this new friendship with Captain Tom, but I do enjoy his company. As with all my male friends, I never know when I'll see him again. But he does happen to have his leave in Germany in October when I'll be playing in Stuttgart. Might be a neat coincidence.

August 11—Mahwah

Hank and I drove up to Mahwah where, on one of those rare occasions, we're staying in private housing. My host for the week, Bill Feehan, and his family couldn't be nicer: They understand that the most important thing is not to treat a pro like she's a goddess. Actually the goddess in the family might be 18-year-old Kim who's an only child and fighting an adolescent's battle against puppy fat. Her dad showed up this morning with enough buns, rolls, cakes, and breakfast pastries from the bakery to sink a ship.

When Hank and I checked in at the tournament site, I found Elise Burgin in the locker room. She told me the best clean joke I've heard in ages.

"Why don't the Chinese have phone books?"

"Why?"

"Because they have so many Wings and Wongs that they might Wing the Wong number."

Isn't that a great joke?

August 12—Mahwah

I beat Ros Fairbank six and four in a difficult first-round match. Ros plays slowly, even stalls at times, and she's beaten me, so she has confidence against me. My toughest matches are the ones I'm expected to win. I'll take playing Chris and Martina any day. Those are the matches I live for. There's no pressure and I have such a great time. Somehow, I've got to have that loose feeling in all my matches.

Then I had some endorsement business to take care of. Equipment endorsements make up a large part of a player's income, and I haven't had a shoe or clothing deal since the spring. In April, Fila, the Italian clothing company, dropped me after a six-year association. Although Fila's decision wasn't personal—the growing strength of the dollar vs. the lira made my contract 60 percent more expensive for them—I was hurt. I'm a loyal person and I build relationships to last. Then when Nike didn't renew my shoe contract, I was beginning to get a little panicky.

But Prince signed me to a new racket contract recently, and now I may go with Prince for clothes and shoes as well. My contract is actually a pay cut for me, but I'll be the only one wearing their stuff and it will be for three years. I love to be different, and I like the idea of being an all-Prince girl.

The endorsement market is getting much tighter because manufacturers have been stung by whiz kids who burst on the scene with one or two great tournaments, gobble up huge guaranteed contracts, then fade to No. 40 or 50 in the rankings. I wouldn't mind having a contract based on my performance and my ranking: If I'm in the Top Ten, I receive X amount; if I fall out of the Top Ten I get docked, and if I fall out of the top twenty I get docked some more. This kind of deal would be fair to both sides.

The kids and their agents are messing things up for consistent players like me. I've been in the Top Ten for over four years. I'm also one half of the No. 1 doubles team in the world. I'm personable and love to do appearances and cocktail parties, but still no contract. Maybe Anne White had the right idea after all.

August 13—Mahwah

There's a lot of loose change to be pocketed during the Grand Slam tournaments. A few weeks ago, ProServ came to me with a patch deal for two weeks at Flushing Meadow. I'd receive a ridiculously large amount of money from Audi—ridiculous when one considers my only job is to sew a 2-square-inch patch on my sleeve (my sewing is not worth beans). I told ProServ I couldn't do it because Ford had spoken to me at Wimbledon about a $25,000 deal to act as spokesperson for their Ford Challenge Cup, a four-woman special event in the spring. It's just not right to wear an Audi on your sleeve in September and then work for Ford in April. Especially if you still drive a BMW. But now Sara has to track down the status of the Ford deal.

I also have the watch contract with Guy Laroche. They make beautiful clothes, too, so I drove into New York City to meet with their president, Stan Schwartz, and to ransack their showroom. Good. My wardrobe needs a lift and the price is certainly right.

August 14—Mahwah

Housing at tournaments is a little like roulette. You just never know what the chemistry will be between you and your temporary family.

But the Feehans have turned out to be really great. Bill is excited by our stay; he's a tennis nut and hasn't missed a night at the matches yet. His wife, Jill, is taking us in stride, but she can't do enough for us either.

The funniest thing about Bill is his morning run to the bakery. To help with Kim's diet, I've been stuffing my face with doughnuts, coffee cake, Danishes. This morning it was bagels. Actually, bagels are a good source of carbohydrates and I had three before my match.

God, I just read that another plane went down—520 dead—and it was that same JAL Tokyo-Osaka flight that I had my worst flight experience on.

I'm not too happy with my attitude this week. Actually, I've been in a pissy mood because the weather has been so humid and in the back of my mind is that stupid Riggs-Gerulaitis challenge match next Friday. I just can't seem to get concentrated on my tennis. If I'm not thinking about endorsement deals or Bobby Riggs, I'm thinking about my family and wishing I were home.

My little sister Eleanor had her foot operated on today. She was born without a joint in her foot so Dr. Silberstein fused together three joints. I haven't seen Eleanor since I left for Paris in late May because she's been away at camp. I miss her. She misses me and wants me to lose so I'll be home earlier. If I don't snap out of this cranky attitude, I might be home earlier than I want.

August 15—Mahwah

I beat Helen Kelesi, a Canadian, in miserable heat. She's one more 15-year-old baseliner. She pounds the heck out of the ball off both sides and runs down a lot of balls, but she argues line calls way too much. They're already beginning to call her Hurricane Helen, but at least she has some character and spectators will remember her.

Talking of questionable calls, Hank's girlfriend, Kim, called tonight while Hank was at the movies with Carina Karlsson. Kim wanted to know where Hank was and since I didn't know their current status I had to fib a bit. The truth is Hank finally got up the nerve to ask Carina out. If their relationship grows, it could get sticky for Hank and me because it presents a conflict of interest: He's my coach and he's going out with another player on the tour.

We've discussed it and he said, "Well, I don't think Carina is that much of a threat to you." At this point, that's true, but she's starting to play better and it could become a problem. But I guess we'll cross that bridge to Peyton Place if we come to it. I certainly don't ever want to say to him that he can't go out with someone on the tour. That's just not fair. On the other hand, hey, I'm the boss.

I meet Sabatini next and if I win I could play my third 15-year-old in a row. That prospect chills me. All these kids that start on the tour are baseliners with little instinct for the net. The more I think of my accomplishments at that age, the more special they become. When people remember that I'm the youngest finalist in U.S. Open history I wish they'd add an asterisk: *And she served and volleyed.

August 16—Mahwah

Crap! I lost again to Sabatini. This time in straight sets, five and four. What's worse, I was up 4–1 and serving in the first set. I was in a pissy mood from the start. Don had come up for the match, and when I warmed up with Hank before the match, Don started saying things to help me. It was the same old story: I just didn't want to hear it from him. I was nervous and I got more and more aggravated. Besides, things weren't clear in my mind what I should do on court. The courts were too slow to serve and volley, yet on hard courts I feel that's what I should do.

I didn't play particularly well or intelligently, but the slow courts, heavy-duty balls, night play, and three overrules were all in her favor. And the crowd was on her side!

Can you imagine the crowd cheering for a foreigner in any other country but the good old USA? Still, if these people want to cheer for a 15-year-old, raven-haired South American beauty instead of a Fourth of July-born, 23-year-old, damn-proud-to-be-American girl, that's OK with me. It's a free country. I'll just take myself off to the bar for a couple of Midori melonballs, thank you. These drinks have kind of become a losing tradition at Mahwah, so Don, Hank, Carina, and I drank several to ease the pain. God, I don't want to make a habit of drinking after my losses. I lose too much.

I hate tennis now. I can hardly wait to hit the New Jersey Turnpike and head home.

August 17—En route

I hardly slept a wink last night, but I never do when I combine a late loss with a few drinks. Carina came back with Hank for a while, and I went to bed worried about the back door not being locked. The Feehans had received crank calls throughout the week and were extrasensitive about the doors being locked. Since we were the last ones home and Hank's habits are not exactly stellar in this area, I got up to check the doors at about 3:15 a.m.

The back door was not only unlocked, it was ajar. I shut it and locked it, muttering something about Hank and his "open-door policy." Ten minutes later the doorbell rang. I heard Bill go and answer it. This morning I found out it was Hank. He'd gone outside to walk Carina to her car and I'd locked him out. So Bill and Hank ended up having a nice little chat at 3:30 a.m.

August 18—Lutherville

When I got home yesterday I made a beeline to the hospital to see poor Eleanor. She's at Children's Hospital, where, coincidentally, my sports medicine clinic is located. It was great to see her, even if she's a little bloody and a little bowed. Just being with my family can make me feel so much better.

August 20—Lutherville

Elise and I practiced for two hours before our hunger forced us to stop. I've lost 6 pounds in the last two days by exercising hard and eating dull (salads, sigh). I weigh 157 pounds. I'm sure 157 sounds like a ton to most people but I hide it well (there's got to be *some* benefit to being 6 feet tall).

After practice, Elise, good egg that she is, came to Children's Hospital with me. Only Elise's good humor could get Eleanor out of her crabby mood. I almost walked out on her before Elise's laughter began to work its miracles. After we left Eleanor, I went across the hall to visit Lorie. Lorie has lived at the hospital all her 22 years. She has a horrendous skin-and-bone disease that has left stumps where her arms and legs used to be. I was afraid of Lorie until I found out that her mind is so sharp, clear, and brave. I gave her one of my tennis rackets, which she adores, and we're friends now. Still, she can be a shock to see and Elise was a bit upset by the sight.

August 22—Lutherville

For the first time since April I feel stale. I haven't had more than one week off in a row since I returned to the tour. I'm a bit worn out, and here it is the week before the Open. This is not what you'd call good timing. Today I lost four straight practice sets, one singles and three doubles, and my attitude was pitiful. Tomorrow Hank and I drive up the coast to the Jersey shore to practice doubles with Martina and Mike. The dumb Riggs-Gerulaitis match is interrupting my tournament preparation. Who needs to worry about a doubles challenge of the sexes four days before the U.S. Open begins?

August 23—Atlantic City

This Riggs-Gerulaitis thing is more disorganized than I ever imagined it would be. When Hank and I arrived to practice, the court hadn't been laid down yet and the huge, drafty Convention Hall looked seedy as hell. We disappeared into the casinos for an hour and I shook off some of my depression by relieving a one-armed bandit of ninety-nine quarters.

I still can't figure out who's losing his shirt on this match. There are 100 different chiefs and no Indians. The ticket prices range from $25 to $500, and the $25 seats are 4 miles away from the court. Martina and I asked for upgrades into the $150 seats for the tickets we bought. When the promoters said no, Martina threatened not to play and that seems to have brought them around. I've had to buy twenty-five tickets for friends and relatives—including John, who's coming up from Dallas—and I know Martina has at least that many supporters. If the seats around the court aren't filled, the atmosphere is going to suffer, and the atmosphere ain't exactly Wimbledon to begin with.

We beat R & G easily, 6–2, 6–3, 6–4, never losing serve, but I've had more fun going to the dentist. Martina and I tried to keep it light. We entered the arena wearing coordinated T-shirts (given to us by Kathy Jordan, Liz Smylie, and Marcella Mesker, who were in attendance): "15–0, 30–0, 40–0, GAME," said mine. Hers: "WOMEN DO IT 4 WAYS." But we were too nervous to enjoy any of the hoopla.

The rules allowed both teams to have as many coaches as they wanted on court so Don, Hank, and Mike were all there. Then when we discovered we'd run out of tickets for friends, we smuggled anyone without a ticket onto the court. We needed a traffic cop by the time the ninety-minute fiasco was over.

I knew that if anyone was going to blow our chances it was probably going to be me, so I was even more uptight than normal. I remember one time coming to the changeover and hearing Mike go into some really technical piece of advice. I just put my head down between my hands and said, "I'm just going to play the way I feel comfortable." The strategy was pretty simple after all: Hit everything to Bobby.

It worked like a charm. We hit to him relentlessly and he'd react about five minutes later. Vitas tried to cover as much as he could, and he was trying to line up his forehand all night. That was the only shot that gave us any trouble. I got around on Vitas's serve really well, and I had no problem finding his backhand with my serve.

We knew we had the match when we broke Vitas's serve in his first service game, but we still never loosened up. I hope it was more fun to watch than it was to play, but I have my doubts. In the end, we weren't even challenged.

In the postmatch press conference Bobby never shut his mouth (and he has horrible halitosis). He kept telling anybody and everybody that "it's no disgrace to lose to the best women's doubles team in the world" and how he was "the best 65-and-over player in the world." God, the guy is incredible: He never stops selling.

I guess playing one of those sex challenges every fifteen years or so would be OK. When the time rolls around again, I'll be raising babies and Bobby will be "the best 80-and-over player in the world." I can't wait.

I'm exhausted. I need sleep. I don't like my Open preparation one bit. I've decided to go try to get a solid day of practice indoors at home instead of fighting the predicted rain and shortage of courts in New York. This means I'll have to skip the most important WTA board meeting of my three-year tenure: We're picking our new executive director. But I've got to think of myself and my tennis right now. Don would be proud of me.

August 24—Lutherville

Why is my arm acting up? Is it the heavy-duty balls or the rain? Or have I been neglecting to pace myself properly? I certainly don't feel fresh, and maybe I haven't been as good with my shoulder exercises as I could have been. However, I've entered tournaments not feeling top-notch before and played well. If I can't get up for the Open, then I'm a poor competitor.

I need to slow down in the next two days and concentrate on getting ready for the first match. Atlantic City and Riggs are behind me. I've successfully defended the honor of women tennis players from the big mouth of a 67-year-old hustler. Everyone who came up to watch seemed to have a good time (how, I'll never know). John met a friend of his from New York in Atlantic City and won $600. I hardly saw him between the hoopla and the nerves and the match, but he seemed happy.

Hank and I practiced at Mom and Dad's today for two hours. Right in the middle of our session, my mother brought out the cordless phone and said I had a call. It was the Vice President—just calling to find out the inside dope on the Riggs match. Then an hour later I was dressed and off to the wedding of a friend. John came with me, and I must say, it was nice having a date for a change at these affairs. Marion, Fred (Marion's boyfriend), John, and I have made tentative plans to take a week's vacation together in the Bahamas after Christmas. I wasn't sure I wanted to go ahead with it, but John *is* special and I'd like to have some time with him without tennis defining our schedule and my emotions.

August 26—New York City

When you play the Open, you can spend most of your life on a bus going to and from the Tennis Center. Hank and I were stuck in a traffic jam on the 59th Street bridge for an hour on our way to the courts. Then we had to wait for some kids to squeegie the Grandstand court, and we still played target practice with the puddles.

While we were hitting, Frank Chirkinian, the executive producer of the Open broadcasts of CBS, dropped by and asked me when I was "going to stop all this and come to work." I'm not ready yet, but broadcasting does appeal to me as a neat thing to do after I retire. Like next week.

I was in an edgy mood all day because of menstrual cramps, but I feel lucky to get the crampy day over with before the tournament begins. Your coordination and your timing are off that fraction of a second, and if you hit a tough opponent on your bad day your tournament could be over. Cramps are a serious problem, but, I admit, sometimes we use them as a convenient excuse.

Roy Emerson told me the best period story I've ever heard the other day, and it's too good not to let Emmo tell it verbatim:

"I coached Martina in Team Tennis for the Boston Lobsters in the early '70s," he began in that familiar gravelly Aussie twang of his. "Martina wasn't as receptive to hard work in those days as she is now. She was definitely in the 'before' stage in her fitness training, so I would try to get her into shape by running her hard for big matches.

"I'd begin the practice and say, 'OK, Martina, we have a tough match in four or five days, let's do a lot of work today.' So, I'd run Martina back and forth, side to side, and encourage more than a casual serve and volley, but pretty soon she'd stop running and say, 'How would you like to serve and volley with a period?' "

(At this point in the story, Emmo's eyebrows arched in that quizzical, now-how-should-I-know? kind of look. And then he continued.)

"Giving Martina the benefit of the doubt, I'd lighten the workout, but I'd write down in my little book: July 14, Martina, period. Then, ten days later, I'd say, 'OK, Martina, big match against BJK in three days, let's run you around hard for an hour.' Well, not too far into the workout, Martina would shoot back at me, 'How would you feel running around with your period?'

"I tell you," Emmo finished in mock seriousness, polishing his punchline and arching his eyebrows again, "I would look at Martina and think, 'This woman has more periods than any female alive.' "

August 27—New York City

Last night at the WTA awards banquet to benefit the March of Dimes, I got a good needle into Chris. She had received our WTA Service Award, and truthfully, no one has given more of her time than Chris. She was elected to a record fourth term as WTA president yesterday, but I couldn't let her head get too big, could I? So, when Martina and I received the Doubles Team of the Year Award, I opened my speech by saying, "I'd like to congratulate Chris on finally winning an award for her service." Broke up the house, too, except for Chris: She had gone to the bathroom. Wouldn't you know? I can't ever get the best of her.

August 28—New York City

I got through my opening match against Tine Scheuer Larsen, the Danish No. 1, 6–3, 6–3. My arm felt better than it has in days. I was wearing a patch for Carrera sunglasses on my sleeve for less than the amount Audi offered but it's still more than my sewing is worth. I look at it as a down payment on my hotel bill for Hank, Don, and me for two weeks in New York. That will come to $3500. Now if Carrera would just supply me with glasses so I can stop feeling guilty about wearing my Vuarnets. Remember that Ford deal? Well, it fell apart so I could have worn the Audi patch during the Open.

The first excerpt from my diary in *Sports Illustrated* came out today. Chris thought it was funny. I only hope she thinks so next week after "Shriver, Second Blood" appears. I don't want to offend anyone, but sometimes it's tough not to step on a toe or two.

August 29—New York City

Hank, Don, and I fought through two hours of traffic and a swarm of bees on the courts to get an hour and a half of practice at the Hamlet, a club out on Long Island. The practice-court situation at Flushing Meadow is just pitiful.

Marion came up from Baltimore to stay over for my match tomorrow. We went shopping at I. Miller, among other places. I. Miller is my favorite shoe store because they carry size 11s. It's not easy, you know, wearing a size 11.

Speaking of 11, on a scale of 1 to 10 that's how I rate my favorite New York restaurant, Jim McMullen's on Third Avenue. I've been eating at Jim's since my first U.S. Open in 1978, which was also Jim's first full year in business. Marion and I enjoyed another great meal there tonight.

August 30—New York City

Rain, wind, and hail pounded Flushing today, leaving the courts underwater and the Tennis Center strewn with wind screens, chairs, umbrellas, tree branches, and electrical wires. The joint had to be evacuated, and it looked as if Kevin Curren's wish that "they drop an A-bomb on the place" had come true. Curren's remarks were made in anger after an unexpected first-round loss, but the press is always more sensitive to comments at major events. I've made a couple of PR disasters in my time, but nothing compared to what Kevin did. After all, he just became an American citizen so that he might move about the world more easily with a U.S. passport instead of a South African one. And then, it's just terribly ungracious of him to turn around and dump on the new country that welcomed him in.

Speaking of disasters, my second set was a beauty! I lost serve four times against Hu Na, and she served twice for the set. Hu Na, or Na Hu (which she says is the proper form of address in China), is sort of a poor woman's Martina.

She defected from a Communist country as a teenager, leaving her family behind. She has improved tremendously over the last year while living and training in San Diego. I think she has a bright future, which is more than anyone would have said a year ago. She was composed and competitive in her first time on the Stadium court, even though she choked twice when serving for the set. With time she'll be able to serve out a set against a top player.

Thank heavens her time wasn't today or Marion would have killed herself. Poor Marion. You see, last night she had a coughing fit at 2:30 a.m. that lasted for hours. Of course, I woke up and couldn't get back to sleep, so I asked her to go to the front desk and get another room. She sat up in the corner of the room for hours suppressing her coughs. And today as I struggled through my match, Marion said she felt like throwing up. "Every time you swore, I swore," she told me.

Oh, one more funny thing. I tried to take a few pictures of the storm damage with my new camera. It's one of those automatic things that rewinds at the touch of a button. Somehow I just couldn't get that button to rewind the film. After several minutes of pushing, prodding, and poking, I discovered there was no film in the camera to rewind. All those nifty pictures I thought I had are now only in my mind's eye. What a dummy! The funny thing is, too, that I've been trying to take up black-and-white photography as a hobby. Mel DiGiacomo, my favorite tennis photographer, is my teacher, but he's obviously got to have me repeat lesson 1: Put film in the camera.

In a way, it's strange to be interested in photography when photographers can be such a distracting presence on the court. I'm aware of all the cameras clicking just as I'm about to serve, especially in a big match. It's just another thing you find so difficult to put out of your mind, and when you're losing, those cameras clicking sound like grenades going off.

August 31—New York City

Martina and I finally got our new streak started, winning the first sixteen points and eight games against two very nervous girls we hardly knew. At 6–0, 5–2, 40–15, one of them hit a great return and Martina missed the volley. Always the perfectionist, she stooped in disgust. I went over and patted her on the back. Deadpan, I said, "It's OK, we can still do it." She laughed and we wrapped up victory No. 1 three points later.

After the match, I saw Rod Laver and he told me that young Richard Laver, Ian's son who was hurt in that plane crash outside Dallas four weeks ago, was out of the hospital. Richard has recovered exceptionally well from his injuries. I'm so glad.

I'm living on those upbeat moments right now because I'm really worried. My shoulder is tired and my Achilles tendon is so sore that I've had to take Motrin, an extrastrength aspirin, three times a day. Plus, I'm doing all the icing, stretching, and ultrasound treatments I can fit in. It doesn't seem to be helping. This morning when I woke up I had trouble putting weight on my toes.

September 1—New York City

The Open is the only Grand Slam tournament that requires the top seeds to play in both bright, hot daylight and damp, dark night conditions. I routined Anne Hobbs tonight so I think playing under the lights is just dandy, but I'm sure Bjorn Borg takes a much dimmer view of the practice. Bjorn never won the Open and twice had his Grand Slam bids stopped under the lights here.

I just found out Hana Mandlikova doesn't think too much of my diary. She came up to me in the locker room today and asked if we were still set to play doubles in Stuttgart this fall. I said sure and told her the story in the *SI* article was just meant to be funny. Hana said, "I don't think it's so funny when you call somebody 'wacko.' "

Well, she had me there. I just smiled lamely and shrugged.

September 2—New York City

I've never had an opponent serve four straight double-faults against me the way Alycia Moulton did today. But, hey, I'll take 'em any way I can get 'em. Alycia seems to be in a little bit of a trough now. A year ago she was really clocking the ball and seemed to have gained a lot of confidence and consistency. That's when she beat me and got to a semifinal and a final, before losing to Chris and Martina. But lately she seems to have lost that edge and has been plagued by the streaks of wild hitting that she was prone to in the past. It's funny how sometimes when your peers are just beginning to show how much they respect you, both on and off the court, your game goes AWOL. Alycia was just elected to the WTA board for the first time a couple of days ago. I think the players realize that anyone who graduated from Stanford must be pretty smart. She's quiet and well liked and today, thankfully, she was a little off. As I said, that's OK with me.

Next up is Steffi Graf, the kid I nipped 6–4 in the third at Wimbledon. My arm is feeling stronger, but I'll have to be able to throw in my kick serve against Steffi. She eats up the pace of my fast one.

This talented 16-year-old stands between me and a Grand Slam semi-final, a place I haven't been in nearly two years. I *need* this win badly.

September 3—New York City

Only doubles today. Martina and I beat Smith and Reynolds to reach the quarters. I also met with three guys from Pringle's potato chips. They're looking for a spokesperson for their chip, but I don't think I'm their gal. I don't like the idea of wearing silver (the Pringle's color) tennis clothes. It smacks too much of wearing a leotard at Wimbledon.

September 4—New York City

Never have I poured so much into a single tennis match as I did today. The muscles in my legs, arms, and hands are still twitching from the torturous three hours I spent in the inferno of the Grandstand court. I can honestly say I pushed myself to the absolute limit for the first time ever on a tennis court. In the end, I ran out of shots, ran out of luck, ran out of gas, and ran out of courage. Steffi Graf beat me in three tiebreaker sets.

The court surface felt like the top of a stove and inside the deeply banked Grandstand it *was* an oven. I've never played in heat and humidity this bad; I even changed my skirt during a changeover early in the third set. If I could have done it discreetly I would have changed my shirt, too. Later, I found out that the conditions had forced Anders Jarryd to default his match against Mats Wilander just a few yards away, over in the Stadium. Heck, it's more open in there and they had a breeze. And they could change their shirts!

I seldom feel that I need to change my clothes during a match. I just don't sweat that much. During this match I wanted to change everything. I was soaked to the skin, so I had Sara Fornaciari go and get me another skirt and shirt. A couple of the girls have changed their shirts on court; I remember Virginia Wade and Claudia Monteiro both did it during their match last year at the Federation Cup in Zurich and Candy Reynolds has done it before. Candy went behind the tarp screening at the back of the court, and Virginia and Claudia sort of finessed it in the shadow of the umpire's chair. I debated about a shirt change today because, in a match as close as this, if you're that little bit more comfortable, heck, you might win one or two more points. That's all it would have taken today.

But I just didn't feel comfortable about undressing in front of 6000 people. With my skirt, I just slipped the dry one over the wet one, unzipped that and discarded it. I think there should be some way—either a nearby changing booth or one "sweat time-out" per match—to allow the women to change shirts. After all, the guys can do it.

Anyway, I never even considered giving up, even after I lost the first set, even after Steffi came back from 0–3 in that first tiebreaker to win seven of the next eight points for the set. I remember sitting down, my head pounding in the airless furnace, and thinking about the effort I'd have to make to win the match. I wanted this match as much as I've ever wanted any match in my life. It's all a little blurry now, but I stretched and chased and lunged for more shots than ever before. I even dove (or rather tumbled) after a netcord in my best Boris Becker imitation. I've never done that in a match before.

Obviously, almost every point in a 7–6, 6–7, 7–6 match is a big point, but it felt as if something distracting happened on each big point. Pieces of paper, napkins, and assorted junk kept falling from the upper levels surrounding the court. At one point, a whole Ritz cracker box came down! The debris falling on the court was incredible. Once I was about to serve and a moving shadow caught my eye. I knew it was a piece of paper, but I couldn't serve until the damn thing finally finished floating down from the heavens. A ballboy grabbed it to the sound of applause. This must have happened about five more times. At first, the delay to walk over and towel off was a welcome respite from the heat and humidity, but after a while the floating crud became a pain in the neck. Besides the intrusion of this "air force," the trains, birds, crying babies, and buzzsaws (!) were enough to drive us bonkers, but for the first time in my life I concentrated through an entire match.

I lost a service break advantage in the second set, but gutted out the tiebreaker, 7–4. Then I jumped to a 3–1 lead in the third set, with my serve to come, when I felt the first leg cramps I've ever had in my career. Each time I pushed off on my serve, my hamstrings and then my quads would tighten. I served two aces to win that game and go up 4–1, but I knew I'd have to win the points quickly or be literally crippled by the cramps.

I had to come to net on everything: first serves, second serves, hers and mine. I found myself wanting to hit aces, realizing that if I didn't Steffi would eat up the pace. I did serve for the match at 5–4 but her returns were just too good. I did have 30–all in two of her service games late in the match, but she served her only two aces of the day then. Unbelievable!

Somewhere in those games I missed my only overhead of the match—an easy one, but my legs were gone and I mistimed it. I don't remember much from the third tiebreaker except for two volleys that clipped the top of the net and fell back, and then the last backhand volley that floated a fraction too long.

I was crushed, defeated. Once again, I had come up short in a Grand Slam event. I sat down and cried, cried for an effort that wasn't good enough, cried for the leg cramps that gripped me. I didn't really care if people saw me cry. If they couldn't understand the emotion, then it was their problem. When I finally left the court, Don hugged me and said, "Pammy, I've seen you play lots and lots of matches and I've seen you determined and fight hard, but never have I seen you fight like you did today."

Two good friends, Susan Whitney and Liz Nuttle, also helped me through the tough hours after the match. Susan and I were Junior buddies, and now she is getting her Ph.D. in history at Rutgers. Liz is my next-door neighbor. After the match she said, "If I'd wanted to suffer from this much anxiety, I could have stayed home and picked a fight with my mother."

Although the laughter and the affection helped, it will take me a long time to get over this loss. The cramps in my legs, feet, and hands continued for hours, bitter reminders of the toughest match I've ever played. And once again: a quarterfinals loss in a Grand Slam tournament, with only the doubles to look forward to.

September 6—New York City

I did some TV commentary and interviews for CBS today. I wanted to be at the courts to support Martina, but Don thought I should stay away from the Tennis Center, and we had one of our typical spats. It didn't help, I'm sure, that there was an article in one of the New York papers about how I was being groomed for Congress by the Republican party in Maryland.

Anyway, Martina handled Graf easily and I aced the postmatch interview. Now I'm sitting in the hotel watching Chris and Hana's semi. The cameras keep showing Collette Evert; I've never seen Mrs. Evert scream so much for Chris. She needs it: Hana's up a break in the third set, 4–2. Hana just held for 5–2. Hana's two points from the match. If she holds on, she'll lose a big part of that "wacko" tag.

It's match point No. 1. . . . It's match point No. 2. . . . It's match point No. 3, and Hana just played a stupid backhand up the line wide. It's Chris's ad. Chris's game, 5–3 Hana. Hana's serving for the match. I'm nervous. Hana's puking. Hana's 30–0. Hana just blew an overhead that would've given her triple match point. . . . It's 30–all now. Hana's lost three straight points. Deuce. I'm dying. Ace, Hana. Match point No. 4. A match like this is great for women's tennis.

Hana just won it with another huge serve. Chris, ever the gracious one, patted Hana on the back. A new finals in a Grand Slam event: Mandlikova and Navratilova. Could this finally be Hana's tournament?

September 7—New York City

A U.S. Open should not be decided on a tiebreaker. For the second time in five years, Martina lost the Open 7–6 in the third. I've got to hand it to Hana, though. She never folded. Hana has been a sleeping volcano for years, ever since she won the French Open and the Australian Open in her teens. She has been an inconsistent player and a moody person for the last several years, but her talent has always been undeniable. God help the rest of us now.

I've never seen Martina so upset after a loss. She barely managed to get through the awards ceremonies. In the deserted locker room, she flung her rackets at the wall and burst into tears. I never saw her like this before. I tried to console her by getting drinks and putting cold towels on her face, but she was just devastated. Martina feels the most pressure when she plays a fellow Czech, and if there's anyone in women's tennis who is a better athlete than Martina, it's Hana.

Besides, no matter how much you've won, losing always has a way of erasing all the great moments in a career. The winning is never as sweet as the losing is bitter.

As I warmed Martina up for our doubles semifinal against Turnbull-Mandlikova, I was worried about how *I* would play. Martina always bounces back in these situations, but I feel a pressure to play exceptionally well to lift her spirits. It's a different kind of pressure. We came through three and four, but I still felt lousy. You see, I'm one of the few players who always wants Martina to win. She's my partner.

September 8—En route

I couldn't help Martina out there today because I couldn't help myself. We lost the doubles final in three sets to Kohde-Kilsch and Sukova. I knew Martina was down, but I was down, too. After my loss to Graf I tried hard to stay up for the doubles, but I couldn't do it. My mind is as tired as my body.

After the finals, I finally told Martina flat out that I'm not comfortable playing on the ad side. She's got to be on that side because she can return big serves from there much better than I can. I never wanted to change sides, but when Martina suggests these things I can only resist so much before I give in. Maybe I should have fought her harder on this, or maybe we were just bound to lose some matches.

As I write this, Team Shriver—Moppie and Gaga, Marion and her boyfriend Fred, Eleanor, Mom and Dad—is on I-95 heading south for Lutherville. We're listening to the men's final on the radio and Lendl is pounding McEnroe. The Europeans have dominated this Open. I swear the heavy-duty balls have something to do with it. Lendl just won. That's two Czechs, both getting a monkey off their backs.

September 10—Lutherville

The press has adopted an interesting attitude toward me in the aftermath of the Open. Now I'm a tennis misfit: I'm more intelligent than the average player but less dedicated than Martina and Chris and less talented than Mandlikova, Graf, and Sabatini. One local writer even said that I've gone as far as I can go in the sport. Well, I guess I better pack it in. . . .

I find it sickening how everybody harps on being No. 1 in America. I feel more pressure and inadequacy as the No. 4 player in the world than I would as No. 25 because who the hell cares about No. 25? In my heart I know how well I've done, but to the press I'm a failure. There's no way I should be considered a failure, not in any shape or form.

At 23, I'm seven years younger than Martina and Chris and about seven years older than Graf and Sabatini. Hana and I are the same age, but I know I'm nowhere near the talent she is. I have no illusions about my tennis. I will never be consistent enough to be a No. 1 player. However, I know I can win three of the four Grand Slam events with a little luck. The French is my only impossible dream. I'm sure I will win a major title before I'm through, but even that probably won't satisfy the media.

The thing about this No. 1 syndrome is that it's smothering America's tennis talent. Europeans seem to be more realistic, more understanding about this business. Why are the Swedes, the Czechs, the Germans, and the French showing us up now? I'm sure it's because a player like Joakim Nystrom is well respected in Sweden for being No. 8 in the world. Over here, Nystrom would be castrated. Over here, everybody's always asking what's *wrong* with Arias and Krickstein and Rinaldi and Rehe and Gurney. American kids grow up with this pressure to be No. 1 even if they don't have the talent, and if they do have the talent, the expectations crush them before they know how to handle the pressure.

I'm just waiting for the day a writer comes up to me and says, "Wow, No. 4 in the world!" and writes what a success story I am. That will finally mean that sportswriters are living in the real world. Unfortunately, I think I've got a long wait.

September 11—Lutherville

Last night I attended my first McDonogh Alumni Directors meeting. I love that school so much. At dinner I sat next to Jeff Cook. He graduated a couple of years ahead of me and then led Johns Hopkins to at least one national title in lacrosse. He's in his last year of law school now. Anyway, he dropped the hint about us getting together sometime, and I think I'll pick him up on it. I'm starting to get more invitations from guys than I used to.

I wish I had two weeks off to recharge, but I've barely had two days. I'm off to Hilton Head tomorrow for the DuPont All-American Tennis Classic on clay. It's an exhibition and I'm guaranteed of winning about the same amount as I would for a medium-sized tournament, so financially it's worthwhile, but I'm pooped. Then from Hilton Head I fly to Chicago. I wouldn't be playing there except I'm the defending champion. I like to defend titles; it's not like I've had that many titles to defend in my career.

September 12—Hilton Head

Tonight Stan and Margie Smith had a welcome dinner for all the players in this exhibition and I got to see some of the younger guys away from the courts. Most of them are antisocial drips, but I'm sure the feeling is probably mutual. God, I wish I hadn't committed to play this event. What a negative attitude!

The people connected with the tournament are nice and it's well organized, but the last thing I want to be doing now is playing tennis. Heck, I would've come down here just for the parties.

September 13—Hilton Head

Exhibitions must be taken for what they're worth: money and socializing. If I had won today, I would've picked up another $3000, but I couldn't see practicing two more days on clay for an exhibition when I'm defending a tournament title indoors on carpet next week. So I have to live with losing to Gadusek four and love. I didn't get upset until she turned common midway through the second set. When I served what I thought was an ace, the linesman first called it out, then reversed himself, and the umpire then called a let. I appealed to Bonnie's sense of fair play:

"Could you have reached that?"

She nodded.

"With what?" I was really hot.

If this had been a real tournament, I wouldn't have put Bonnie in the position of having to make a call against herself. I should have known Bonnie would play this one as if it were the finals of Wimbledon.

September 14—En route

I figure I spend a good part of my life on planes, but even with all the recent accidents, flying doesn't bother me. I find it one of the few times when I can get away from all the responsibilities and hassles of my life. The only bad part is when the guy sitting next to me wants to talk . . . about (groan) tennis. Like now.

"Do you play tennis?" he asks pleasantly.

"Yes," I answer tersely.

"Professionally?" Conversationally.

"Yes." Abruptly.

"I'm sorry, I don't know your name. What is it?" Inquisitively.

"Pam . . . Shriver." Reluctantly.

"Oh, my God . . . I'm sorry I didn't know." Obsequiously.

"That's OK." Condescendingly.

"Didn't you beat them all in 1981?" Proudly.

"No!" Give me a parachute!

September 15—Chicago

Something is wrong with me. I think about money all the time. About the money I earn, the money I spend, the money I save, the money I waste. I received a healthy amount for three days in Hilton Head and already I'm worried about the $3000 I'll spend here in overhead alone. Hank's room and mine will come to $1400 for the week, plus I pay Hank a weekly salary *and* his expenses, plus a bonus if I get to the semis and beyond. Meanwhile, Don is at home and I'm still paying him a percentage of my prize money, although a smaller one than when he traveled full-time with me.

I'm single and I have more money than I can possibly spend now, but here I am wondering whether I should ask Hank to room with JoAnne Russell's coach this week. Would I want to room with JoAnne? No, I'm more comfortable in a room of my own. If I could only rationalize my expenses as the perfectly acceptable 20 to 25 percent of my gross earnings, I'd feel better. But I can't. I don't have a set salary. I earn my week's wages by how well I play each week. I've got to stop thinking about money. . . . Let's see, if I win this week I net $15,000. Maybe Hank and I could hitchhike home.

September 15—Chicago

Great news! John Bassett is here with Carling this week and his tumors have almost disappeared with the treatments. He's still thin, but he looks much better than he did this spring. And he's been upbeat and full of laughs all week.

This may just be one of those instances in which the power of positive thinking has curtailed the power of disease. Carling and the whole family have had such a good, hopeful attitude throughout her father's illness. She's been amazing.

September 16—Chicago

I had breakfast with Steve Stone, the former Oriole pitcher who's a baseball announcer here, and we talked about the drug scandal that's rocking baseball now. Steve says cocaine is just the tip of the iceberg; he says many players use amphetamines because of the physical beating they take during the season. As an ex-pitcher, he should know. He asked me about tennis, and I told him that I don't really travel in the circles where drugs are evident and that as far as I knew drug use is not very widespread at all in the sport.

You just can't take drugs and play tennis because there's no way you can send in a substitute to play for you. The same things about the sport that make tennis players so susceptible to burnout also make it relatively drug free: year-round play, no breaks, no substitutes, no time-outs during matches, etc. Players in team sports don't have burnout; players on the tennis tour don't do drugs.

September 18—Chicago

I had dinner last night with Bill Von Dahm, the Virginia Slims PR affiliate here, and dinner tonight with Hank and his former college roommate, Mark. I feel so much better about myself when there are guys around to go out with.

September 20—Chicago

I played like crap and lost two and three to Kathy Jordan. These are really the dog days of the tour, and I'm finding it difficult to motivate myself. I tried to get myself pumped up for the match, but nothing happened. I seldom lose easily to a player ranked lower than I am, but tonight I was absolutely dead on the court. The strange thing is that I've been playing well in practice, but the juices just ran dry during the match. Maybe my newly active social life is sapping my strength?

September 21—Chicago

Boy, am I ticked. Apparently, I wasn't the only one having dinner with Bill Von Dahm the other night. He was also feeding a local gossip columnist. A few tasty morsels in the paper yesterday had us "holding hands" and being "close friends" for years. "Bullbleep," as they say in the newspaper business. Mr. BVD (Bill's new nickname in the locker room) even had the gaul to tape the item on the wall in the players' lounge. I tore it down. I know this tournament needs publicity, and he's in charge of the P.R., but I hate being used this way.

And my insomnia has returned with a vengeance. I've taken a mild sleeping pill every night this week, but they haven't helped much. The past few mornings I've resorted to calling Mom and Dad at 6:40 a.m. their time. Thank heavens they're early risers and understand their nutty daughter.

September 22—Chicago

Gadusek and Rinaldi, a couple of baseliners, are in the finals here. What a joke on all the serve-and-volleyers. People think that hard courts are fast, but they don't understand that most of the carpets in the indoor arenas are slow and cater to the baseliners with lots of topspin and great passing shots. I should have played in the '50s.

They're going to end up killing women's tennis with these slow surfaces. Here's what happens: You hit a serve, you hit a volley into the corner, some fleet-footed little monster runs back and hits a passing shot up the line, you barely spoon it back crosscourt, she runs up and knocks it by you. Then on the next point, you have a backcourt rally, you run side to side, you finally hit a deep, biting approach, the little deer runs over and tees off on it as the court holds it up for her, you volley it into the corner, she runs over and hits a great lob. And you're dead. You can't win. The matches are all lasting $2^1/_2$ hours and if you have two baseliners, you can go get a hot dog, read a few chapters of *War and Peace*, and still be back in your seat at 1–0, 30–15 in the first.

September 24—New Orleans

It doesn't seem to matter where I am, insomnia follows me. I've spent three nights here in three different rooms trying to escape the ear-splitting blasts of riverboats on the Mississippi River outside my window, plus the sweet music of jackhammers (!) down the street. And now John is coming in for the weekend, and I know I'll be more nervous than a cat, especially if I'm still in the singles.

Our new executive director, Merrett Stierheim, sat in on today's board meeting even though Jerry Diamond is still our director until January. Merrett used to be the Dade County commissioner before our search firm recommended him for our top spot. He certainly should be able to handle our budget problems (after all, he handled Miami's), but will he be able to juggle all the tennis politicians and still keep the WTA strong, unified, and independent?

September 26—New Orleans

I ran into Chris at Saks today. She's fun to shop with because she makes sure I spend lots of money. I must have had twenty things in the changing room when Chris drifted off with Ana Leaird. Then, as I was trying on one of my choices, I saw someone walking toward the changing room I was in. Someone with a full head of wavy black hair. Someone who looked like Carmen Miranda walking like Chris Evert Lloyd. Well, of course it was Chris. I was hysterical. Ana and I pleaded with her to wear the wig on the court, but she'll never do it. She saves these glimpses of her zanier side for us, which is kind of neat when you think about it.

September 27—New Orleans

All week my game has been positive, concise, and thoughtful, a welcome reversal of last week's listless performance. Tonight I was awesome, clobbering Turnbull love and two. At 33, Wendy must wonder where her game is going. Once a perennial member of the world's Top Ten, she's slipped to No. 13 and doesn't look to improve. She's won over $2 million in prize money and is in the top five on the women's all-time money list, but how long will she hold on? Please God, don't have me hanging on into my 30s.

September 28—New Orleans

John arrived in time to see most of my win over Wendy, and he saw me comfortably beat Anne White tonight to reach the finals. This is a landmark for me: I've never asked a boyfriend to come to a tournament before. The night was wonderful but I couldn't help wondering how I would have reacted had I lost. This relationship hasn't been tested until he sees me when I lose. John has to spend time with me at a tournament to understand the demands made by my lifestyle. He doesn't get it yet. Before he arrived, he called and asked me if he should make dinner reservations for the weekend. I told him rather bluntly that I wouldn't know my schedule, and we'd have to play everything by ear.

Last night he told me he'd forgotten that he was coming to visit me *and* a tennis tournament, not just me. It's good for John to see what this lifestyle is all about. My schedule for today was forty-five minutes of practice and then the rest of the day in my room conserving my energy for the match this evening. He seems to have adjusted: He's still out sightseeing, and he should be back around 3:00 so we can have lunch together.

September 29—New Orleans

In the locker room before the finals, Chris and I jabbered away like a couple of magpies. Unlike Wendy and Anne "Never-Take-the-Walkman-Off" White, who didn't say a word to me before or after our matches, Chris feels comfortable talking to an opponent before a match. So does Martina, and believe it or not, Chris and Martina have no problem chatting together before a match. They might get a little quieter before a Grand Slam finals, but they never ignore each other to plug into a higher level of concentration or anything.

Anyway, once our finals got started tonight all that friendliness disappeared. We had lots of close calls and this time Chris used more than her eyes to protest. Once she told the umpire how close the calls were, and another time she muttered under her breath about how quickly I walked to the changeover after a dodgy service call went against her. Bad luck, Chris, it was 40–0 for me anyway, and it was too close for me to give you the call.

She finally won four and five, but a volley here, a first serve there, a passing shot somewhere and I could have won. Afterwards Chris told me, "You're a good sport, Pam." She obviously didn't agree with the umpire who gave me a warning for kicking the ball out of the court enclosure. I didn't agree with him either: It was a great boot. Three points!

September 30—Lutherville

Win or lose, I never know quite what to say to my opponent at the net right after the match is over. I hate to say, "Good match," especially if I beat somebody one and two or something. I mean, that sounds so phoney. Obviously, they didn't play a good match, and they know it. If I win and I think I've played well, I will say that instead: "Sorry. I played well, today." Obviously, if you've just gotten whipped it's at least nice to know that your opponent didn't cream you with less than her best. It seems to me, too, that if I get beat, I also want my conqueror to know—if it's true—that they took me at my fullest. I'd never say anything like, "Well, congratulations, but of course, I really didn't play very well."

I remember one time I played a close match against Chris, although, as always, she beat me; so at the net, I said, "Gee, I had a lot of opportunities today." After all, that was a compliment. I was saying, in effect, I couldn't beat you even when it was close. But, of course, Chris was terribly offended. She took it as if I were disparaging her victory, and she gave me one of those looks she usually reserves for linesmen. Then later, to top it off, she went to Don and let him know what bad form I'd exhibited.

By the time I plopped my suitcases down in my house last night, it was midnight. My room was just as I'd left it $2^1/_2$ weeks ago—a mess. But I've got two whole weeks to pick it up, the first time since I returned to the tour that I've had that many days off in a row. I'm a little arm-weary, but I feel happy and healthy enough to try to go for third place in the Virginia Slims bonus pool. I'll have to play often and well to make it, but the bonus is worth $100,000.

John's coming to New Orleans was a good decision. We got along beautifully after the dinner-reservation gaffe. He *is* special, and I'm looking forward to the vacation we're taking with Marion and Fred in the Bahamas in December.

October 1—Lutherville

Yea! Martina said she'll do the exhibition for CF in Baltimore, but I think we'll have to put it off a year because we need the time to organize the sponsorship package. That's OK. I've got all the ingredients: top players who care and the inspiration of Alex Deford.

October 3—Lutherville

Poor Marion. Whenever I'm feeling sorry for myself I remember how lucky I am to be gifted in a profession that pays very well. Marion earns $24 a day teaching 5-year-olds the classroom fundamentals, and she also works in a dress shop part-time. She makes about $600 a month and her expenses include $150 to rent the ground floor of my house and $150 to keep her beloved horse in a neighboring field. We've never argued about money, but I know it bothers her that she's always struggling. Usually, though, we end up laughing about our economic outlooks—like yesterday when we collapsed in giggles while comparing the price of toilet paper. We had both instinctively started counting sheets per roll, and the ludicrousness of a millionaire saving 16 cents on a $79 grocery bill struck our funny bones. (I just hope the discount toilet paper is soft.)

October 4—Connecticut

A day in the life of Pam Shriver, tycoon. I went to New York to shoot a print ad for an investment firm today. Everything went smoothly, and the tagline is great: "I thought I was too small for Drexel Burnham." I hear Wilt Chamberlain has done an ad for them, too. Pretty neat, eh?

Then I took the train out to Connecticut for a "corporate day" with a company called the Greenwich Capital Group. I haven't done many of these corporate deals, but I think this one was a little different than most. You see, I was hired to settle a bet.

It seems that the firm's employees, who average about 31 years of age and are a pretty athletic bunch, got into a big debate about whether a good male club player could beat a top woman pro. So, being entrepreneurs who trade government securities and bonds by the billions, they decided to put their money where their egos were. Somehow they got to Sara and she put a solid fee on my services to see if they were serious. They were serious.

After lunch and a tour of the company's computers, we went to a tennis club and got down to business. Ted, who told me all about his bad back, was first up. He was a good, solid club player and had chosen challenger's rights to serve first and last in our three-game minimatch. Luckily, Ted wasn't a big server and I moved him from side to side, breaking his serve to love, and then held mine to love, serving at only two-thirds pace. I had mixed feelings about winning twelve straight points, but I wasn't going to give it away. When I finally made a forehand error in the final game, Ted said humbly, "Thank you, Pam." Then I closed out the match.

After I'd played $1\frac{1}{2}$ hours of doubles with some other employees and customers of the Greenwich Capital Group, Rick arrived for the main event. He told me all about his tendinitis in the shoulder, but we decided to play a full set anyway. His serve was a weapon, better than most of the girls on the tour, and he had three game points (two on my serve), but I held to win 6–0, playing 75 percent.

So, if anyone asks you how a woman pro would do against a good male club player, tell him Pam Shriver won her second and third battle of the sexes of 1985 against a couple of hotshots from the Greenwich Capital Group without losing a game. Of course, you can also tell him that I'm no ingrate and that I finished the day by losing two doubles matches 3–2. I also offered to return for free if I win Wimbledon next year.

October 7—Lutherville

What do you get a soon-to-be-29-year-old multimillionaire who has traveled all over the world? Martina's birthday is next week and I've been combing the area for ideas. I always try to give Martina things that reflect me and my home state in some way. Last Christmas I found her a large watercolor painting of some black Labrador puppies at the beach. Today I found her a hand-carved Baltimore oriole (the state bird, not a baseball player). At least I know she won't have anything like it.

I don't know if any of the other players make a practice of exchanging gifts, but Martina and I have been doing it for about two years. I don't give any other players things at Christmas or birthdays, but Martina and I have such warmth for each other. It would be unnatural for us not to exchange gifts. She's given me jewelry and a leather evening bag, all in the best of taste. My first gift to her was a specially inscribed gold charm. We'd won three legs of the Grand Slam at that point and there's an Australian saying—"bob's your uncle"—meaning "keep it up, we're home free now." As in, "If we win this game we're up two breaks and bob's your uncle." So I had this charm made up with three diamonds and "B.Y.U." It worked too: We won our fourth leg and the Grand Slam. Bob's your uncle, Martina!

October 8—Lutherville

Poor Don. Once again he took the brunt of my anger while I was practicing with Hank. Don has always been my personal chopping block, but now that he's no longer involved in the day-to-day routine, it's unfair to keep abusing him. I'm finding that three is a crowd at my workouts. Hank is more confident in giving me instructions now, and I know Don feels insecure about where he and I go from here. The Australian tour next month should go a long way in clarifying our future working relationship. Don and I will work one on one there, and Hank will get a long-deserved vacation. It'll be interesting what becomes of Don and me: We've had more ups and downs, ins and outs, than a rocky marriage.

October 9—Lutherville

A couple of days ago I played tennis again with Vice President Bush at the Naval Conservatory in Washington. Mr. Bush helped me out of a fix. I was wondering whether to accept another invitation to a White House dinner, this one for the Prince and Princess of Wales next month or keep my traveling date for my tournament in Australia. People will probably think I'm crazy, but I've decided to turn down the invitation to the social event of the year. After all, as the Vice President says, tennis is my career and I've got to honor my commitments. Australia takes two days to get to and a couple more to get acclimated, and my scheduled flight is cutting it close as it is. Tennis is the reason I'm being asked to these dinners in the first place, so I'd better keep my priorities straight. Don would be really proud of me today.

October 10—Lutherville

These two weeks at home have flown by. I've been madly visiting old friends, practicing, working out at Children's, putting Orchard's house in order (e.g., handling complaints about not enough towels, about too much hair in the drains, etc.), watching Maid to Order put *my* house in order (What am I going to do when I get married and have kids of my own?), stocking up on groceries for Marion, and keeping up with McDonogh's alumni association affairs.

I made a special trip to see Nan Taylor the other day. Nan was my gym teacher in the fifth and sixth grades at Garrison Forest School. She's been paralyzed since my seventh-grade year when a back operation somehow went wrong. I've visited her periodically ever since. She has covered the wall of her hospital room with clippings—some yellow with age—about me and my exploits. My career is one of her hobbies, and some people tell me it helps keep her going. . . . After I left Nan, I drifted up I-83 to visit Bubba who was our maid for twenty-five years, until last spring when she inadvertently discovered she was 80 and retired on the spot.

The official White House invitation to The Dinner came in the mail today. I heard through the grapevine that John Travolta has replaced Robert Redford on the guest list. Imagine that: Robert Redford and Pamela Shriver are the only ones to decline, with regrets, to dine with Prince Charles and Lady Di at the dinner of the year in Washington!

Speaking of dinners, tonight was the first time I've used my oven in a year and three months. I fixed dinner for Jeff Cook, Marion, and Fred. The highlight of the menu was my apple-oatmeal dessert, which I'd made earlier that afternoon. I'd almost been stymied by a squadron of little brown bugs that had invaded some of the oatmeal packets. I poured the defiled packets down the drain and started again with debugged ones. As I told my guests at dinner, "If there are any of the little varmints left, it's OK because they've been at 375° for half an hour." It was OK. Nobody died.

October 11—En route

This morning I tied together the last loose end: the board of PHS, Ltd., met to check my finances. My accountant showed me an overall balance sheet so that I could see my income, expenses, and taxes since 1980. I'm a wealthy person from one look at the numbers. Champagne for Hank and me in Stuttgart!

After a 2½-hour delay, my World Airways flight finally got off the ground to Frankfurt. During the delay I bumped into Eddie Murray, the Orioles first baseman and in my unbiased view the best all-around player in baseball. All I read is how shy and introverted he is, but we've met before at a couple of sports functions in Baltimore and we had a great chat today. We talked about our social lives and about how difficult being a public personality in a traveling profession is on relationships. It simply isn't true that Eddie Murray is reserved and private; he's just selective.

Stuttgart

What do you know, we did have champagne! When Hank and I returned from a light workout at a club in nearby Filderstadt, we found a little complimentary bottle of the bubbly in each of our rooms. I devoured mine before the ice had melted. Then I settled down to watch the Blue Jays and the Royals playoff game on the Armed Forces Network before falling asleep. What a life.

October 12—Filderstadt

My foot is getting worse, which I didn't think was possible. I've had my orthotics adjusted a half dozen times, and I'm doing the torturous contrast-bath routine and popping anti-inflammatories three times a day. The hard courts here (an indoor carpet laid over something hard, probably cement) haven't helped matters. I can hardly wait to get to the soft grass courts of Australia.

October 13—Filderstadt

The tournament officially begins tomorrow but there might be some delay of selected first-round matches. The Federation Cup is being played in Japan this week, and not only is it tough to get from Nagoya to Stuttgart in any direct way, but the matches have been held up by rain there. I'm hoping I can start tomorrow.

The Federation Cup is the women's answer to the Davis Cup, our international team competition. The Czechs have won it the last two years and they're probably going to do it again this year. Hank just heard that Elise lost a tough three-setter to Helena Sukova in the No. 2 singles and Kathy Jordan is down a set and 0–3 to Hana in the No. 1. Since the Fed Cup matches consist of three points—No. 1 singles, No. 2 singles, and doubles—it looks as if we're sunk. But it was a darn good showing by the American team, especially since Martina and Chris chose not to play, Barbara Potter dropped out at the last minute, and Zina Garrison couldn't play in the last two matches because of a sudden kidney infection.

Elise was a last-minute substitute for Potsie. I know she didn't expect to actually play in Nagoya, but she had to fill in when Zina got sick. If Elise had been able to pull out that match in the finals against Sukova, she could have been the heroine of the event and she would've nailed me.

You see, I've never played Fed Cup because it's been on clay a couple of times, and this year I felt a jaunt to Japan was just too impractical, especially since I'm playing for the United States in the

Wightman Cup against Britain in two weeks. But as one of the three highest-ranked Americans who chose not to play, I should at least have kept my mouth shut. It's not as if I made any public statement but I did make a tacky reference, in private, to Elise a couple of days before she was chosen for the Fed Cup team. "It looks like we're sending the 'B team' again," I said, or words to that effect. Boy, did she let me have it! And rightly so; I felt a little ashamed about my remarks.

Martina has told me that she's going to play the Fed Cup next year for sure. The competition will be in Prague, and the trip would be the first time she's returned to Czechoslovakia since her defection in 1975. I won't miss it—even if it's on clay.

October 14—Filderstadt

This evening Hank and I went into Stuttgart and celebrated part of their folkfest with some of the locals. We were just digging into the frighteningly large steins of beer at a noisy hofbrau haus when a drunk German tumbled off his bench and fell right on top of me. I was just sitting on my bench minding my own business and wham! I was stunned. A little bruised, too. I moved to the other side of the large table, out of harm's way, and two minutes later a lady did a back somersault off her bench and landed smack on our table. People must hurt themselves all the time in the beer halls. By the end of the night, we were dancing on our bench, too. But we didn't fall off. Better balance or hollow legs, I guess.

October 15—Filderstadt

I showed more inspiration at the beer hall last night than today against Amanda Brown. She's a qualifier, and qualifiers can be dangerous because they have had to play and win three matches just to get into the main draw. So they're familiar with the balls, light, and court speed. Although I never lost serve, I found the court and the balls heavier than I'd like. I won three and four but the conditions would seem to favor the heavy-hitting Europeans.

Elise came to my room for a chat and told me all about Japan. She called the Americans "a real melting-pot team" because KJ and the coach, Tom Gorman, are of English and Irish descent, Elise is Jewish, Zina's black, and Sharon Walsh is Californian-American, which is an ethnic group just like any other. Elise said that the Japanese were really enthusiastic and wanted her to sign everything they owned, including expensive suede handbags. Elise stunk up my room with her curling iron: Her hair was actually sizzling and smelled terrible. It's great to have such a good friend on the tour.

P.S. The Czechs did win, 2–1, so Martina will have something extra to prove in Prague next summer. Maybe I will too.

October 16—Filderstadt

The highlight of the day was my doubles match with Hana. It was our first tournament together since that fiasco in Florida in March. Moreover, it was my first match playing on my old side (returning serve from the deuce court) since last December. Hana teased me again about the "wacko" comment in *SI*, but we only got confused once on overheads and beat Bonder and Ruzici 6–1, 6–2.

Not that there weren't a few moments worthy of the Marx Brothers out there. On a changeover towards the end of the match, I heard Hana say something about "the boss." I didn't quite understand what she was referring to, so I said, "What?" Once again she said, "Boss," so I said, "Sure, you're the boss." Hana looked at me and laughed. "No, not boss," she said. "New balls." Her Czech accent had dropped the els.

Luckily, that was our only communication problem the entire evening.

October 17—Filderstadt

I'm the top seed here but the press hasn't bothered to ask me one question. They're all hot about Susie Mascarin, who spent last week in Monte Carlo "practicing" with Boris Becker. Sue insists she was "working out" with Tiriac and Becker, but the press is stirring up the romance plots. "Nothing's going on," Sue keeps telling reporters and players alike. But something is going on; I just don't know how involved Boris and Sue are. Sue has a habit of going out with tennis players: Chris Lewis and Mel Purcell are two that I know about. Now she's going out with the Wimbledon champion who's four years younger than she is.

Sometimes I wonder what a high-profile romance would be like, but I don't think I'm the type.

Every once in a while I get damn lonely on the road. Overseas, it hits me the hardest. The baseball games and a couple of eventful visits to the masseur have kept me from getting really depressed here. Massages are an important part of every player's tournament routine. The further you go in a tournament the more you rely on those magic fingers.

Every masseur has a different style and Rossario's here is unique. His fingernails seem as long as the ones Howard Hughes was supposed to have had. A few of the girls have complained that he's scratched them. Yesterday I had Leza Hatch, our WTA trainer, go after him with a set of fingernail clippers. Then today, halfway through my massage, a photographer comes into the locker room and asks if he can take a few pictures. Talk about feeling vulnerable.

October 19—Filderstadt

When I first woke up this morning and turned on the TV, I was welcomed into the new day by a gruesome wilderness documentary. My eyes still blurry with sleep, I watched a lion stalk and then tear apart an orphan water buffalo. I quickly switched off the set, but minutes later I thought to myself: That's what I'm going to do to Graf, pounce all over her as if she was a helpless baby.

Revenge is oh, so sweet! I pounced on Steffi just like that lion pounced on the defenseless calf. She didn't have a chance. I did just what I wanted to do, rallying some from the back but coming to the net with a purpose. My volleys were strong and my serve thoughtful. I was proud of the way I played and of the score: 6–4, 6–2.

Steffi and her father caused a stink about how the crowd didn't get behind her enough. Welcome to the club, Steffi. Now you can imagine what it's like to be an American player. I must say I played the crowd like a crafty veteran. At one point in our match, Steffi bounced a ball hard on the court and it came over the net toward me. I turned around and bounced it back towards her. Not exactly Abbott and Costello stuff, but the crowd laughed. From then on they were pretty balanced in their affections.

After the match, Steffi barely shook my hand and stormed off the court before I had gotten a chance to get my rackets together. It's a courtesy that an opponent usually waits for the other player and they walk off court together. It's amazing how short Steffi's memory is: Only six weeks ago at the Open, in a match that meant the world to me, I swallowed my pride and was as gracious in defeat as I've ever been.

The problem isn't Steffi as much as it is her father. If he doesn't watch it, he's going to destroy the respect her peers might have for his daughter. She's a nice girl and I'd hate to see that happen. Why don't these parents ever learn to ease up a little?

In tomorrow's finals I play Catarina Lindqvist of Sweden. I've never played her before but I know she has a wonderful backhand. Her serve can be attacked, however. I must string my volleys and serve well and the Porsche, the grand prize and golden reason for playing here, will be mine.

October 20—Filderstadt

My seventh final of the year proved to be a lucky one. I beat a plucky Lindqvist 6–1, 7–5, thanks to my serve and some good pressure tennis. I had to climb back from 2–5 in the second and recovered from a double-fault on my first match point. I almost doubled on my second one too, but plopped a second serve in and watched gratefully as Catarina lifted a backhand over the baseline. This was my first tournament victory ever in continental Europe.

Tom left this morning. He had a great time watching the tennis, but he didn't get to see much of Stuttgart. Tennis tournaments can do that to the people involved.

Wacko Hana and I had a blast playing doubles together. Last night we laughed a lot and beat Elise and Andrea Temesvari, the two doyennes of the makeup mirror, in the semifinal and today we easily beat Tine Scheuer Larsen and Carina Karlsson. What a difference between yesterday's match and my last doubles against Elise in Eastbourne where we acted like cranky, spoiled children. Last night we laughed so hard we almost wet our tweeds, as the Brits would say.

In the beginning of the match, Elise went back for an overhead, lost the ball in the lights, and mishit it, whereupon it landed on her head. I heard her start to laugh and immediately I lost it, too. Two games later I was still chuckling to myself.

Then late in the second set I was serving to go up 5–2. They pulled back to deuce, then earned a break point. The umpire mispronounced Elise's last name so that it sounded like "Advantage, Virgin." I turned around, raised my brows, and said questioningly, "Virgin?" Everybody cracked up, especially when Elise retreated to the back wall in embarrassment, hiding her face against the backdrop. It took ages for Virgin to regain her composure enough to play.

Then she broke me.

October 21—En route

This trip home seems endless because every seat is taken, the flight was a couple of hours late taking off, and World Airways has no first class (but they do fly direct to Baltimore from Europe).

I'm stiff as a board from having to play nine matches this week, but you know, I haven't had to pull out of a single tournament in 1985. I've reached more finals and won more tournaments than in any other year in my career. And I've signed several non-tennis business contracts.

The two most important matches were against Fairbank in Australia in May and Jordan in Chicago in September. It is an accurate reflection of my year that I won one and lost one, but both helped my professional attitude. That loss in Chicago to Jordan woke me up again. From that day on, my workouts have taken me to a higher level—with special thanks to Hank's influence. Interestingly, I never spoke to Don once during this victory in Stuttgart. I was so confident I didn't need his reassurance. A year ago, Don *was* my tennis.

Financially, I'm sitting pretty because by winning this week I created a gap between me at No. 3 and Claudia Kohde-Kilsch at No. 4 in the Virginia Slims bonus pool. Also, my win in the doubles put me close to the top in doubles. If I finish No. 1 in doubles and No. 3 in singles, I'll receive a $135,000 bonus. Not peanuts.

Socially, I've never felt better. Besides John, whom I adore, I've met three or four other nice guys. I'm too young to have one solid attachment yet, so the variety has been fun.

In short, life couldn't be better. Now if this stupid plane would just get me home. . . .

October 22—Lutherville

Well, bliss can't last forever. John just phoned and seemed a little miffed that I hadn't phoned him when I got home last night. This is the darndest relationship. In some ways we act as if we're seriously involved and in other ways we don't. I haven't spent more than a week with him in over a year. Four days here and there is hardly conducive to passionate romance. But there is enough chemistry and potential between us to keep the doors open.

I don't know if I should tell John about Tom's being in Stuttgart for three days. I don't think I should, at least not until I see John. Hank blew it the other day and called Tom, John. He'd better watch it or I'll call Carina, Kim.

I'm not sure what's happening with Hank and Kim and Carina,

and I'm not sure Hank knows. But that'll sort itself out. These things always do, at least that's what Dr. Ruth says.

October 23—Lutherville

People around here are going crazy because I won a Porsche at the Stuttgart tournament. I'm going to sell it. Boy, when people find out I'm selling the Porsche I won and turned down a White House invitation for dinner with Prince Charles and Lady Di, they're going to think *I'm* wacko. Maybe I am.

October 24—Lutherville

Laura DuPont, Don, and I met with Dr. Mules, the headmaster, and Tommy Kiegler, his assistant, at McDonogh about a Tennis Daycamp at the school. I'm a little gun-shy about the idea because McDonogh and I go back a long way. It's almost as if I would be entering into a business relationship with an old friend. I don't want to jeopardize this special feeling for a place that has always meant learning and pleasure to me. It's scary. But the camp would be a good use for the school's facilities in the summer.

Don and I had a forty-five minute workout yesterday, which was tremendous. He took a bag of forty balls and ran my little behind all over the court. He'd try to run down my balls, but in case he didn't, he always had another ball to rifle back at me. I looked as if I were competing in a lobster look-a-like contest when it was over, but he had hardly worked up a sweat. Amazing what forty balls and a clever Aussie coach can do.

I read the funniest story in the paper about an Aussie-rules football team. The story caught my eye because this team, Footscray, was one of the teams I'd watched when I attended my first Aussie-rules game Down Under back in May. I almost feel as if I know the players personally. Here's what the story said:

"Players from Footscray were put off a Qantas airliner Thursday for rowdiness on a flight from Melbourne to Honolulu. Players raced wheelchairs during a stop in Nadi, Fiji, and on the plane they threw food, broke 12 seat backs and tore off a female flight attendant's jacket."

Way to go, boys, you animals!

October 25—Lutherville

No account of my tennis life would be complete without mention of Jeff Lamborn. Jeff has been a close friend since I was 8 or 9. As a matter of fact, Jeff is the unsung hero of my career. When I was 10, 11, and 12 he was the one who took a keen interest in my tennis. At the time, Don was busy playing and coaching the Baltimore Banners of World Team Tennis, so Jeff was the one who picked me up at school to take me to practice, drove me to tournaments, and taught me every day during the summers. It seemed as if he had dinner at our house just about every night one summer. He didn't do it for the money; he did it because he saw potential in me.

The year I turned 13, things turned sour between Mom and Jeff. Jeff is an intelligent, opinionated, and oversensitive guy, and I guess the combination began to rub Mom the wrong way. Anyway, I went back to Don at Orchard. Being loyal and true-blue I tried to have both Jeff and Don as coaches, but I soon found out you couldn't have two drivers steering the car.

The lesson was brought home quite painfully. I had my first write-up, no big deal, just an interview in *Middle Atlantic Tennis* magazine. My name was in the headlines and there were pictures. Gosh. I mentioned my two coaches, Don and Jeff, in the article, but his wife Elaine later told Mom how disappointed Don had been that I'd said I had two coaches. When Mom told me, I burst into tears and felt sick. It was the first time something I'd said in all innocence to the press had gotten me in trouble; little did I know it would foreshadow the pattern of my career.

Anyway, through all the good times and all the bad, Jeff and I have remained good friends. The reason I'm thinking of him now is because he and his fiancée Becky have asked me to be in their wedding. I can't go because I'll be in Australia. This is the first time I've ever been asked to be a bridesmaid. Shoot!

October 26—Lutherville

I went up to Princeton to shoot a commercial for Prince and pick up my racket contract. When I walked into the Prince offices, all the employees showed up at the entrance with a big welcome sign congratulating me for winning Stuttgart. This was the nicest and most personal thing Prince has ever done for me—and I've been with them since I was 14 years old.

October 27—Lutherville

Tom Gilroy wrote to me. The letter served many purposes. He thanked me for the great time he had in Stuttgart and congratulated me on winning. Ace! He told me how much fun he had with me and how nice I was. Forehand winner! He also told me that in the last two or three months he'd been seriously dating someone. Fault. He wasn't sure he should have gone to Stuttgart because he didn't want to lead me on. Double-fault. He explained that, although he thought we could develop a fun relationship, our jobs would always make a serious relationship difficult. Dropped shot.

I'm no dummy and had sensed that Tom had a girlfriend, and I wasn't looking for a serious relationship. I'm touched that he took such care to make the words come out right. He's an honest and honorable man. A true Marine.

October 28—Lutherville

Why do I feel I've come to the beginning of the end in my relationship with Don? Anything that changes something has to hurt, I guess, but this morning we went to my lawyer's office to draw up our agreement for next year. We've never had a written contract before, but since the relationship isn't as clear now, he felt we needed something in writing.

Eventually, Don wants to go back on tour with someone else. We've discussed this before, but I'd have emotional problems seeing him coach another girl. I hate to even think about it. On the other hand, I'd love for him to gain the full respect he deserves from the tennis community. He could do that if he took someone else into the Top Ten. But I can't handle that emotionally right now. So I will pay him to continue as my non-traveling coach/consultant through 1986. Then he'll be free to do what he wants.

While Don was explaining all this to my lawyer, I couldn't stand it. I started to cry. I can't imagine my career without Don. Someday it will happen, but not next year. He'll probably go to Australia with me in May, to Wimbledon in June, and to the U.S. Open in September.

October 30—Williamsburg

Mom came with me to the Wightman Cup here. She's a William and Mary alum, so this is her second trip to this event with me. She loves it.

This morning after devouring a huge breakfast buffet, I played a set and a half with Chris. I've never thrown up on court, but after several gritty Evert Lloyd points, the thought crossed my mind. She won the first set 7–5 and was leading 3–1 in the second. Then we played a tiebreaker, which Chris won 8–6.

While I was showering, Chris wrote the following on the top of my *Washington Post*: "Dear Pam: Remember the score, 7–5, 3–1, 8–6 tiebreaker. For you to enter into your journal. Lots of love, Chris."

At our team dinner tonight we all shook off our good manners and had a fine old time. Without much trouble, the conversation turned to sex. We decided we should do a skit spoofing Dr. Ruth Westheimer's show, *Good Sex*. That would be the entertainment for the black-tie gala dinner on the last evening of the event. Hey, let's put on our own show! Yeah, let's call it *Good Strokes*. Yeah, and Chris and Kathy (Rinaldi) will discuss their two-handed grips, and yeah, Pam doesn't need both hands! Yeah, and. . . . Well, you get the drift. Chris is one of the funniest people, but almost no one knows that.

October 31—Williamsburg

Chris and Kathy Rinaldi got the United States off to a rousing 2–0 start. But the best action of the evening came in the opening ceremonies, where we tried some Halloween slapstick, blackening a tooth here and there, then turning outrageous grins to a stunned audience.

The evening also featured one of those rare times when Chris allows herself to say something funny *during a match*. She was wearing a Tinling-designed sundress with two American flags on the skirt. She obviously hadn't worn it in a while because it was form-fitting and a tad short, but with Chris's figure it looked great. The dress must have been choking off some of her shots though, because she lost the first six points of the match before she recovered to lead 5–1. At this point, she walked toward our team box in the corner and said sotto voce: "Is this dress tight enough?"

Not tight enough for Jo Durie; Chris beat her 6–2, 6–3.

November 1—Williamsburg

For the second time in six weeks I won a match 6–0, 6–0 (the first one was against Jenny Klitch in Chicago), but this was the Wightman Cup. This was for the USA. This was the English. Poor Annabel Croft never knew what hit her.

Anne White and Betsy Nagelsen clinched the Cup tie by winning their doubles. That's forty-seven American victories in fifty-seven years.

November 3—Williamsburg

Well, we didn't put on our skit, but the closing banquet did have its ribald moments. Chris had some good lines accepting the Cup. Chris and I played the final doubles and lost the only U.S. set of the week before closing out a 7–0 victory. I forget what Chris said to the assembly, but I'll never forget the note she gave me later. She told me what a good time she'd had playing with me this week, how she felt we'd both come to understand each other, how she hoped I'd always feel I could come to her if something was troubling me. Then she finished by saying that she might even let loose and "swear at an umpire" for me. Ah, true friendship.

But the story of the week belonged to Nancy Jeffett, the chairman of the Wightman Cup committee for the U.S. Tennis Association. To really appreciate the story you've got to understand that Nancy is a very distinguished and courteous lady from Dallas. But underneath all that honey and sophistication is the soul of a free spirit and a pioneer. Anyway, Rosie Casals invited Nancy to her player party during the tour stop in San Francisco a number of years ago, and Nancy gobbled up four of Rosie's brownies along with her usual cocktail intake. Little did Nancy know that the brownies were laced with marijuana. When it finally came time to leave, Nancy went stumbling in search of her black fur coat and came instead upon Rosie's sleeping black German shepherd, Midnight. The next thing anyone knew, Nancy was picking up Midnight and trying to drape the poor animal across her shoulders! I love Nancy for telling that story on herself.

November 4—Lutherville

Chris and I drove to Washington together for a WTA board meeting. I feel that we've really turned a corner in our friendship. Oh, we might still have a few odd problems on the court, but I think we'll always be able to clear things up without all the sturm and drang we've gone through before. I feel we're friends for life.

The board meeting was long and tedious. After five hours I tried to hang myself with my belt. After seven hours of sitting around a table, I thought I'd succeeded and gone to hell. We did accomplish a few important things, like changing our computer ranking system to eliminate the part of the program that devalues a result if it's more than six months old. Now results for a whole year will count for the same amount in the computer rankings, no matter how old they are. I don't really understand how the computer works, and I don't think many others do either, but Chris and Martina both felt strongly about changing the computer and they carry quite a bit of clout. Still, the motion barely passed.

By the way, remember my warnings in Birmingham (verbal obscenity) and New Orleans (ball abuse)? Well, I've gone over the limit of four for a year and that transgression cost me $500. Criminy! Joaquin Andujar was only fined $1500 for almost attacking an umpire in the World Series!

November 6—Lutherville

Another busy day before my flight to Australia: sports clinic at Children's, practice, and a meeting with Sara and Hank Butta of C&P telephone company. He's been one of our most ardent supporters in my Cystic Fibrosis exhibition tournament. Although we've had to postpone the event until next November, it's been an education for me in the red tape involved in corporate decision making.

Tonight I had an early Thanksgiving dinner to celebrate the holiday with my family. The best part of the evening was the company: four girls (Marion, Eleanor, me, and my next-door neighbor, Liz) and four guys (Marion's boyfriend, Fred, Hank, my parents' neighbor, Michael, and my date, Reid) flanked Mom and Dad at the dinner table. Dad toasted the men and thanked them for evening out the Shriver gender imbalance. The ensuing conversations were as plentiful as the food. Never let it be said that a Shriver dinner is a quiet, formal affair.

We all ended up deciding we'd heard enough about Charles and

Diana and the royal visit. Marion, reacting like any jealous nursery school teacher might toward the fortunes of Lady Di, a former nursery school teacher herself, said, "Why couldn't it have been me? I'm a schoolteacher with blonde hair and a pleasant personality." I caught Liz's eye and mouthed across the table, "*Diana* was a virgin." Fortunately, Marion didn't see me.

November 7—Lutherville

It pays to advertise. Remember how I wrote about the time in San Antonio when a guy snuck into the locker room and stole my underwear? Well, that part of my journal appeared in the *Sports Illustrated* articles, and because I mentioned the brand name of my unmentionables, the Olga Company has written me a letter offering to replace the hot pants and bra. I disclosed my bra size, but in the letter, from the vice president of marketing, I was asked to report my pants size and the style I wanted. They even sent me a whole catalog to choose from.

Gee, I should have also mentioned the time my $100,000 DeBeers diamond tiara was stolen.

November 8—En route

Don and I are on our way to Australia again. This is the first flight we've shared since we flew to Australia together in May. What a change from the previous six years when we hardly ever traveled anywhere without each other. Hank dropped us off at the airport. I was sad that he wasn't coming, but Don wanted to go it alone and I agreed. Australia's a long way to bring two coaches. After an uneventful stopover in Fiji (no Aussie footballers, no racing wheelchairs), we're nearing Sydney. It's now been twenty-six hours since I left my house. Oh, here the stewardess comes with a hot towel. Things like a hot towel are a major happening on a flight this long.

I figured I've been to Australia eleven times; at this rate I'll make twenty trips Down Under by the time I'm 29. I should be ready for an ambassadorship by then.

I love Australia. I really don't look forward to going to Europe for five weeks in June and July. There's too much pressure riding on Wimbledon and the weather is always abominable and the people can sometimes throw a wet blanket on you, too. But in Australia the weather is usually glorious, and the Aussies I've met in my six years here have become more than good friends. Nobody knows how to have fun like an Aussie, and I fit in like a true Sheila.

November 11—Brisbane

Tonight Don and I went out to dinner at our favorite seafood restaurant here. One of the hazards of being a recognizable tennis player is that people sometimes notice me and start talking about tennis. I thought that had happened tonight when six people at a table behind us started to talk about the matches that had been on TV today. Suddenly my name came up. I perked up my ears, expecting a compliment or two.

"She walks like a duck," said one diner. Then they all had some fun discussing Pam Shriver's funny walk. Needless to say, they didn't know I was one table away.

November 12—Brisbane

I've been hitting with Charlie Fancutt, an Aussie who's played the men's tour on and off for years. Yesterday, I beat him 6–3. To be perfectly fair to Charlie, he was doing his best to play like a girl. If he wanted to cream me, he could. It's ridiculous that the talk ever got started that Martina could beat the No. 100 guy. I think Martina realizes that now, too. I think Martina was just curious to know how she'd do against a man on her best surface, grass—against a man who had no idea how to play on grass and who didn't serve well or know how to approach or volley.

Basically, any guy ranked in the top 300, even if he didn't know how to play on grass, would easily beat the top woman. I think that it was kind of unnecessary to call attention to a thing like that.

For a while when I first hired Hank, I was beating him in practice sets. But then he began to feel a little more comfortable in his role and realized that I needed him to beat me for me to get better. Charlie probably felt some of the same things today, but I bet I surprised him with my serves and returns.

November 13—Brisbane

Martina and I creamed two young qualifiers. One of the girls, Lisa O'Neil, has ballgirled for me in Sydney. That made me feel old: I don't think I've ever played against someone who was a ballgirl for me. It reminded me of how I felt when I first introduced myself to Stephanie Rehe about a year and a half ago. Stephanie is 16 now, lean and tall like me and she's played her way into the top thirty. But at that time she was 14 and traveling with Robert Lansdorp to one of her first pro tournaments. When I introduced myself and asked her to hit, she said, "Here, Robert, take a picture of me with Pam Shriver." I almost freaked out. Here was a teenager in the same situation I had been in not too many years before. And now I'm only 23 and I'm playing my ballgirls. God help me.

On the news I saw Prince Charles playing polo in Palm Beach. He was playing at the same club, Palm Beach Polo, that had courted me for their touring-tennis-pro job last spring. Bill Ylvisaker, the man who owns the place, was rubbing mallets (or whatever you call it) out there on the pitch with the Prince.

My deal with Mr. Ylvisaker and the club never panned out. These resort liaisons can work a lot of ways; the place can pay you in real estate, in cash, or both. I already have a condo in Florida, so when Palm Beach Polo offered me real estate the deal began to look less inviting. Besides, they wanted seven to ten days a year, and while that doesn't sound like a lot of time, it's really more than I have at the moment. But I still hope Mr. Ylvisaker teaches me how to play polo some day.

November 14—Brisbane

Last night I had a rare dinner with Martina *without* her tribe. As I've mentioned, Martina loves traveling with friends, family, coaches, and dogs, and the more the merrier. People think that Martina and I spend a lot of time together off court because we spend so much time together on it. They're wrong. Martina is usually in the middle of planning dinner for ten. But tonight we laughed and had a fine old time. Martina's great for a laugh, just like Chris, but Chris has an earthier sense of humor.

And, most important of all: Martina and I have gone back to our original sides in doubles. I'm returning again from the deuce court, my better side. We never really discussed it. I had told Martina after we lost the U.S. Open finals in September that I thought we should switch back. When we walked out for our first match here, she looked at me and said, "Well, what side?" I shrugged and told her, "You know what I want to do." And without another word we went back to our old sides. One small step for Shriver, one giant leap for Navratilova-Shriver (I think).

Another interesting thing happened at the courts today. I rarely watch matches on the outside courts unless I'm scouting a future opponent, but Elise was playing Robin White so I ambled over. Elise had won the first set but then lost eleven of the next twelve games to go down 0–4 in the third. What's worse, some of the ballkids were cheering loudly for Robin. I went over to them and said, "Do you all have a problem?" They looked up at me in shock. "As long as you're in your ballgirl uniforms you really shouldn't be so biased," I said, feeling a little like a schoolteacher. But it worked: The kids toned down their act and Elise clawed her way back from 0–5. I kept telling her to hang tough because I've seen players like Robin blow big leads before. And what do you know? Elise won from 0–5 in the third!

November 15—Brisbane

I played my first singles match against a Russian today. I climbed all over Larissa Savchenko (is that Russian or what?) to go up 6–2, 2–0, but then she started to have loads of fun with my serve. She broke me three straight times with beautiful backhand returns and feathery drop shots, but I broke her three more times and won 6–4. Larissa's a dandy player; if she lost 20 pounds, she could be a real force on the tour. She's also a character; her facial expressions and mannerisms on the court are a stitch. I swear she's a cartoon character waiting to happen.

Tomorrow I play Helena Sukova and Martina plays Claudia Kohde-Kilsch in the other semifinal. Interestingly, Martina is the shortest of the bunch by over 4 inches. If Martina had lost today to Britain's Sara Gomer (who's 6′2″) we may have had the tallest semifinal lineup in the history of tennis—men or women. Remember, McEnroe and Connors are only 5′11″ or so, and Lendl's only 6′2″.

There are a lot of tall players on the women's tour. Kohde's 6′0½″; Sukova's 6′1½″; Jo Durie's 6′; and Alycia Moulton, Marcella Mesker, Anne White, and Andrea Temesvari are all a shade under 6. We're all a little clumsy compared to someone like Martina who's 5′7½″, but for tall people it's more important how well you cover the net. When I'm really into a match and can read where the ball's going, I know I'm as tough as anyone in the game to pass. And people don't lob me that much; it's amazing. I think it's because I don't tend to crowd the net; also, for a period of about two years I hardly missed an overhead. My overhead isn't as good anymore because I haven't been able to practice it as much with my sore shoulder. Still, players don't lob me.

More players should use the lob in women's tennis, because most women don't know what they're doing on the overhead. That's one of the shots Martina's improved on the most but has probably gotten the least amount of credit for. I used to be able to get six or seven lobs over her backhand shoulder on huge points during a match because she crowds the net so much. But now she moves back incredibly well. It's tough to get anything over her head, and if you do, she's so fast she can run it down and more often than not hit a passing shot by you.

November 16—Brisbane

I won a tough three-setter from Sukova in the semis today. There were no service breaks in the first set, and I hit some great shots in the tiebreaker for the set. But then I blew the next five games in a row, reverting back to my old self, glaring at Don. I even smacked myself on the leg with my racket. It hurt, but it worked. I broke her midway through the third, then broke her again. So, tomorrow it's the big one again: Martina.

P.S. Martina and I beat Hana and Wendy 6–1, 6–3. We're playing much better on our old sides.

November 17—Brisbane

Crap. I lost again. This time 6–4, 7–5. I'm so damn sick of losing to Martina and Chris in close matches. They both get psyched up to play me, which seems kind of unfair. I played a fine match but Martina's serve was unreal. She played one bad game and that was when she served for match at 5–4, 30–0. Damn, these are the matches I need to win.

This is no excuse, but my left foot is a mess. I've got a case of athlete's foot between my two smallest toes; my little toe has developed a soft corn from the pressure I've been putting on it to take the weight off the ball of my foot. Stuffing the foot inside a sweaty sock for five hours a day isn't exactly promoting the healing process. I might have to pull out of Sydney next week.

November 18—Brisbane

Martina and her big mouth. Get this scene: She wins the singles and doubles, and then at her press conference she drills the sponsor for having too much white in the signs at the back of the court. You would have thought she could keep her gripes to herself, especially since Panasonic is the most loyal sponsor of women's tennis in Australia. Sure, there's a rule against white in the signs behind the court because sometimes a player has a hard time picking up the ball against that background, but Martina didn't lose a set in the singles all week and we only lost one set in the doubles.

To understand why Martina persisted in this petty complaint you've got to understand what a person of principle she is. She plays by the rules and expects others to as well. It's just that principle got in the way of common sense here.

I wouldn't be surprised if Panasonic pulled the plug after Martina's remarks and after Gigi Fernandez's performance at the player party the other night. They must think we players are a bunch of ingrates. Panasonic has given us generous gifts here the last couple of years. Last year they gave us 35-mm cameras, and the years before we got portable stereo stuff. Well, this year we got a wet-dry shaver and Gigi yells out, "Oh God, last year we got a camera." We all just about died. Talk about tactless. Talk about ungracious. If you're a smart player, you realize that you're spoiled and you don't draw anybody's attention to it.

November 19—Sydney

I've officially pulled out of the tournament. The doctor told me that salt water helps, which is the best excuse I've ever heard for taking the week off to go to the beach. I haven't had to pull out of a tournament in well over a year. Who would have thought a little toe could cause such a big problem?

November 20—Sydney

I'm feeling even more awkward than I usually do at the beach, and it isn't my tan (or lack thereof) that's bothering me. The only ones wearing suits besides me are the guys. Bondi Beach is Titsville, Australia. Milestone: my first visit to a nude beach.

Everyone's upset with Martina about her comments last week. I think Martina is feeling the pressure to regain her No. 1 ranking. She's never been one to like being No. 2, but there are probably also a lot of year-end endorsement bonuses riding on finishing No. 1. She's motivated by pride more than anything else, as is Chris, but it's difficult not to think about the financial rewards, too. If Martina wins Kooyong next week, she'll overtake Chris for No. 1.

November 23—Sydney and Melbourne

Wendy Turnbull had her annual birthday party, and for the first time in five years I wasn't invited. Oh, well, maybe Rabbit still holds a grudge about the comments I made after she beat me a year and a half ago in the U.S. Open. Or maybe she remembers the love-and-two drubbing I handed her in New Orleans. Whatever, *I'm* not going to hold it against her.

Elise, Trish Faulkner of the WTA, and I had dinner at an American barbeque joint. Our dinner conversation revolved around the players who have had serious emotional problems on the tour this year. Remember the player who had bulimia in the spring and summer? She's since dropped off the tour and now is getting treatment in a hospital. Elise had tried to help her out during Wimbledon, but the girl became so furious when Elise even suggested there might be something wrong that she dropped it.

And the player who has had plenty of physical problems the last couple of years is now suffering from depression. I'm talking not about mild depression but almost manic. Last week she defaulted in the middle of a match because she couldn't handle the pressure. She needs professional help but first she's got to admit she has a problem. This life is just too difficult for a woman, unless you're Chris or Martina and you win all the time.

November 25—Melbourne

Yesterday I attended a player meeting and almost got drawn and quartered by the lower-ranked players for the board's decision to do away with the diminishing return in the computer rankings. Nobody understands the computer anyway, and I was just voting with Chris and Martina because they felt strongly that the diminishing return allows much more sudden movement in the computer rankings than is reflected in year-long performance. The diminishing return gives more weight to recent results by diminishing the value of tournaments over six months old. It's a classic argument between the "haves" and the "have nots," and I guess I'm a marked person because I've been a "have" my whole career. Anyway, as I was trying to explain Chris and Martina's arguments, Barbara Gerken cut in from the first row, "I guess we're all playing for Martina." I shot back, "Don't be a wise ass. You all asked me to explain what happened in the board meeting."

The lower-ranked players always think they're getting the fuzzy end of the lollipop in these things, and the top players always think they're giving away too much to the lower ones. It can get pretty testy at times, and this time I was thinking to myself, "Where's Chris? Where's Martina? Why am *I* the one taking the heat?"

Things like this always seem to come up during the pressure of Grand Slam events. I've felt blue the past few days and have been a pain in practice. Today I even cried like a spoiled brat because my toe hurt, I wasn't hitting well, I hadn't played a match in ten days, *and* it was raining. I'm nervous and worried that my Grand Slam preparation hasn't been good enough because of my foot injury. I think I'll just cut my little toe off and throw it away!

November 26—Melbourne

Chris is so sensitive! She must read every word ever written about her because she picks up on every quote that puts even the slightest dent in her professional ego. Yesterday there was a quote from Martina that I knew would nibble away at Chris's insecurity. Martina supposedly said, "All things being equal, Hana is a better player than Chris. She has more power and more shots."

Now let's dissect this quote. (I feel like Martina's defense attorney.) What does Martina mean by "all things being equal"? If she means "if Hana was mentally tough and not a wacko on the court sometimes," Chris should feel better already. And what about Martina's comment, "Hana is a better player than Chris"? That statement is absolutely ridiculous: One glance at the record books shows that Chris's record on all surfaces is nonpareil. I know Martina doesn't consider Hana a better player than Chris, unless she's speaking of raw talent and shot-making ability, which leads us to the last part of the quote: "She has more power and more shots." OK, Hana has more power off the forehand, overhead, and volleys than Chris and she definitely has more shots than Chris, but Hana has more shots than any woman who ever played. So, case dismissed: Chris shouldn't feel threatened by this innocent remark, which was probably taken out of context anyway.

But she does. She's hurt and angry. Martina and Chris will have to mend this small tear in what is really an amazing friendship. But they will. We all get sensitive about what our fellow players say about us. Earlier this year, for instance, Martina went on a tirade because she felt JoAnne Russell had implied that her glasses weren't really necessary and might be a psychological ploy. JoAnne, who was doing commentary on TV at the time, has an irrepressible sense of humor, and all she said was something like, "Just think about what Martina did half-blind without her glasses, going 99–1 one year. It's a wonder she was even able to hit the ball!" But Martina got all bent out of shape.

November 27—Melbourne

Rain, rain, rain and no matches yesterday. But the day wasn't a total washout. I met the nicest male player in my seven years on the pro tour. We were standing next to each other in the lunch line at Kooyong, and he actually started talking to me.

"Is the food nice here?"

"Not bad. Better than the U.S. Open anyhow," I said.

He laughed and then said, "Pam, I don't think we've met. I'm Bud Schultz."

I nearly fainted. A male player introducing himself to me? Then when he said, "You probably don't remember, but before I started to play the tour, I drove you all over the place when you played Boston one year," I knew he was special. Imagine a guy being secure enough to admit that he drove transport for a women's event.

"Was that the year of the blizzard or the year I lost to BJK in the first round?" I asked. (I wasn't going to let this conversation end, no sir.)

"The year you lost to Billie Jean in the first round."

"The fish is pretty good here." (Good, Pam, what are you going to talk about next, the weather?)

"I really enjoyed your *Sports Illustrated* articles." (Maybe he was trying to keep the conversation alive too?)

"Oh, thanks."

Finally, we'd gotten our food and we headed off to separate tables. But when I'd finished lunch with Don, I went over to his table where he was sitting with Tim Mayotte and Bob Green, a.k.a. Team New England. I chatted a minute or two so that Bud Schultz would know that I appreciated his friendliness. (These guys have to be reinforced, you know.)

Tomorrow I play my first match in ten days and with one sore toe. I'm worried.

November 28—Melbourne

No reason to worry so much. I served eight aces and crunched Andrea Holikova two and three.

Tonight Martina had her annual Thanksgiving dinner for about twenty of us. We had turkey with all the trimmings in her suite. It's interesting that Martina has made it her tradition to put on the quintessential American holiday for all of us who're 12,000 miles away from home.

Boris Becker lost in his first match yesterday in five sets to the No. 188-ranked player in the world. He may be the Wimbledon champion, but he's only 18 and he's going to have these ups and downs for awhile. Since he's staying in this hotel I sent him a note telling him not to worry. It began: "Take it from someone who lost in the final of a U.S. Open only to go back the next year and lose first round to a qualifier. . . ." I know that when you're young the losses weigh too heavily on your mind. I wanted to spare him some of the pain I'd felt. The kid will never again play pressureless tennis the way he did at Wimbledon this year.

November 29—Melbourne

Ion Tiriac came up and pinched me on the cheek as I was walking out to practice today. "You're a very nice girl," he said. "Thank you." Ion is a formidable-looking guy but a softie at heart, although I'm sure Boris doesn't think his coach's practices are so soft. Anyway Boris looked up from practice and said, "Thank you for your letter. It was very nice."

Boris has a great personality and he seems to have bounced back from his defeat. He was having a good time in practice today. He certainly is popular with the girls. Susie Mascarin isn't the only one who's been "practicing" with him. Now Lisa Bonder is on the work-out-with-Boris tape.

Martina and I played our first doubles here and defeated two young Aussies, Louise Field and Michele Turk. They're decent players but Field has an annoying habit of yelling, "Go!" to Turk on almost every point. Finally I'd had enough and told her to stop with the go stuff already.

December 1—Melbourne

Depression. I lost to Catarina Lindqvist in the third round after leading a set and 3–1. My last chance for a Grand Slam singles title is gone for the year and I've still got another week here. I can salvage the trip by taking the doubles with Martina, so I won't do anything to hurt our chances. But I definitely feel a few late nights are in order!

Still, I'm down. I honestly don't think Catarina ever played as well on grass. I know *I* didn't think she could play that well on the turf. She just started knocking off winner after winner. She won ten straight games from 1–3 in the second to 5–0 in the third. Apart from Chris, I haven't lost on grass to a baseliner in six years.

December 2—Melbourne

Despite a fun date last night with an Aussie-rules football player named Jason, I can't put the Lindqvist match out of my mind. I'm trying to put it in perspective. She went into the zone for awhile and I don't think Rod Laver could have stopped her, but my serve wasn't firing the way it should have. I hadn't hit groundstrokes on grass for two weeks, so I felt unusually uncomfortable from the backcourt, and whenever I tried to come in she loved the target. She hit lines, angles, corners, everything. No, I didn't play well, but I was snakebit by my foot problems for two weeks before the event. This was the year of poor preparation for the Grand Slam events.

Next year I promise the Grand Slams will get my highest priority. No distractions. No press conferences. No lengthy board meetings. No state dinners. Well, maybe one or two.

December 3—Melbourne

In five years together Martina and I have only lost once before the semifinals, and that was a quarterfinal $4^1/_2$ years ago. Today we nearly lost to the No. 1 Australian junior team, Janine Thompson and Jenny Byrne. They were out of this world and didn't lose serve in the first $1^1/_2$ sets. We were a little lucky to win the first-set tiebreaker. We finally squeaked through 7–6, 4–6, 6–3. I guess our invincibility is gone for good; people now believe they can beat us.

For the first time in my life, I have a problem fitting in my social engagements. There's Jason, the Aussie footballer, who turns out to be only 21 (but he looks older). And then there's Bud Schultz, who's made me revise my opinion of male tennis players. He's friendly, intelligent (B.A., Bates College; grad school, Boston U.), athletic (basketball and tennis for Bates), industrious (he worked his way onto the pro tour by trading his services as a teaching pro for the coaching of Bill Drake, Barbara Potter's former coach), and he's obviously got great taste (he likes me). We've had some great talks.

December 6—Melbourne

The press has been down on John McEnroe ever since he set foot in Australia, and he's evidently feeling a lot of pressure, but the guy hasn't behaved like a champion here. A couple of days ago he just gave up against Slobodan Zivojinovic, just didn't try, and it showed. I feel sorry for John. He feels so persecuted right now. Everybody's against him, or at least that's how he sees it. He's gone through stages like that before but I think he's worse now. He really needs a break.

I've asked him, "Isn't there anywhere you can go where you can get away from it all and not be under as much pressure?" And he's answered, "There isn't anywhere. The only place that's close is New York." Can you imagine any place less conducive to getting away from it all than New York City, where 9 million people are all over you all the time? But it must offer a comfortable anonymity for public personalities like John and Yannick Noah. I remember that New York was the place Yannick came to find his peace after he found himself living in a fishbowl in Paris.

That's really tough when you have to go to New York for peace and quiet. That's like going to Siberia for the sun.

December 7—Melbourne

Martina and I won our twelfth Grand Slam doubles title today by beating Kohde-Kilsch and Sukova three and four. Martina desperately wanted to catch a flight to Honolulu at 7:30, and she kept reminding me that we had to win in straight sets. It seems that every year in the Australian doubles final we're rushing to catch a plane. There's enough pressure in a Grand Slam finals without having to worry about the time. Jeez.

December 8—Sydney

I came here to look into some business opportunities and do some radio promos. I also saw Bud Schultz win his singles match at White City. The men's tour continues through the end of the year without a break, so all the guys who haven't gotten enough match play through the year pack up and go on. I couldn't go another step on a tennis court right now. Thank God the women's tour takes a three-week break for the holidays, and I don't have to feel guilty about missing anything.

Don and I left each other on horrible terms. He drove to Adelaide last Saturday without saying a word. Obviously he's upset with me and my attitude, but through all the years and all the ups and downs he's always said goodbye. I wonder what will happen for next year?

I spoke to Don's mother, Molly, several times, and I finally got up the nerve to tell her about the problems Don and I are having. She knows he may not be coming back with me next May but she told me, "You come back and stay in my unit and bring whoever you want. The place is yours." Oh, Molly, you're a brick, you are.

December 9—En route

So, here I am, a year later, 40,000 feet up again, leaving Australia for home again, writing my last entry in this journal.

Don and I had an honest conversation. We admitted to one another that we just haven't worked well together down here. God knows he tries so hard for me, but my attitude toward our professional relationship has deteriorated after all these years. Emotionally I just can't handle the criticism that a player must accept if the coach is going to be of any benefit to her. Really, I don't think there's much profound that I can offer, except to say that familiarity breeds strain. Nobody's to blame, but I guess after awhile sometimes you have to change just because there's nothing left to do *but* change. Don and I have been with each other for so long—and cared for each other for so long—and now we have to both step back away from one another if I'm to move ahead.

What I wish for him is that one of those stupid guys on the men's tour would get smart enough to hire Don. Then I wouldn't ever have to play another Don Candy player, and I could even cheer for another Don Candy player—besides myself. Me, I'll always think of myself as a Don Candy player, no matter what happens, no matter how many coaches I work with.

I also feel that it's probably all over for John and me. I'm going to see him after Christmas in the Bahamas, with Marion and Fred, but unless something extraordinary happens, I'm sure that we're finished as a romance.

Anyway, 1986 will surely begin with much more stability than this journal's year did twelve months ago. Hank is in place now across the net, and I'm set with ProServ for my management off the court, and Martina and I will be starting our sixth year together (which must be some kind of a record just by itself), and I'm not depressed, and I even have two healthy arms, like real people.

Only, of course, none of that necessarily means anything, because as injured and confused as I was when '85 started, it turned out, all around, to be my best year ever. I made eight finals and won four of them, and Martina and I not only took two more Grand Slam championships, but we also hit our century—109 in a row. I made an embarrassing amount of money, and I saw more of the world and more of the interesting people in the world than almost anybody else ever does in a whole lifetime.

Well, Martina and I already have a new streak going—ten down, only an even hundred to go to beat our old record. And I'm still, as ever, just a lousy one away from all I ever wanted in singles—a Grand Slam title. I'm back where I belong, in Martina's right court and on Chris's right side. Now all I have to do is beat those two girls.

I've got a window seat confirmed all the way back to Baltimore, and then I can take a couple days off from tennis and try to learn to sleep some again.